Cinema and Soft Power

Cinema and Soft Power

Configuring the National and Transnational in Geo-politics

Edited by Stephanie Dennison and
Rachel Dwyer

EDINBURGH
University Press

Edinburgh University Press is one of the leading university presses in the UK. We publish academic books and journals in our selected subject areas across the humanities and social sciences, combining cutting-edge scholarship with high editorial and production values to produce academic works of lasting importance. For more information visit our website: edinburghuniversitypress.com

© editorial matter and organisation Stephanie Dennison and Rachel Dwyer, 2021, 2023
© the chapters their several authors, 2021, 2023

First published in hardback by Edinburgh University Press 2021

Edinburgh University Press Ltd
The Tun – Holyrood Road
12 (2f) Jackson's Entry
Edinburgh EH8 8PJ

Typeset in 11/13 Monotype Ehrhardt by
IDSUK (DataConnection) Ltd

A CIP record for this book is available from the British Library

ISBN 978 1 4744 5627 2 (hardback)
ISBN 978 1 4744 5628 9 (paperback)
ISBN 978 1 4744 5629 6 (webready PDF)
ISBN 978 1 4744 5630 2 (epub)

The right of the contributors to be identified as authors of this work has been asserted in accordance with the Copyright, Designs and Patents Act 1988 and the Copyright and Related Rights Regulations 2003 (SI No. 2498).

Contents

List of Figures, Charts and Tables vii
Notes on Contributors ix
Preface and Acknowledgements xii

   Introduction: The Soft Power of Film 1
   Stephanie Dennison
1 Soft Power and Cinema: A Methodological Reflection and Some Chinese Inflections 17
   Song Hwee Lim
2 Building BRICS: Soft Power and Audio-visual Relations in Transnational Context 38
   Stephanie Dennison
3 The Global Animation Market: Opportunities for Developing Countries 58
   Alessandra Meleiro
4 *(Masha and) the Bear* Diplomacy: Soft Power as World-building and Russian Non-governmental Agency 74
   Vlad Strukov
5 The Limits of Hollywood as an Instrument of Chinese Public Diplomacy and Soft Power 95
   Chris Homewood
6 The Second World War, Soviet Sports and Furious Space Walks: Soft Power and Nation Branding in the Putin 2.0 Era 119
   Stephen M. Norris
7 Popular Geo-politics, Strategic Narratives and Soft Power in *Viking* (2016) and *Guardians* (2017) 140
   Robert A. Saunders
8 The South African Soft Power Narrative, Cinema and Participatory Video 169
   Paul Cooke

9 New Myths for an Old Nation: Bollywood, Soft Power and
 Hindu Nationalism 190
 Rachel Dwyer
10 Soft Power and National Cinema: James Bond, 'GREAT' Britain
 and Brexit 210
 Andrew Higson

Index 236

Figures, Charts and Tables

Figures

2.1	Tradition and modernity meet in Jia Zhangke's 'Revive China'	47
2.2	Elizaveta Stishova's 'imagined' Russian village in 'Catfishing'	48
2.3	Real-life landslide wreckage as backdrop to Walter Salles's 'When the Earth Trembles'	49
4.1	The Bear enjoying afternoon tea. *Masha and the Bear*, episode 1	78
4.2	Masha making 'kasha' (porridge). *Masha and the Bear*, episode 17	79
5.1	Film grab from Roland Emmerich's *Independence Day: Resurgence*	100
5.2	Grab from Steven S. DeKnight's *Pacific Rim: Uprising*	103
5.3	President Trump tweets about what he terms the 'Chinese Virus'	108
5.4	A Chinese censor amends Stan's film script in the *South Park* episode 'Band in China'	112
6.1	Members of the famous Panfilov's 28 come together and prepare to defend Moscow in *Panfilov's 28*	126
6.2	A Russian team forms on the Eastern Front. Members of the Women's Battalion of Death head into battle in Dmitrii Meskhiev's *Battalion*	128
6.3	The 1972 USSR hockey team defeats the Canadians because of their iron will, in *Legend No. 17*	130
6.4	The recreation of the last three seconds of the game in Anton Megerdichev's *Going Vertical*	133
7.1	Opening credits of *Viking* – 'Pagan Europe, 977'	146
7.2	Major Larina comes to recruit Ler at the Khor Virap monastery in Armenia	148

7.3	The Mass Baptism of Kyivan Rus' in the Dnieper river	152
7.4	*Guardians*' 'faceless enemies' as a stand-in for the 'opposition forces'	156
8.1	The low angle-dominated world of *Heaven Hugged Me*	184
8.2	Twinky's enigmatic smile in *Heaven Hugged Me*	185
10.1	A film made for the opening ceremony of the London 2012 Olympic Games	212
10.2	One of the posters produced for the Bond/*Skyfall* tie-in with the GREAT campaign in 2012. Source: VisitBritain	215
10.3	'Oh, Mr. Bond . . .'. Raoul Silva to James Bond, in *Skyfall*	217
10.4	The title image from a promotional film produced by the British Film Institute as part of the GREAT campaign in 2016	229

Charts

3.1	More common services/jobs	65
3.2	Origins of resources and intellectual property ownership	66
3.3	Distribution platforms in the animation segment	67
3.4	Export of content and animation service provision to overseas companies	69

Tables

7.1	Potential sources of soft power in *Viking*	147
7.2	Guardian team member characteristics	149

Notes on Contributors

Paul Cooke is Centenary Chair in World Cinemas at the University of Leeds and is part of the Centre for World Cinemas and Digital Cultures. His main research focus is on the use of participatory arts as a tool for community-led research and advocacy, with a particular emphasis on the use of participatory filmmaking. He has run projects in South Africa, Nepal, India, Germany, Cambodia, Kosovo and Kenya, and is currently the principal investigator on the Arts and Humanities Research Council/ Global Challenges Research Fund Network Plus project 'Changing the Story: Building Civil Society with and for Young People in Post-conflict Countries'. This is a four-year project currently running in twelve countries across the Global South.

Stephanie Dennison is Professor of Brazilian Studies and Director of the Centre for World Cinemas and Digital Cultures at the University of Leeds. She has published books on Brazilian, Latin American and World Cinema. Her latest monograph, *Remapping Brazilian Film Studies in the 21st Century*, was published in 2020. She was primary investigator and director of the Arts and Humanities Research Council-funded international research network Soft Power, Cinema and the BRICS (Brazil, Russia, India, China and South Africa).

Rachel Dwyer is Professor Emerita of Indian Cultures and Cinema at SOAS University of London. Her most recent cinema book is *Picture Abhi Baaki Hai: Bollywood as a Guide to Modern India* (2014) and she has recently co-edited (with Prashant Kidambi and Manjiri Kamat) *Bombay Before Mumbai: Essays in Honour of Jim Masselos*.

Andrew Higson is Greg Dyke Professor of Film and Television at the University of York. He has published widely on British cinema, from the early silent period to the present, and on the concepts of national and transnational cinema. He is currently the Director of the Screen Industries Growth Network (SIGN), an industry-facing research and knowledge exchange project, funded by Research England and designed to support the screen industries of Yorkshire and Humber (https://screen-network.org.uk/).

Chris Homewood is Lecturer in German and World Cinemas at the University of Leeds. He is also Subject Leader for the JH Film Studies programmes in the School of Languages, Cultures and Societies. His most recent publications include '"Directed by Hollywood, Edited by China"? Chinese Soft Power, Geo-imaginaries and Neo-orientalism(s) in recent U.S. Blockbusters', in Robert Saunders and Vlad Strukov (eds), *Popular Geopolitics: Plotting an Evolving Interdiscipline* (2018), and 'Politics in, and of, the Berlin School: Terrorism, Refusal, and Inertia', in Marco Abel and Jaimey Fisher (eds), *A Transnational Art-Cinema: The Berlin School and its Global Contexts* (2018). Currently, he is co-editing, with Jaimey Fisher, a forthcoming volume about German film stars.

Song Hwee Lim is Professor of Cultural Studies at The Chinese University of Hong Kong. He is the author of *Tsai Ming-liang and a Cinema of Slowness* (2014) and *Celluloid Comrades: Representations of Male Homosexuality in Contemporary Chinese Cinemas* (2006). He is the founding editor of the *Journal of Chinese Cinemas*. He is also the co-editor of *Remapping World Cinema: Identity, Culture and Politics in Film* (2006) and *The Chinese Cinema Book* (2011; second edition 2020). His latest monograph on Taiwan cinema and soft power is forthcoming.

Alessandra Meleiro is Associate Professor at the Universidade Federal de São Carlos, in Brazil (Department of Arts and Communication). She holds a postdoctoral qualification from the Media and Film Studies Programme at SOAS, University of London. She is the author of *The New Iranian Cinema: Art and Social Intervention* (2006) and editor of the book series 'World Cinema: Industry, Politics and Market' and 'Brazilian Film Industry'. She is President of FORCINE (Cinema and Audiovisual Education Forum) and of the Cultural Initiative Institute.

Stephen M. Norris is the Walter E. Havighurst Professor of Russian History and Director of the Havighurst Center for Russian and Post-Soviet Studies. He is the author of *A War of Images: Russian Popular Prints, Wartime Culture, and National Identity, 1812–1945* (2006) and *Blockbuster History in the New Russia: Movies, Memory, Patriotism* (2012), as well as editor or co-editor of six other books. He is currently working on a biography of the most significant Soviet political caricaturist, Boris Efimov.

Robert A. Saunders is a Professor in the Department of History, Politics, and Geography at Farmingdale State College, a campus of the State University of New York. His research explores various intersections of popular culture, geo-politics and national identity, and has appeared in *Politics, Millennium, Political Geography, Geopolitics, Nations and Nationalism, Slavic Review* and *Europe-Asia Studies*, among other journals. He is the author of five books, including *Popular Geopolitics and Nation Branding in the Post-Soviet Realm* (2017) and *Geopolitics, Northern Europe, and Nordic Noir* (2021).

Vlad Strukov is a London-based multidisciplinary researcher, curator and cultural practitioner, specialising in art, media and technology cross-overs. He is an Associate Professor at the University of Leeds and a researcher at Garage Museum of Contemporary Art (Russia), working on global visual cultures. He is currently carrying out a major research project, funded by the Swedish Research Council, on contemporary queer visual culture. He is the author of many research publications, including a monograph on contemporary Russian cinema (2016).

Preface and Acknowledgements

The present volume is one of a number of outputs of the international research network Soft Power, Cinema and the BRICS (2015–18), funded by the UK's Arts and Humanities Research Council (AHRC). The network built on the connections established, and the research findings of a World Universities Network-supported project entitled Film Policy, Cultural Diplomacy and Soft Power, which ran from 2012 to 2014 and which brought together scholars working on cultural policy issues relating to soft power (the power of nations to attract in contradistinction to coercing) in a number of countries, including the UK, China, South Africa and Brazil, with a focus on how policymakers seek to achieve soft power objectives, and how they negotiate artistic, economic and political networks. A key output of this initial project was a seminar entitled Film Policy, Cultural Diplomacy and Soft Power, held in Leeds in 2013. The kinds of policymakers we engaged with at the seminar were linked to tourism, film institutes and government-linked thinktanks.

From our discussions at that seminar it became clear that nations such as Brazil and South Africa had a very different 'story' to tell, compared to countries such as the UK and China, and those tasked with communicating the stories were also very distinct. Thus, in our follow-on AHRC research network project, our focus shifted to the relationship between both state *and* non-state actors in the cultural industries of the BRICS countries (Brazil, Russia, India, China and South Africa) and national soft power strategies, with a particular focus on the nature and function of the film industry. We looked comparatively at the engagement by filmmakers, producers, Ministries of Culture and so on, with the soft power and nation-branding agendas of their country, in order to ascertain whether this engagement is explicit or implicit, what forms it takes, and with what results. We wanted, then, to investigate the competing pressures across the BRICS that shape the ways its members understand film as a vehicle of soft power, and exploring the role that soft power plays along the industry's entire value chain, from production to consumption, as well as the way it influences the types of films that audiences around the world get to see.

Individual members of the BRICS group, most obviously China and Russia, had already been discussed in some detail in relation to their (widely criticised) attempts to wield soft power in order to increase their profile on a global stage. However, the diverse and often competing ways that the group as a whole engages with film as a medium of artistic expression, on the one hand, and as a soft power 'resource', on the other, along with the wider implications for world cinemas of its members' very different, and dynamic, positions within the global media landscape, remained to be investigated comparatively. Thus we felt the time was right to explore in greater detail the employment of soft power strategies by emerging nations, in order to nuance discussions on what successful soft power 'looks like' in different parts of the globe, and by providing analysis from the perspective of film culture.

Our ambition was and remains to steer World Cinema research in a new direction, taking as a starting point an analysis of both on- and off-screen stories. And it is both on-screen and off-screen stories that are captured in the essays in this edited volume. Many of the ideas developed in the individual chapters were first presented at an academic conference in 2017 in Leeds entitled Cinema, Soft Power and Geo-Political Change, which, while continuing to focus on BRICS nations, took discussions to other filmmaking contexts, such as the UK. We are grateful to all the network members and conference and event attendees across the life of the research network for their input and contribution, either directly or indirectly, to this volume.

An earlier version of Chapter 1 was delivered as a keynote speech at the conference on 'Cinema, Soft Power and Geo-political Change' at the University of Leeds in June 2017; the version here was presented, in brief, at the conference on 'Transmedia Storytelling: Digital Creativity in TV, Film, Internet and Multi-Media' at Seoul National University in June 2019 and at the conference on 'Affect and Critique: Language, Body and Politics in Modern Literature and Culture' at Taiwan's Academia Sinica in December 2019. Song Hwee Lim would like to thank Stephanie Dennison for inviting him to the Leeds conference and to act as a steering committee member on the AHRC international network 'Soft Power, Cinema and the BRICS', and Jaeho Kang and Yu-lin Lee for their respective invitations to Seoul and Taipei. Thanks also to his colleagues Chung Peichi and Tan Jia for their helpful feedback on the chapter; his research associate Roberto Castillo for collating and digesting scholarship on China's soft power;

research assistants Chen Zhengheng for summarising materials on affect theory, Lu Xin for compiling information on China's film industry and cultural policies and Zhang Zongyi for sharing his knowledge on Chinese leaders' use of cinema as a diplomatic tool. The work described in this chapter was substantially supported by a grant from the Research Grants Council of the Hong Kong Special Administrative Region, China (Project No.: CUHK 14606815).

Rachel Dwyer would like to record her thanks to the AHRC for funding this project; Dr Shashi Tharoor (Lok Sabha) and Dr Swapan Dasgupta (Rajya Sabha), the latter serving on the committee for Report (2016a) which the former chaired, for granting interviews about India's soft power today (see Chapter 9 for references).

Stephanie Dennison and Chris Homewood would like to thank the School of Languages, Cultures and Societies of the University of Leeds for supporting research trips in relation to this book to South Africa, Brazil and China.

The following people have supported this project in a variety of ways and we extend our gratitude to them: Lorraine Blakemore, Michael Dwyer, Alessandra Scangarelli, Daya Thussu, Dunja Fehimovic, Ashvin Devasundaram, Cesar Jimenez Martinez, Xiaoning Lu, Yanling Yang, Juily Mangharmalani, Russell Hlongwane and Rafael Luna. Thanks also to Richard Strachan and staff at Edinburgh University Press for their assistance in bringing this volume to fruition.

Introduction: The Soft Power of Film
Stephanie Dennison

Coined by political scientist Joseph Nye in 1990 in an attempt to rethink the USA's position and future in global politics, soft power refers to the ability of a country to influence through attraction rather than coercion, whereas coercion, or hard power, consists of military intervention, economic sanctions and so on (Nye 1990). It implies recognising what those from other countries already find attractive about a given country, creating new and attractive features (as a way of countering unattractive features associated with one's country) and producing a coherent narrative that incorporates these attractive features, so that they might be mobilised in an effort to gain favour.

Although Nye revised his theorising in light of the challenges in international relations in the twenty-first century (2004; 2011; 2019), and most notably in 2004 when he argued that a combination of soft and hard power, or what he termed smart power, was needed to produce effective foreign policy, it is the neat but simplified conceit of 'attraction rather than coercion' that has tended to dominate discussions of soft power to date. It is little wonder, then, that it is often dismissed as a woolly concept, as 'mushy, over-boiled, fuzzy, and irrelevant [. . .] in a fluid, multipolar, and increasingly challenging world' (Sarukhan 2016). Thus, despite the impressive volume of texts that have been produced purporting to discuss soft power, as Naren Chitty (2017) has argued, 'the compressed but broad account that one finds in the soft power narrative of Nye (2011) has not been sufficiently unraveled and analyzed'. Furthermore, while culture is regularly identified as a potential source of soft power, there has been relatively little meaningful discussion of the role that audio-visual culture, and film specifically, might have in its generation.[1] This book, then, sets out to fill this gap, and thus to 'unravel and analyse' soft power in relation to film culture.

With the exception of one chapter, which examines the soft power of the UK's James Bond franchise, the contributions in this book focus on film and national visibility among the countries that make up the BRICS nations. This grouping, which, for many commentators, heralded a potential geo-political shift away from the 'West against the rest' to a 'rise of the rest', emerged around the same time that the concept of soft power began to make an impact beyond the merely academic terrain. The existence of an implicit association between these two forms of geo-political reframing was recognised, for example, in the sustained curiosity of the UK government between 2011 and 2015 in interrogating the soft power trajectories and potential of BRICS members China and Brazil, through a series of initiatives designed to find out more about soft power and how the UK might best take advantage of its own 'attractive' assets to stake a stronger claim in the new world order in the twenty-first century. These initiatives included a series of high-profile conferences on soft power run by Wilton Park, an executive agency of the Foreign and Commonwealth Office, including one held in Brazil, and regular features sponsored by the British Council. Crucially, a House of Lords Select Committee report was produced, looking at the UK's soft power potential (HM Government, *Persuasion and Power in the Modern World*, 2014), and rather than seeking the views of representatives from powerhouses such as the US and Western European countries, it took evidence from specialists in Chinese international relations and the Brazilian Ambassador to London, among others.

By far the most discussed case study of the uses (and abuses) of soft power, by academics, by the international press and in diplomatic circles, is China. The concept of soft power was legitimated early on (2007) by the Chinese Communist Party (Albert 2018) and has featured ever since in China's five-year plans. Scrutiny of China's soft power objectives has tended to involve the country's media footprint (the penetration of China Global Television Network in Africa, for example), public diplomacy initiatives such as the Confucius Institutes, and the perceived takeover of Hollywood by Chinese film production concerns. While one collection of essays has recently been dedicated to the soft power of Chinese cinema (Voci and Luo 2018), as Chapters 1, 2 and 5 attest in this volume, there is still much ground to be covered in relation to the reception of Chinese films, to the analysis of Chinese co-productions, and to the role of non-state actors in the instrumentalising of Chinese film culture as public diplomacy.

China presents a unique case, given the extent of the buy-in of the Chinese government in the soft power agenda, and the degree of criticism that has been aimed at its attempts to develop soft power. Together with fellow BRICS member Russia, another BRICS country to have embraced

Nye's term directly in its international relations strategies, China's soft power was critiqued by Matt Johnson in a short essay written for *Foreign Policy* in 2013 and entitled 'What China and Russia Don't Get About Soft Power'. In it, Johnson argued that both the Chinese and Russian governments 'stepped on their own message', and that for them to succeed, 'they will need to match words and deeds in their policies, be self-critical, and unleash the full talents of their civil societies' (Johnson 2013). The implications of this observation will be returned to presently.

Both China and Russia offer examples of a use of soft power that is closely bound up with vigorously promoted public diplomacy efforts. But what about emerging countries, where a soft power strategy is either non-existent, incipient or not particularly ambitious? Take, for example, the case of Brazil, a country with a recognisably attractive culture and growing geopolitical importance in the twenty-first century. While a certain buzz may have developed around Brazil and its soft power capacity within international relations circles, in Brazil itself the term soft power has had relatively little purchase, and certainly when we compare it to other BRICS countries and the UK, for example. If anything, it has been viewed as part of the Workers' Party (PT) national project, given that the term was almost exclusively engaged with by two key PT members: Celso Amorim, Foreign Minister in Luis Inácio Lula da Silva's two administrations (2003–10), and Marta Suplicy, Minister of Culture in Dilma Rousseff's first term of office (2011–14). Both the hosting of the FIFA World Cup 2014 and the Summer Olympics 2016 were secured by Brazil during Lula's administration, which also saw Brazil, via Lula and Amorim, further stake a claim for being taken seriously on the global stage through its involvement in finding a peaceful solution to Iran's impasse with the United Nations over its nuclear arsenal.[2] Crucially, these soft power-generating initiatives coincided with a period of impressive economic growth, whereby Brazil rode out the world financial crisis of the first decade of the twenty-first century on the back of a commodities boom, enabling the country to overtake the UK (briefly) in 2012 to be the world's sixth strongest economy (Inman 2012). With the collapse of the Brazilian economy in 2013, the impeachment of PT president Dilma Rousseff on corruption charges, the dismantling of the South–South diplomacy with which Brazil's soft power ambitions were closely associated under Lula, the victory at the polls of a far-right president, Jair Bolsonaro, and his catastrophic handling of both the COVID-19 pandemic and the threat to Brazil's forests from 'wildfires', it is no coincidence that Brazil has plummeted in the soft power rankings.

The Brazilian case demonstrates a number of problems relating to how soft power works in practice. The first of these, which Brazil amply illustrates, is the lack of a level playing field among countries with regard to the separation of government and civil society when discussing soft power. While chastising China and Russia for failing to practise what they preached when it came to their soft power visions, Nye (2004: 11) recognised that 'a residual soft power helps to cushion a fall', thus implying that (other) nations with a long tradition of attraction have the ability to ride out storms produced by unattractive governments or government actions.[3] Secondly, the Brazilian case reveals the extent to which soft power success is bound up with a perceived financial stability. And thirdly, Brazil's failed attempt to produce a lasting soft power edge through what could be described as a textbook generating of soft power assets (two successfully managed mega-events, peace-seeking diplomacy in the Middle East, and the international projection of a very popular and charismatic leader [Lula]) points to expectations of sustainability of the message: expectations, one might argue, which are hampered in the case of a great many emerging nations by rapid shifts in political direction.

Sustainability can also be hampered by the existence of competing (negative) narratives. This was witnessed, for example, in the relentless criticisms in the international press of the organisation of the Rio Olympic Games, despite the fact that they were ultimately 'successful' (Davis 2016) The competing narrative of Brazil was of an unsafe, corrupt and therefore badly managed country with a weak democracy. A number of chapters in this volume attest to the existence of such competing (and negative) narratives, many of which are generated abroad, and linked to film culture. As nation brander Simon Anholt (2010) has argued, it is always risky to underestimate the appeal of negative stories.

Joseph Nye (2004: 11) points out that soft power depends on 'the existence of willing interpreters and receivers'. Brazilian cinema (and most others, regardless of the volume of production and state support and investment) is arguably not well enough known to produce the volume of willing interpreters and receivers needed to translate into soft power. As Vanita Kohli-Khandekar (2013) has argued, even the success and reach of India's Bollywood film phenomenon, which Nye first suggested in 2005 as a candidate for India's flagship soft power asset (Murthy 2017: 358), has been overplayed when it comes to describing the soft power of film. We thus need to take care not to make grand claims regarding the power of film to convince publics to re-examine foreign cultures in a 'positive' light.

By way of illustration, when Bong Joon-ho took home the Best Picture Oscar in 2020 for *Parasite*, the international press was quick to frame his success as a victory for Korean soft power (Kim and Lee 2020; Lee 2020; The Times 2020). But there was no such link forged the previous year between the film *Roma* and Mexican soft power when Alfonso Cuarón picked up three Academy Awards, including Best Director. Put simply, despite a certain familiarity with and attraction to its culture, Mexico does not have *hallyu* (Korean wave), a strategic narrative bolstered in large part by the all-conquering K-pop. National cinemas, then, when they are not part of a wider strategic narrative, risk serving only as window dressing for public diplomacy activities carried out by embassies.

But as Janet Harbord (2002: 1) posits in her analysis of film culture, there are many ways that film enters our lives. Roy and Huat (2012: xxi) have described Bollywood as a 'free-floating signifier': while most people will not, despite the hype, have seen a Bollywood movie, many can claim to have a sense of the attractive features of the Indian nation that Bollywood has come to symbolise. We might also consider the co-optation of film-makers (Zhang Yimou, Danny Boyle, Fernando Meirelles and Takashi Yamazaki) in the production of Summer Olympic Games opening ceremonies since 2008, in a recognition of their ability to tell visual stories that 'sell' national/regional cultures to a potential global viewing public of billions. In brief, we can find further potential soft power impact from film culture more broadly in a variety of guises, from high-profile directors strongly identified with a national brand (such as Spanish director Pedro Almodóvar), to the hosting of A-list film festivals (such as Cannes in France), and film training and exchange initiatives such as the US State Department-sponsored American Film Showcase.

It is no coincidence that a number of the chapters in this volume engage with Roselle, Miskimmon and O'Laughlin's singular take on soft power in the twenty-first century as 'strategic narrative' (2014). For a start, the narrative aspect of this interpretation of soft power resonates with the uniquely placed story-telling abilities of audio-visual culture. Matt Johnson (2013) recognised the increasing importance of narratives when he quoted Arquilla and Ronfeldt (2001: 328), and defined the race to top the soft power rankings as 'whose story wins', while Chinese President Xi Jinping has acknowledged the importance of the story-telling aspect of soft power in various addresses (Kim and Lee 2020). There is also a clear convergence between this interpretation of soft power and the work of public diplomacy and nation branding, both in terms of public diplomacy's reliance on state-led directives, and nation branding's strategic (re)orientation toward the market (Fehimovic and Ogden 2018: 3–4).[4] After all, national cinemas do not exist merely to tell situated stories for posterity: they also function (and gain state support and finance) to lay claim to a stake in the increasingly lucrative culture industries market. As the chapters in this volume demonstrate, on-screen and off-screen film stories can, with varying degrees of success, be state-led via directives and funding, and they can be 'cajoled', to use Roselle et al.'s term (2014), whereby a successful product deemed to fit a strategic narrative can be taken advantage of.

As both the volume of scholarship on soft power and the investment that nations make in improving performance in soft power rankings increase, so too do questions relating to the ethics behind soft power measurement. Consider, for example, Zhang and Wu's recent (2019) accusation of implicit bias in Western models for calculating soft power that make it difficult for emerging nations such as those of the BRICS to challenge the domination of Western erstwhile 'first-world' powers. Naren Chitty (2017:19) also recognises that Western normative soft power ultimately comprises 'the distillation of European heritage values', while Simon Anholt, creator of one of the first nation-branding indexes (the Anholt-GfK Nation Brands Index) has shifted his focus (and methodology) away from soft power per se to humanitarian actions (the Good Country Index). Meanwhile, the noticeable shift to the right of a number of soft power success stories (for example, the UK, Brazil and India) and their attendant hardening of attitudes with regard to foreign relations, as well as Donald Trump's declaration in January 2020, in the light of the growing crisis between the US and Iran, that 'American strength, both military and economic, is the best deterrent' (BBC 2020), appear to point to a wholesale rejection of soft power as having little purchase for many nations going forward.

Notwithstanding this seeming undermining of the ethos of *attraction* associated with soft power, what remains implicit in relation to the governments of the countries under examination in this volume is the urgency of projects of (trans)national visibility in an increasingly competitive and globalised world, and a recognition of the ability of film to contribute to such projects. Contributors to this volume therefore discuss, apply and frequently challenge a range of interrelated concepts (soft power, smart power, strategic narratives, public and cultural diplomacy, popular geopolitics and nation branding), whose ultimate purpose is to understand the relationship between culture and the desires of nations and supranational groupings to raise their visibility and prestige on the international stage.

Soft Power, BRICS and the COVID-19 Pandemic

It is likely that the BRICS nations will be particularly hard hit in terms of their image abroad as a result of the COVID-19 pandemic. As Nilsen and Von Holdt (2020) have observed, four of the five countries worst affected by COVID-19, and thus open to fierce criticism for their handling of the health crisis, are from the BRICS grouping: Brazil, Russia, India and South Africa, while Wuhan in China was the source of the virus. China, then, is where a great number of irresponsible national leaders and social media warriors have laid the blame for both the loss of life and the economic impact that the pandemic has had worldwide, thus increasing the already existing suspicion of China's intentions on the global stage, to which a number of chapters in this volume refer. Tensions are running high, especially between China and the US. As Gill (2020: 97) comments,

> The COVID-19 crisis has injected an already-inflamed US–China relationship with new levels of ill will as each side blames the other for the disease's spread and struggles to spin global opinion in their favor. The stakes grow ever higher as the blame game further aggravates US–China competition over matters of governance, values, and ideals.

The pandemic has provoked a more extreme version of existing regime politics (Nilsen and Von Holdt 2020), with Joseph Nye (2020) fearing that the novel coronavirus will simply accelerate existing trends toward nationalist populism and authoritarianism. As Jonathan Clory, founder of the Soft Power 30 Index recently put it, 'For soft power, the glue that holds countries together and enables them to convene and work together, it hasn't been a great couple of months' (British Council 2020). Pre-eminent commentators on soft power, such as Joseph Nye, Henry Kissinger, Simon Anholt and Jonathan Clory, all agree that opportunities for international co-operation have been squandered (Nye 2020; Kissinger 2020; Anholt 2020; British Council 2020). And as countries such as China, Russia, the US and the UK all invest heavily in finding a cure for the coronavirus, it is clear that vaccine diplomacy will play a central role in soft power generation going forward.[5]

The relationship between film and soft power is likely to be impacted significantly by the pandemic, film content on subscription video on demand (SVOD) and the shift of major film festivals to online platforms being two areas already ripe for future analysis. Film production and distribution have been severely affected by COVID-19 isolation and quarantine measures, with popular streaming services such as Netflix being one of the few examples of the industry bucking the spiralling downward trend. Film production was put on hold in February/March 2020, and many film cultures have been very slow to return to business post lockdown for financial reasons. Industries that rely on international co-productions are particularly hard hit, given continued travel restrictions (Guerini 2020). Beyond the Hollywood studios, whose decision to hold back a number of blockbuster international releases has been widely discussed by the media, other significant film-producing cultures are being impacted by both cinema closures and audience fears of returning to watch films in public. A number of A-list Bollywood movies are having straight-to-digital premieres while cinemas remain closed (Gupta 2020), and most of the traditional audience for such films in South Asia does not have access to the internet. And in Russia, cinemas are being encouraged to avoid screening 'dramas', and to focus instead on films likely to raise the mood of spectators (Merz 2020).

The financial support offered to out-of-work film industry personnel varies considerably across the globe, with most funds being managed via national film agencies. In South Africa, for example, the National Film and Video Foundation set up a COVID-19 relief fund (with grants of up to 10,000 rands) to support and assist independent freelance practitioners and technical and production crew in the film and TV industries (NFVF 2020). Private and public funders appear to be moving away from capital funding projects to crisis grants (Forwood 2020): in Russia, for example, funding designated for film theatre and other digitisation upgrades has been moved to the national disaster fund (Reuters 2020). And if, despite its more generous national arts relief funding, the UK's oldest and much-loved film theatre (Birmingham's Electric) has been unable to open at the time of writing (August 2020), then there can be little hope for most of Brazil's independent film venues, which were already struggling pre-COVID as a result of withdrawal of investment in the arts from both private and public sources.

Despite the gloomy outlook, Jia Zhangke, the Chinese director and executive producer of the BRICS compilation films discussed in Chapter 2, is hopeful that the current situation will lead to creative renewal within the film industry:

> On a personal level, as filmmakers, I don't think that this epidemic will somehow dent our passions or our eagerness to continue making films. This epidemic has caused us to stop and think about our society and a lot of issues that we haven't been reflecting on for a long period of time. So on a creative level, we may find a lot of sources of inspiration as a result of this epidemic (Kohn 2020).

While we await, then, the outcomes of this much-hoped-for creative renewal, and the longer-term impact of COVID-19 on international relations, this volume offers reflections on soft power and film culture in the BRICS and the UK in a pre-pandemic twenty-first-century global political landscape.

Organisation of the Book: Film and Soft Power Stories

The opening chapter of this collection, Song Hwee Lim's 'Soft Power and Cinema: A Methodological Reflection and Some Chinese Inflections', provides an interrogation of the term soft power and a meaningful demonstration of its potential methodological usefulness in relation to film. Recognising the difficulty in quantifying the results of soft power, Lim provides, through a case study of the China/US co-production *The Great Wall* (dir. Zhang Yimou, 2016), one model for evaluating the soft power impact of film, 'introducing affect as a missing but crucial factor in mediating soft power transactions'. Taking an affective approach to reading a film like *The Great Wall* (as opposed to focusing, for example, on agency, such as the much-discussed acquisition of Hollywood film studios by Chinese interests, or on effect: box office, reviews and so on), Lim spells out 'the mediating environment in which not only this particular Chinese film circulates but also the affective intensities that all things Chinese might generate'. The result of this, Lim reflects, is that

> *The Great Wall* – both the film and the architectural structure after which it is named – is [seen as] symptomatic of China's soft power ambition to conquer the US film industry and box office; it no longer stands as a historical, militaristic structure to keep out invading barbarians but rather a present-day, metaphorical platform from which China expands far beyond its borders. The affective 'message' becomes: the Chinese are coming, with their armies, weapons and gunpowder.

While acknowledging that China has an image problem that creates challenges for the promotion of its soft power, Lim reminds us that audiences for soft power are not homogenous. In Chapter 2, Stephanie Dennison continues this line of enquiry with an analysis of film relations between BRICS countries, among which China's soft power kudos is arguably accrued and displayed in a more palatable form. In 'Building BRICS: Soft Power and Audio-visual Relations in Transnational Context', China, through its proactive attitude to the annual BRICS film festival and BRICS co-production initiatives, emerges as 'facilitator, promoting a wide range of cultures as well as its own'. At the same time, Dennison questions both the extent to which other BRICS nations have benefited in soft power terms from hosting the film festival, and the ability of such festivals to create genuine intercultural interaction between quite disparate countries.

Dennison highlights some of the tensions around culture and diplomacy in Brazil that have resulted from the recent abrupt shift to the far right within government. Alessandra Meleiro in Chapter 3, 'The Global Animation Market: Opportunities for Developing Countries', takes as her focus the market for animation films in Brazil and their soft power potential, and she too acknowledges the 'confusing signals' about the effective direction taken by Brazilian foreign policy that complicate such discussions. Meleiro reminds us that, writing with animé and manga in mind, Joseph Nye highlighted the soft power potential of animated films. She argues that animation has achieved strategic status in the production chain of the creative industries in Brazil, but that without government (that is, state actors') steer and investment to internationalise production, Brazilian animation's soft power potential will remain unrealised.

Meleiro draws attention to an issue in relation to soft power highlighted above and by a large number of the contributors to this volume: the risk of an audience failing to appreciate the origin/identity of a cultural product and thus attribute kudos accordingly. This is a major issue for film genres such as animation, whereby a number of producers seek to imitate successful models from elsewhere (such as animé). Likewise, through dubbing into different languages, cultural references can easily be erased or altered to suit different consumers.

In his analysis of the hugely successful Russian online cartoon series *Masha and the Bear*, Vlad Strukov in Chapter 4, '*(Masha and) the Bear* Diplomacy: Soft Power as World-building and Russian Non-governmental Agency', demonstrates how this animated series does manage to function as a soft power asset for Russia, but at the same time, 'in terms of circulation, it is trans- and multinational, advancing a sense of multipolar and multidirectional globalisation'. In this chapter, Strukov provides an in-depth critique of Nye's conceptualisation of Russian soft power from the perspective of poststructuralist theory. For Strukov, Nye erroneously discusses Russian soft power through the framework of Soviet soft power, bound up with readings of Russia as still somehow part of a Soviet, communist ideology. Strukov here understands soft power agency, of the kind demonstrated by the success of *Masha and the Bear*, as 'ongoing, networked and cross-platform', allowing him to theorise (Russian) soft power in the twenty-first century as that of world-building: 'a way to create and sustain long-term engagement of users with a fictional universe which extends beyond existing notions and forms of cultural exchange'.

Continuing the discussions of transnational filmmaking and complementing the analysis conducted by Lim in Chapter 1 on the soft power impact of China's foray into co-productions with US-based majors, Chris Homewood in Chapter 5, 'The Limits of Hollywood as an Instrument of Chinese Public Diplomacy and Soft Power', explores China's recent attempts to utilise the soft power potential of Hollywood by using a strategic narratives approach. Citing Roselle et al. (2014), Homewood determines that 'Strategic narrative *is* soft power in the 21st century', but that in the case of China, when it comes to co-productions, its story is not winning. He concludes that big-budget films may accommodate and even endorse Chinese strategic narratives but they renege on the idea of a major reorganisation of global political space, ultimately operating to contain China in a dependent role vis-à-vis the United States. China is accepted and promoted as a responsible stakeholder in global affairs but *under* US leadership, which these films work to persuade audiences is still needed most to advance global security and prevent international system chaos.

For Homewood, too, the credibility of this positively framed (yet safely contained) understanding of China and its place in the world faces mounting competition from other Western sources of China information, few of which seem to share Hollywood's affirmative stance.

Returning to the Russian context and state-driven soft power initiatives, Stephen Norris in Chapter 6, 'The Second World War, Soviet Sports and Furious Space Walks: Soft Power and Nation Branding in the Putin 2.0 Era', points to the dual purpose of government-endorsed filmmaking: international recognition and, more importantly, the playing of a key role in domestic soft power exercises. Norris thus identifies a 'recalibration' post 2012 of the role that film plays in building a positive image of Russia, and particularly under the influence of Culture Minister Vladimir Medinskii, who is seen to interfere directly in film production and distribution, with a view to promoting a positive image of the nation.

In Chapter 7, 'Popular Geo-politics, Strategic Narratives and Soft Power in *Viking* (2016) and *Guardians* (2017)', Robert Saunders continues the analysis of Russia's use of big-budget films. Specifically, Saunders considers how the adaptation of profitable Western cinematic styles, such as the neo-noir superhero film and the medieval soap opera, is part of a project to revivify Russia's role as a major force in the world. As he explores, however, the films in question also invite counter-readings that could undermine their ability to influence.

In 'The South African Soft Power Narrative, Cinema and Participatory Video' Paul Cooke in Chapter 8 argues that 'as the country's economic power has faltered, the soft power of this narrative, as well as the concomitant set of values it communicates to the world, has become all the more important'. Like the UK, India and a number of other countries beyond the scope of this volume, South African soft power is discussed and developed within a national branding scheme ('Brand South Africa'). Like the more forcefully orchestrated and more generously funded nation-building pretensions of the Russian historical films discussed in Chapter 6, these South African soft power initiatives are designed to play a significant role in national cohesion. Cooke's chapter highlights a number of structural issues that make using film as a soft power tool challenging. These include a focus on the part of government film agencies on foreign investment in so-called runaway productions, and self-censorship on the part of film-makers who are encouraged to avoid impacting the nation's strategic narrative of progress, the overcoming of adversity and the rainbow nation.

While ostensibly tied only to tourism, India's equivalent government-led 'branding' initiative, Incredible India, has proved to be very successful, yet in Chapter 9 Rachel Dwyer highlights how India's soft power has been most successfully channelled through non-state organisations, film being the leading example. In 'New Myths for an Old Nation: Bollywood, Soft Power and Hindu Nationalism', Dwyer recognises that India is 'an easy country to market in terms of soft power', but, at the same time, its 'view of itself and that from outside changed with Prime Minister Narendra Modi's election in 2014 and his subsequent landslide victory in 2019'. Like Brazil, it has witnessed a dramatic shift to the right, a rejection of a socialist vision, and the promotion of reactionary views on gender, sexuality and religion. How, then, Dwyer asks, can soft power handle the current negative images of India overseas? In her chapter, Dwyer ponders the ruling government's failure to embrace Bollywood for the purposes of soft power projection. Perhaps, she argues, 'it is because it expends more energy in an almost obsessive zeal to tame it, especially where depictions of the nation and Muslims are concerned'. Like Russian, Chinese and South African cinema, then, film in India is recognised as playing a role in domestic cohesion (and that of the important diaspora, in the case of India), which has implications for film's use as (external) soft power asset.

In the final chapter in this volume, our focus shifts away from the BRICS countries to one of the world's soft power superpowers. In 'Soft Power and National Cinema: James Bond, "GREAT" Britain and Brexit', Andrew Higson analyses the use made by the UK's GREAT branding campaign of the globally recognised film franchise James Bond, most recently starring Daniel Craig. As Higson argues,

> Despite the evident investment by Hollywood in the films and the transnationalism of their production, the Craig/Bond films [are] repeatedly mobilised as national totems in political debates about global Britain, co-opted into a soft power play that was designed to promote a persuasive and attractive image of the UK as a leading global player.

Higson demonstrates how Bond can be seen to represent a post-Brexit vision of Britain, ready to branch out in new directions beyond the European Union. Higson then highlights issues discussed in other chapters in this volume which serve to challenge the seemingly watertight case for soft power effectiveness of the 'Bond is Great' campaign, such as the impact of the use of 'reductive, non-complex images and narratives of the nation for consumption', the uncertainty of attribution (do global audiences always identify Bond as British?), and the ever-present possibility of alternative readings of national narratives as presented on screen.

Notes

1. A number of authors in the volume contributed to a special issue of *New Cinemas* film journal entitled 'Soft Power, Film Culture and the BRICS' (Cooke 2016). See also Dennison (2018).
2. The sought-after but still elusive soft power goal was a much-coveted permanent seat on the UN Security Council. See Stuenkel and Taylor 2015; Spektor 2016; Amorim 2017.
3. Nye cites, by way of example, US actions in Iraq at the time of writing, but the argument could equally apply in the present day to the unpopular aspects of the Trump administration.
4. The relationship between soft power and public diplomacy has been presented in contradictory ways. For Chitty (2017: 1), soft power and public diplomacy are 'conjoined twins', while Louw (2017: 305) describes soft power as 'outsourced public diplomacy'. For the purposes of simplicity, we see successful soft power as the *end result* of a process that can include assets generated by non-state actors, as well as state-driven nation branding and public diplomacy strategies.
5. See Wee (2020) and Ramscar (2020).

Works Cited

Albert, Eleanor (2018), 'China's Big Bet on Soft Power', *Council on Foreign Relations*, 9 February, <https://www.cfr.org/backgrounder/chinas-big-bet-soft-power> (last accessed 11 November 2020).

Amorim, Celso (2017), *Acting Globally: Memoirs of Brazil's Assertive Foreign Policy*. Lanham, MD: Hamilton Books.

Anholt, Simon (2010), 'Editorial: What Makes a Good Story?', *Place Branding and Public Diplomacy*, 6, 263–7.

Anholt, Simon (2020), Tweet, 27 March, <https://twitter.com/simonanholt/status/1243489717347368960> (last accessed 11 November 2020).

Arquilla, John, and David Ronfeldt (2001), *Networks and Netwars: The Future of Terror, Crime, and Militancy*. Santa Monica: RAND Corporation.

BBC (2020), 'Trump: Iran "Standing Down" After Missile Strikes', *BBC Online*, 9 January, <https://www.bbc.co.uk/news/world-us-canada-51039520> (last accessed 11 November 2020).

British Council (2020), 'Soft Power and COVID-19', May, <https://www.britishcouncil.org/research-policy-insight/insight-articles/soft-power-COVID-19> (last accessed 11 November 2020).

Chitty, Naren (2017),'Soft Power, Civic Virtue and World Politics', in N. Chitty, L. Ji, G. D. Rawnsley and C. Hayden (eds), *The Routledge Handbook of Soft Power*. London and New York: Routledge, pp. 9–36.
Cooke, Paul (ed.) (2016), 'Soft Power, Film Culture and the BRICS', special issue of *New Cinemas*, 14:1.
Davis, Wyre (2016), 'Has the Olympics Been a Success for Brazil?', *BBC News Online*, 20 August, <https://www.bbc.co.uk/news/world-latin-america-37133278> (last accessed 11 November 2020).
Dennison, Stephanie (2018), Film: *Film and Soft Power*, UK, <https://www.youtube.com/watch?v=Z8dWQNPDcXk> (last accessed 11 November 2020).
Fehimovic, Dunja, and Rebecca Ogden (eds) (2018), *Branding Latin America: Strategies, Aims, Resistance*. Lanham, MD: Lexington Books.
Forwood, Thomas (2020), 'UK Arts Funders Unlock Crisis Grants After Coronavirus – But at What Cost?', *The Art Newspaper*, 5 June, <https://www.theartnewspaper.com/analysis/uk-arts-funders-unlock-crisis-grants-after-coronavirus-but-at-what-cost> (last accessed 11 November 2020).
Gill, Bates (2020), 'China's Global Influence: Post-COVID Prospects for Soft Power', *The Washington Quarterly*, 43:2, 97–115.
Guerini, Elaine (2020), 'Brazil's Filmmakers Face Double Challenge as Covid Compounds Funding Crisis', *Screen Daily*, 24 July, <https://www.screendaily.com/news/brazils-filmmakers-face-double-challenge-as-covid-compounds-funding-crisis/5151788.article> (last accessed 11 November 2020).
Gupta, Vivek (2020), 'Digital Bollywood: Can Amazon and Netflix Save Indian Cinema?', *Nikkei Asia*, 31 July, <https://asia.nikkei.com/Business/Business-Spotlight/Digital-Bollywood-Can-Amazon-and-Netflix-save-Indian-cinema> (last accessed 11 November 2020).
Harbord, Janet (2002), *Film Culture*. London: Sage.
HM Government (2014), *Persuasion and Power in the Modern World*, <https://publications.parliament.uk/pa/ld201314/ldselect/ldsoftpower/150/15002.htm> (last accessed 11 November 2020).
Inman, Phillip (2012), 'Brazil's Economy Overtakes UK to Become World's Sixth Largest', *Guardian*, 6 March, <https://www.theguardian.com/business/2012/mar/06/brazil-economy-worlds-sixth-largest> (last accessed 11 November 2020).
Johnson, Matt (2013), 'What China and Russia Don't Get About Soft Power', *Foreign Policy*, 29 April, <https://foreignpolicy.com/2013/04/29/what-china-and-russia-dont-get-about-soft-power/> (last accessed 11 November 2020).
Kim, Sohee, and Jiyye Lee (2020), Shock 'Parasite' Oscar Showcases Korea's Soft Power, *Bloomberg*, 10 February, <https://www.bloomberg.com/news/articles/2020-02-10/shock-oscar-for-parasite-showcases-korea-s-growing-soft-power> (last accessed 11 November 2020).
Kissinger, Henry (2020), 'The Coronavirus Pandemic Will Forever Alter the World Order', *Wall Street Journal*, 3 April, <https://www.wsj.com/articles/

the-coronavirus-pandemic-will-forever-alter-the-world-order-11585953005> (last accessed 11 November 2020).

Kohli-Khandekar, Vanita (2013), 'Hard Facts About Soft Power', Paper presented at the University of Westminster, September.

Kohn, Eric (2020), 'Jia Zhangke's New Movie Delayed by Coronavirus, Talks Outbreak's Impact on China's Film Industry', *Indiewire*, 21 February, <https://www.indiewire.com/2020/02/coronavirus-jia-zhangke-berlin-1202212612/> (last accessed 11 November 2020).

Lee, Claire (2020), '"Parasite" Oscar Success Opens New Era', *yahoo news*, 11 February, <https://uk.news.yahoo.com/parasite-oscar-success-opens-era-085522675.html> (last accessed 11 November 2020).

Louw, P. Eric (2017), 'When Soft Power Success and "Attractiveness" Cannot Be Sustained: Zimbabwe and South Africa as Case Studies of the Limits of Soft Power', in N. Chitty, L. Ji, G. D. Rawnsley and C. Hayden (eds), *The Routledge Handbook of Soft Power*. London and New York: Routledge, pp. 305–14.

Merz, Theo (2020), 'Russia Will Only Screen "Light-hearted" Films When Cinemas Open', *The Telegraph*, 24 July, <https://www.telegraph.co.uk/news/2020/07/24/russia-will-screen-light-hearted-films-cinemas-open/> (last accessed 11 November 2020).

Murthy, C. H. S. N. (2017), 'Bollywood Enabling India as a Soft Power?', in N. Chitty, L. Ji, G. D. Rawnsley and C. Hayden (eds), *The Routledge Handbook of Soft Power*. London and New York: Routledge, pp. 358–68.

NFVF (2020), 'NFVF COVID-19 Relief Fund', <https://www.nfvf.co.za/home/index.php?ipkMenuID&ipkArticleID=722> (last accessed 11 November 2020).

Nilsen, Alf Gunvald, and Karl Von Holdt (2020), 'BRICS and COVID: Rising Powers in a Time of Pandemic', *The Wire*, 24 July, <https://thewire.in/world/brics-and-covid-rising-powers-in-a-time-of-pandemic> (last accessed 11 November 2020).

Nye, Joseph S., Jr (1990), *Bound to Lead: The Changing Nature of American Power*. New York: Basic Books.

Nye, Joseph S., Jr (2004), *Soft Power: The Means to Success in World Politics*. New York: Public Affairs.

Nye, Joseph S., Jr (2011), *The Future of Power*. New York: Public Affairs.

Nye, Joseph S., Jr (2019), 'Soft Power and the Public Diplomacy Revisited', The Hague Journal of Diplomacy, 14, 1–14.

Nye, Joseph S., Jr (2020), 'No, the Coronavirus Will Not Change the Global Order', *Foreign Policy*, 16 April, <https://foreignpolicy.com/2020/04/16/coronavirus-pandemic-china-united-states-power-competition/> (last accessed 11 November 2020).

Ramscar, Helen (2020), 'Vaccine Nationalism: The Ugly Face of Science and Politics', *RUSI*, 17 August, <https://rusi.org/commentary/vaccine-nationalism-ugly-face-science-and-politics> (last accessed 11 November 2020).

Reuters (2020), 'Coronavirus Outbreak: Russian Cinemas' Proposed Upgrades Stalled as Govt Redirects Funds for COVID-19 Treatment', *First Post*, 9 July, <https://www.firstpost.com/entertainment/coronavirus-outbreak-russian-cinemas-proposed-upgrades-stalled-as-govt-redirects-funds-for-covid-19-treatment-8576971.html> (last accessed 11 November 2020).

Roselle, Laura, Alister Miskimmon and Ben O'Loughlin (2014), 'Strategic Narrative: A New Means to Understand Soft Power', *Media, War & Conflict*, 7:1, 70–84.

Roy, Anjali Gera, and Chua Beng Huat (2012), *Travels of Bollywood Cinema: From Bombay to LA*. Delhi: Oxford University Press India.

Sarukhan, Arturo (2016), 'I Say Poder Suave, You Say Soft Power', *CPD Blog*, 16 June, <https://www.uscpublicdiplomacy.org/blog/i-say-poder-suave-you-say-soft-power> (last accessed 11 November 2020).

Spektor, Matias (2016), 'Brazil: Shadows of the Past and Contested Ambitions', in William I. Hitchcock, Melvyn P. Leffler and Jeffrey W. Legro (eds), *Shaper Nations: Strategies for a Changing World*. Cambridge, MA: Harvard University Press, pp. 17–35.

Stuenkel, Oliver, and Matthew M. Taylor (eds) (2015), *Brazil on the Global Stage: Power, Ideas, and the Liberal International Order*. Palgrave/MacMillan: New York.

The Times (2020), 'The Times View on South Korea's Oscar Win: Prize Fight', *The Times*, 11 February, <https://www.thetimes.co.uk/article/the-times-view-on-south-koreas-oscar-win-prize-fight-gn5vm235d> (last accessed 11 November 2020).

Voci, Paola, and Luo Hui (eds) (2018), *Screening China's Soft Power*. Abingdon: Routledge.

Wee, Sui-Lee (2020), 'From Asia to Africa, China Promotes Its Vaccines to Win Friends', *New York Times*, 11 September, <https://www.nytimes.com/2020/09/11/business/china-vaccine-diplomacy.html> (last accessed 11 November 2020).

Yimou, Zhang (2016), Film: *The Great Wall*, China/USA/Hong Kong/Australia/Canada.

Zhang, Chang, and Ruiqin Wu (2019), 'Battlefield of Global Ranking: How Do Power Rivalries Shape Soft Power Index Building?', *Global Media and China*, 4:2, 179–202.

CHAPTER 1

Soft Power and Cinema: A Methodological Reflection and Some Chinese Inflections

Song Hwee Lim

Three decades have passed since Joseph S. Nye, Jr, proposed the notion of soft power, defined as the ability, which 'arises from the attractiveness of a country's culture, political ideals, and policies', to 'get what you want through attraction rather than coercion or payments' (2004: x).[1] Since then, scholarship building on the notion has grown to the extent that a separate chapter would be needed simply to account for that body of literature. A recent anthology, at nearly 500 pages and with sections dedicated to theoretical and methodological considerations, as well as to case studies drawn from across the world, provides a glimpse into the current state of such scholarship. In the introduction to the anthology, Naren Chitty notes from the outset that the term 'soft power' has had a 'mixed reception, especially in academia', partly because the effects of soft power 'in the hard sense of so many bucks producing so much soft bang are tantalizingly difficult to prove' (2017: 1). It is in this context that this chapter, by zooming in on the exercise of soft power through the specific cultural form of cinema, stages a reflection on methodological issues surrounding the term 'soft power'; it uses as its lens cinema produced in China, which brings with it particular inflections on both the notion of soft power and its deployment.

Among the five countries constituting the membership of BRICS, the People's Republic of China (PRC) can claim to have had a disproportionate amount of attention paid to its relationship to soft power. In a special issue on the BRICS and soft power in the *Journal of Political Power*, the guest editors acknowledge in their introduction that, '[t]hough much has been said about the growing importance of the BRICS, little has been said (outside of analysis on China) about how the bloc members fare in terms of soft power' (Chatin and Gallarotti 2016: 336). The huge amount of attention that China has attracted in the study of soft power cannot be divorced, of course, from the country's staggering rise in the global economic order, as it overtook Japan in 2010 to become the second-largest economy in the world. Moreover, such devoted attention from global observers of China's relationship to soft power corresponds to a rising interest in the discourse of soft power within China itself. Not only has the term been cited, since as early as 2004, as something China should strive for by top political leaders in high-profile meetings (Lai 2012: 2), but its Chinese translation (*ruan shili*) had appeared, by December 2010, on over 14 million websites, a figure generated by a search on Baidu, the most widely used search engine in China (ibid.: 11). Besides the Chinese state's expressed desire to promote its soft power on the global stage, soft power also has 'an internal dimension', as the state can, through its culture industry, 'stabilize internal politics and social conditions' (Fung 2016: 3017).

The specific role that cinema has played (or can play) in the exercise of soft power, however, remains underexplored in academia – until recently. When the international network 'Soft Power, Cinema and the BRICS' was formed in 2015 (under the aegis of which most of the research in this volume was conducted), it might have justifiably envisaged the planned publication of this volume to become the first book on the subject of the relationship between soft power and cinema – not just in the BRICS countries but also in general. Not any more. *Screening China's Soft Power*, edited by Paola Voci and Luo Hui (2018a), has beaten this volume to the finish line. Unsurprisingly, China is the candidate for this academic sprinter, a testament to the currency of conducting research on matters relating to China at this historical juncture. Indeed, the rapidly expanding list of publications on China's relationship to soft power makes the writing of this chapter an increasingly daunting task with each passing month.[2] My aim in this chapter is to provide more than a case study of Chinese cinema's soft power (or lack thereof) by drawing out wider implications for the interrogation of the relationship between soft power and cinema on both conceptual and methodological fronts.

Agent, Affect, Effect: Rethinking Soft Power's Methodology

The first question to ask in relation to the raison d'être for both our international research network and this volume is: why soft power? To what extent and in what ways does the notion of soft power lend a new analytical angle to the study of cinema? In other words, what can the notion of soft power explain and explicate that previous concepts, approaches and methodologies could not? What insights into the production, distribution, exhibition, consumption and reception of films does it offer that are missing elsewhere? More pertinently for my purpose here, what are the methodological advantages and limitations in using this notion? Given that the difficulty of measuring effect is foregrounded as one of the chief methodological discontents in the study of soft power, how can the deployment of the concept improve on existing approaches to audience and reception research in the disciplines of film, media and communication studies?

It is clear that the study of soft power – currently conducted mainly by social scientists – is predominantly interested in tracing the effect of soft power generated by agents' initiatives. Nye, for example, places emphasis on the source of the soft power flow – that is, the role of agents, particularly institutions (both governmental and non-governmental) – thus lending itself comfortably to research fields such as cultural policy studies. Nye locates the resources that produce soft power in 'the values an organization or country expresses in its culture, in the examples it sets by its internal practices and policies, and in the way it handles its relations with others' (2004: 8). However, despite its aims and claims, one critique I would make of Nye's work is precisely that it does not trace the soft power flow of any single cultural product, political value, institution or policy from start to finish; as such, the randomness of and lack of causality in its examples reinforce the impression of the rather slipshod use of the notion of soft power. Counterbalancing an overemphasis on agents, Li Ji, in her overview chapter of the section on 'methodological problems' in the above-mentioned anthology on soft power, calls for a two-directional evaluation of soft power effectiveness that encompasses 'agents' resources, capabilities and behaviors, along with subjects' perceptions, affections and behaviors towards soft power exerted by agents' (Ji 2017: 78). Ji's model complements Nye's work by also paying attention to the reception end of the equation, though I would stress the need to formulate a relationship – and a causal one at that – between agents and effect.

I propose, instead, a three-pronged approach to the study of soft power by introducing affect as a missing but crucial factor in mediating soft power transactions. Whilst Ji's former direction corresponds to Nye's emphasis and my first keyword (agent) in this section's subheading, and whereas her latter direction overlaps with my second (affect) and third (effect) keywords, I have placed affect as a distinct category, not only because it differs in meaning from what Ji calls 'affections' but, more importantly, because, as a form of mediating environment, it underpins the conversion process from agents to effect in a fundamental manner, upon which I shall expand in the next section.[3] If soft power 'rests on the ability to shape the preferences of others' (Nye 2004: 5), my three-pronged model will trace, firstly, the agents, institutions and mechanisms that set out or are deployed to shape such preferences; secondly, the affective environment governing the preponderance for certain preferences; and thirdly, the ways in which these preferences are materialised, and their effects detected and measured.

By bringing the notion of affect into the equation, my contribution from a humanities perspective is to raise the awareness that soft power cannot be studied purely in instrumental and quantitative terms. Moreover, grounding my approach to the examination of cinema as a soft power tool, rather than treating, as many existing practices within film and media studies do, processes of production, consumption and reception as separate entities, my other aim is to link these processes up as a continuous and interrelated flow. In this, I find soft power a useful conceptual holder for a thorough tracking from agent (institutions of production) to affect (interfacing the encounter between text and audience during consumption) and effect (audience response) so that a fuller picture of a film's trajectory from inception to reception can be painted.

Among the three keywords in the subheading for this section, effect needs to be addressed first and foremost because it is, as noted before, the main source of discontent about the employment of soft power as a methodological tool for academic investigation. Two questions immediately stand out: what counts as effects and how can effects be detected or measured? For Ji, effects of soft power practices manifest 'on two parameters (cognition and behavior) of actors at three levels (individual actors, institutional actors and state actors)' (2017: 83). She further suggests three scales for evaluating soft power effects: namely, emotion/sentiment measured by empirical evidence such as poll, survey and questionnaire; perception/opinion revealed through content and discourse analysis; and behaviour studied via big data and framing analysis (ibid.: 84–5). I will address the first question of what counts as effects below, linking it to the conversion process from agent to effect using the example of the Chinese film *The Great Wall* (*Changcheng*, dir. Zhang Yimou, 2016). The second question on how effects can be detected or measured will be dealt with in the next section, where I bring affect in as the mediating factor between agent and effect.

On the first question of what counts as effects, the range of evidence that can be summoned is perhaps a bone of contention for scholars who are wary about the use of soft power as an analytical tool. While Ji maps out a rather comprehensive model for evaluating soft power effects, any study of a soft power strategy, policy or product cannot possibly demonstrate all the evidence corresponding to the myriad parameters, levels and scales she proposes. A political scientist such as Nye clearly favours hard data: the ten bullet-point social indices he lists as examples of US soft power resources are all quantifiable numbers (2004: 33–4). Sociologist

Chua Beng Huat, in his book *Structure, Audience and Soft Power in East Asian Pop Culture*, argues that the effectiveness of soft power 'can only be verified and substantiated by empirical evidence of audience behavior subsequent to reception; there should be evidence of changes in attitude in the audience towards the exporting nation' (2012: 121). The emphasis on hard data and empirical evidence by Nye and Chua betrays a disciplinary or methodological inclination that is alien to a humanities scholar like myself. Yet, discourse analysis such as Ji's use of Erving Goffman's framing analysis (Ji 2017: 85–9) also strikes me as too schematic and instrumentalist, as if every discourse can be explained (away) by a framework and every effect indicated – with remedies recommended, no less. Claims about (or, at least, gestures towards) certainty of findings and credibility of methodologies seem to be the hallmark of such social science disciplines, whereas scholarship in the humanities is typically marked by ambivalence, ambiguity and speculation.[4]

Nevertheless, let me use the example of *The Great Wall* to demonstrate what an analysis in the conventional methodology of tracing the conversion process from agent to effect might look like before venturing, in the next section, to propose affect as an alternative way of mediating soft power. In terms of agent, the film was produced by Legendary East, the Chinese subsidiary of Legendary Entertainment, which was bought for USD 3.5 billion by China's Dalian Wanda Group in 2016 (Brzeski 2016).[5] The group's chairman, billionaire Wang Jianlin, is fully cognizant of the role his conglomerate plays in promoting China's soft power, mentioning the term in a speech he delivered in Beijing in 2016 (Wanda Group 2016). To date, the group's efforts in accumulating soft power resources have been exercised primarily through hard economic power. Prior to buying the production house Legendary Entertainment, Wanda acquired AMC Entertainment, the second-largest theatre chain in the United States, for USD 2.6 billion in 2012, resulting in Wanda owning 432 theatres (including 338 from AMC) with 5,670 screens in the US (Stewart 2012). In 2016, the Wanda-owned AMC bought Carmike, the number-four circuit in North America, for USD 1.2 billion, thus surpassing Regal Entertainment to become the biggest cinema chain in the US (Faughnder 2016). Taken together, the acquisition of a film studio and two cinema chains ensures that the China-owned group can produce films with its desired content and secure market penetration in terms of distribution and exhibition of these films in the US.

In terms of effect, the representative indicators of soft power conversion for cinema would include overseas box-office intake, positive reviews and film awards. With an estimated production budget of USD

150 million or more, *The Great Wall* was, at the time, the most expensive film made in China and the biggest China–Hollywood co-production ever (Brzeski 2016). Directed by the PRC's officially ordained filmmaker Zhang Yimou (who choreographed the opening ceremony of the 2008 Beijing Olympics) and starring the American A-list actor Matt Damon, the film opened in the US (the world's biggest film market) on 17 February 2017 on 3,328 screens, with a weekend box-office intake of USD 18,469,620. A month later, on 17–23 March, its release had been reduced to 439 screens with a weekend gross of USD 456,640; when it closed on 6 April, it took in only USD 98,490 from 104 screens.[6] In total, the film's box-office intake was USD 45,157,105 in North America and USD 334,550,106 worldwide. With China's intake of USD 170,962,106 constituting more than half of the overall figure, it can be concluded that *The Great Wall*, whether viewed as an American or a Chinese film, has failed on the soft power front *for China*.[7] That is to say, viewed as a Chinese film directed by Zhang Yimou, its dismal box-office intake in North America and worldwide (excluding China) would barely cover its production budget; conversely, viewed as an American film starring Matt Damon, its massive intake in China would attest precisely to US rather than Chinese soft power. Both interpretations, however, are complicated by the fact that the film was directed by Zhang and produced by the Wanda-owned Legendary East; thus, the Chinese box-office figure could also be read, in part, as a form of internal soft power consumption.

Two other realms of evidence for soft power effects in relation to cinema are audience response (from formal reviews to informal reactions on social media) and film awards. *The Great Wall* was almost universally panned upon its release, with critics across the Atlantic describing it as 'Zhang Yimou's damp squib of a gunpowder plot' (2 out of 5 stars; Bradshaw 2017) as well as Matt Damon's battle with 'blockbuster-audience boredom' (1.5 out of 4 stars; Travers 2017), making it one of the worst-reviewed films in Damon's career of nearly thirty years (Slane 2017). The film's reception in China was equally negative, despite its box-office result. In fact, the Golden Broom Awards for the worst Chinese films (China's answer to the US Golden Raspberry Awards, or Razzies) not only handed *The Great Wall*'s lead actress Jing Tian the Most Disappointing Actress award, it even had to invent a new category of the Most Heart-breaking Film of the Year for the film itself (Hsia 2017). It is apparent that the film's soft power ambition did not convert into many positive outcomes, whether internationally or domestically.

Affect as Method

Having conducted a more conventional analysis by tracing the conversion process from agent to effect, I propose, in this section, affect as an alternative method for appreciating the operation of soft power. If, according to Nye, 'in behavioral terms soft power is attractive power' (2004: 6), which can be concretised as '*likable features*' that include a country's cultures and values (Voci and Luo 2018b: 2; emphasis in original), there is arguably a 'mismatch between soft power's stated goals (i.e. succeeding in world politics) and some of the key means through which soft power is developed and deployed (cultural practices and values)' (ibid.: 2). As Voci and Luo insightfully point out, 'Cultures and values are neither simply containable nor fully controllable by the state; they are shaped by hybrid local and global belongings that transcend a country's national borders' (ibid.: 2). Thus, understanding how cultures and values are transmitted from country to country – indeed, how likeable features pass from body to body (both individual and collective) – is key to unpicking the underlying working mechanisms of soft power.

I believe the notion of affect can help us explain the mediating environment that fundamentally underpins any cultural flow and communicative process. As such, we can shift the focus of analysis from specific strategies adopted by agents or the measurement of effects to an understanding of affect: that is, how and why people are moved by certain objects. On the notion of affect, Eric Shouse (2005) suggests that 'the pleasure that individuals derive from music has less to do with the communication of meaning, and far more with the way that a particular piece of music "moves" them', generating perceptible bodily effects such as changes in 'facial expression, respiration, tone of voice, and posture'. Affects are, therefore, '[l]iterally moving things – things that are in motion and that are defined by their capacity to affect and to be affected' (Stewart 2007: 4). Nevertheless, 'affects need objects to come into being' (Flatley 2008: 16), and they 'have to be mapped through different, coexisting forms of composition, habituation, and event' (Stewart 2007: 4). Like invisible air permeating an atmosphere, affects 'pick up density and texture as they move through bodies, dreams, dramas, and social workings of all kinds. Their significance lies in the intensities they build and in what thoughts and feelings they make possible' (ibid.: 3).

I will illustrate the implications of affect-as-method for the study of soft power using the same example of *The Great Wall*. Rather than tracing (as I did in the previous section) the film's soft power flow from agent (institutions of production) to effect (box-office intake, review and award), an affective approach would instead spell out the mediating environment in which not only this particular Chinese film circulates but also the affective intensities that all things Chinese might generate. In this vein, a close reading to reveal the 'meaning' of the film text (the hallmark of humanities disciplines) would not be particularly useful because the importance of affect 'rests upon the fact that in many cases the message consciously received may be of less import to the receiver of that message than his or her non-conscious affective resonance with the *source* of the message' (Shouse 2005; emphasis mine). That is to say, it is not the film's message but rather the environment (including the object, its source and communicative events, its bodies of transmission and so on) in which the message is carried that ultimately embodies, emits and transmits affective intensities to the extent that the message itself can often be ignored. To misappropriate a famous construction by media theorist Marshall McLuhan, we might say that it is not the medium, but the affect, that is the message.[8]

Read in this light, for an understanding of how soft power operates, the inherent quality or meaning of *The Great Wall* is less relevant or important than the affective resonances the film has generated. As I noted from the outset, a study of China's exercise of its soft power cannot be separated from the concomitant demonstration of its hard power; indeed, my earlier account of Wanda's acquisition of soft power resources in the US evinces, precisely, that the tissue of soft power is very much predicated upon the muscle of hard power. It is also fair to say that China has an image problem on the international stage in so far as most Western reports on China tend to focus on, among others, the regime's human rights record (its repression of dissidents), its tense diplomatic relations with its neighbours (from animosity towards the Koreans and the Japanese to territorial disputes over the South China Sea), its standoff with Taiwan and its ambitious activities around the world (the 'Belt and Road Initiative').[9] The final aspect is particularly poignant for the US, the undisputed global superpower, as it watches every Chinese move with a combination of fear and trepidation, suspicion and threat, hostility and repulsion – affective resonances that permeate an environment in which a film such as *The Great Wall* would be received.

In her book *Ordinary Affects*, Kathleen Stewart draws on the work of Lauren Berlant to suggest that affects happen

> in impulses, sensations, expectations, daydreams, encounters, and habits of relating, in strategies and their failures, in forms of persuasion, contagion, and compulsion, in modes of attention, attachment, and agency, and in publics and social worlds of all kinds that catch people up in something that feels like *some*thing. (2007: 2; emphasis in original)

One instance in which people have been caught up 'in something that feels like *something*' was a concern voiced by some US legislators about 'the growing scope of foreign acquisitions in strategically important sectors in the US'. In a letter dated September 2016 to the Government Accountability Office, sixteen members of Congress cited Dalian Wanda's aforementioned acquisition of film studio and theatre chains as one example of such a concern, and asked specifically, 'Should the definition of national security be broadened to address concerns about propaganda and control of the media and "soft power" institutions?' (Tartaglione 2016).[10] If to attend to affects is 'to trace how the potency of forces lies in their immanence to things that are both flighty and hardwired, shifty and unsteady but *palpable* too' (Stewart 2007: 3; emphasis mine), in this instance these members of Congress clearly, to put it bluntly, smelled something fishy in Wanda's incursion into the US film industry, a something (foreign acquisition) that felt like *something* (propaganda and control).

Note that this letter, penned by US Congress members, is but one instance in which a particular affective resonance has been voiced, and that it is perhaps a culmination of many other impulses, observations, previously unarticulated thoughts and yet-to-be-named stirrings. It is in this sense that affects can be understood as a kind of permeating environment with a feedback loop,

> always amplifying, dampening, or otherwise modifying some other affect, or drive, or perception, or thought process, or act or behavior, resulting in a well-nigh infinite number of combinations between different affective microsystems and their feedback mechanisms in interaction with their environments. (Flatley 2008: 16)

It is also in this sense that affect is paradoxically both '*prepersonal*' and 'non-conscious' (Shouse 2005; emphasis in original) as well as a 'matter of drill, of learning to inhabit a structure of feeling' (Sharma and Tygstrup 2015: 16). In other words, if affect is 'the body's way of preparing itself for action in a given circumstance by adding a quantitative dimension of intensity to the quality of an experience' (Shouse 2005), it also 'has to do with the attunement of our being' and 'tinges or colours the way in which we take part in the environments we find ourselves placed into' (Sharma and Tygstrup 2015: 14).[11]

To return to the example of *The Great Wall*, regardless of the meaning of its content and the pull (or otherwise) of its director and stars, the very making of the film can be perceived as an occasion in which affective resonances towards the emergence and march of China – in pre-existing, prepersonal, paradoxical forms – coalesce to generate an environment that, to a certain extent, would predetermine the reception of the film. *The Great Wall* – both the film and the architectural structure after which it is named – is symptomatic of China's soft power ambition to conquer the US film industry and box office; it no longer stands as a historical, militaristic structure to keep out invading barbarians but rather a present-day, metaphorical platform from which China expands far beyond its borders. The affective 'message' becomes: the Chinese are coming, with their armies, weapons and gunpowder. Thus the film embodies, emits and transmits a sense of fear and threat (if not quite 'shock and awe') that, however 'unformed and unstructured' (Shouse 2005), is none the less palpable, penetrating the entire cinematic flow from production, distribution and exhibition to consumption and reception. This mode of analysis may not be able to provide empirical evidence or hard data as 'proof', but I hope to have demonstrated that, perhaps more than anything else, it is the intangible, unquantifiable and unverifiable operation of affective intensities that may eventually undermine the efforts of agents and render the measurement of effects a moot point. Failure to appreciate the mediation of affective atmosphere in the soft power conversion process would fundamentally thwart agents' strategies, in turn impacting the effect whose measure is always already circumscribed by affect.

Perception, Policy, Propaganda: Some Chinese Inflections

The affective atmosphere mapped out above allows us to delineate some inflections on the notion of soft power brought about by the specific ways that Chinese agents (in particular, the government) operate, which consequently have a bearing on how effects might turn out. The first inflection that the case of China poses for the study of soft power is perception. That is to say, what are the challenges of promoting soft power when one already has an image problem that stacks up against any such effort? As Nye notes, 'Hard and soft power sometimes reinforce and sometimes interfere with each other' (2004: 25), and the US witnessed a decline in its soft power when the country went to war in Iraq in the aftermath of the 11 September attacks (ibid.: 127). The Chinese inflection, however, shows that soft power efforts might even cancel each other out. One salient example is the establishment of Confucius Institutes, the criticism of which has already led to the closure of some outposts in North American universities (Peterson 2017).[12] Rather than contributing to China's soft power resource, Confucius Institutes have, in fact, been regarded as that 'something else' in the affective atmosphere mapped out above. For its part, the Chinese government is well aware of the need to change Western perceptions of the nation. One strategy is the commissioning of promotional films by the PRC's State Council Information Office and acquisition of airtime slots on public digital billboards in the US. On 17 January 2011, six big screens on New York's Time Square saw one such promotional film featuring, among others, National Basketball Association star Yao Ming and composer Tan Dun of *Crouching Tiger, Hidden Dragon* fame (China News 2011).[13] Change in perception takes time, and China's image deficit on the international stage will continue to undercut the nation's soft power efforts unless perception drastically improves.

The second inflection of the Chinese case is the extent to which the state formulates policies to promote – and, in some cases, intervene in – soft power strategies. Indeed, China's soft power policy formulation takes place at the highest level of government, and one study conflates the notion of soft power in the Chinese context with the notion of public diplomacy, defined as 'the cultivation by governments of public opinion in other nations' in the pursuit of their own 'national interests' (Kurlantzick 2007: 61). In October 2010 the Central Committee of the Chinese Communist Party (CCP) proposed an article under its Twelfth Five-Year Plan (2011–15), calling for 'a great development of culture and an increase in national soft power through inheriting quintessential elements of traditional culture, domestic innovation, exports of cultural products, and external media initiatives' (cited in Lai 2012: 12). So enamoured is China of the notion of soft power that it is now almost inseparable from President Xi Jinping's slogan of 'Chinese dream' (Voci and Luo 2018b: 5).

To zoom in on the specific relationship between soft power and cinema, Chinese political leaders have led the way in using cinema as a soft power tool in diplomatic relations. When President Xi visited Latin America in July 2014, he presented the Argentinian officials with copies of Chinese films and television drama series, including the 2011 box-office hit *Love Is Not Blind* (*Shilian sanshisan tian*, dir. Teng Huatao) (Beijing qingnian bao 2014). At a speech delivered at the Thai parliament during his visit in October 2013, Premier Li Keqiang cited the 2012 top-grossing film *Lost in Thailand* (*Ren zai jiongtu zhi Tai jiong*, dir. Xu Zheng) as an 'advert' for 'Chinese–Thai friendship', noting that Thailand is one of the most popular destinations among Chinese tourists (Phoenix TV 2013). These soft power gestures were, of course, accompanied by hard power treasures. Besides expressing interest in building the host country's high-speed railway, Li declared that China would, in the next five years, import one million tons of rice and more rubber from Thailand (Associated Press 2013). Xi's visit sealed a deal for Argentina 'to borrow USD 7.5 billion from China at a time when the Latin American country cannot tap global capital markets because of disputes over unpaid debt' (Reuters 2014). Hence, soft power and hard power go hand in hand, and it is difficult to ascertain the effects of China's soft power efforts when these are often part of a package sweetened with hard cash and investment.

Furthermore, such high-level attention paid to the role of cinema in promoting soft power can cut both ways. The Wanda Group had had some of its overseas investments – including the planned acquisition of Dick Clark Productions, the Hollywood producer behind the Golden Globe Awards – curtailed by the Chinese government as they were deemed to have breached restrictions (Bloomberg News 2017). Besides, when *The Great Wall* received a less than favourable reaction from netizens – the film scored a 5.2 rating (out of 10) on the film page of the popular search engine Douban (Huang 2016) – as well as negative reviews, official media (led by the CCP newspaper *People's Daily*) condemned these websites and critics as 'seriously destroying the eco-environment of Chinese cinema' (People's Daily 2016). Le Vision Pictures, one of the Chinese production companies behind the film, even sent a warning letter to the poster of an entry entitled 'Zhang Yimou is dead' on Weibo (the Chinese Twitter), threatening legal action if the post was not removed immediately and an apology not issued (Beijing ribao 2016). Official restrictions, condemnations and threats of legal action represent the hard tools that the Chinese government and those with vested interests are all too willing to wield, even in the arena of soft power.

In light of the above, the third inflection of the Chinese case for the study of soft power is whether film-related policies formulated by the state could or should be seen as a form of propaganda.[14] To put it differently, precisely because of the ways in which Chinese officials understand and wield soft power, the very boundary between notions of soft power and propaganda is often blurred to the extent that the two terms may have become indistinguishable from one another. Domestically, the Film Industry Promotion Law of the People's Republic of China, the first law in the Chinese cultural sector, took effect on 1 March 2017 (Chief Editor 2017). Among the five key aspects highlighted by the head of the Film Administration under the State Administration of Press, Publication, Radio, Film and Television (SAPPRFT) is the strengthening of 'exchanges between China and foreign countries to help Chinese films go global', with measures spelled out to 'further expand popularity and influence of Chinese films and elevate [the] international status of China as a film power' (ibid.). On the international front, a 'Great External Propaganda' campaign launched in 2009 (Hu 2017) saw the establishment of an English-language television news channel by the official Xinhua News Agency in 2010 (Dean 2010). In an opinion piece entitled 'Why China Is Weak on Soft Power', Nye (2012) reckons that China's attempt to 'imitate Al Jazeera' had had 'a limited return on its investment', as 'there is little international audience for brittle propaganda'. Global observers concur that China's external propaganda lacks credibility, which is 'key' to the success or effectiveness of soft power (Ji 2017: 77). Moreover, a contradiction exists between the content generated by China's creative industries and the government's censorship and other control mechanisms, the latter undermining the state's attempt to build 'an imitative "Chinawood" with the explicit goal of spreading its version of the China brand' (Fung 2016: 3012). The cocktail of negative perception by Western observers and Chinese government's policies that simultaneously promote propaganda and exercise censorship makes Chinese soft power a rather hard sell on the global stage

Conclusion

We can see traces of the three Chinese inflections to the notion of soft power in the example of *The Great Wall*: how wider perception of the film (not to mention the controversial casting of Matt Damon) and of China undermines the film's reception; how state policies both permit and limit the financial prowess of the non-state actor (the Wanda Group) in its transformation of the landscape of film production and consumption both at home and abroad; and how the state's propaganda machine and other apparatuses will intervene to help contain any negative impact on the nation's soft power venture. Taken together, *The Great Wall* illustrates the reasons that cinematic soft power matters to China as well as the stakes involved. To place it in a broader context, in 2012 the Chinese box office displaced the Japanese one to become the second-largest in the world (after the US) (BBC News 2013); hence, as a US–China co-production, *The Great Wall* is rightly seen as 'designed to bridge the world's two largest box office territories' (Brzeski 2016).[15] The film, however, is but one example of the Chinese ambition to make a global cinematic hit, regardless of the ethnicity of the director or the main actors. More recent attempts include the US–China co-production *Warcraft: The Beginning* (dir. Duncan Jones, 2016) and Chinese productions *Wolf Warrior* (*Zhan lang*, dir. Wu Jing, 2015) and *Wolf Warrior II* (*Zhan lang er*, dir. Wu Jing, 2017). As Aynne Kokas states in her book *Hollywood Made in China*, filmmakers in China 'are under pressure from regulators to produce global Chinese hits' (2017: 64). Therefore, *The Great Wall* is not a one-off but a sign of things to come: indeed, 'the new model for China–Hollywood collaboration' (Bloomberg News 2016).

A major challenge facing China's ambition to produce a global cinematic hit remains the gulf between the box-office intakes of its products in the domestic and foreign markets; or, to put it differently, top-grossing Chinese domestic films simply do not translate into box-office miracles elsewhere. Regardless of their modes of production, the top-grossing domestic films in recent years have been breaking box-office records at home, with Stephen Chow's *The Mermaid* (*Meirenyu*, 2016) becoming, in 2016, the first film to achieve the half-billion USD mark (Frater 2016).[16] This figure is a staggering rise compared to the top-grossing domestic films in the previous two years, whose intakes are around USD 382 million for *Monster Hunt* (*Zhuoyao ji*, dir. Raman Hui) in 2015 and USD 188 million for *Breakup Buddies* (*Xinhua lufang*, dir. Ning Hao) in 2014.[17] However, as an industry insider points out, '80 percent of Chinese box office growth from the past years comes from more movie theaters being built, and only 20 percent from Chinese films' quality improvement' (ibid.). More importantly, the foreign box-office intakes for the three films mentioned above are minuscule as a proportion of their total worldwide intakes, ranging from a mere 0.55 per cent for *Breakup Buddies* and 0.89 per cent for *Monster Hunt* to a slightly more respectable 4.87 per cent in the case of *The Mermaid*.[18] Compared to Hollywood blockbusters whose foreign intakes typically constitute between one-third to over one-half of their total intakes,[19] Chinese films clearly have a long way to go in demonstrating their soft power on a global scale.

Despite the immense efforts of Chinese agents in promoting cinema as a cultural tool and some impressive effects achieved domestically, the affective environment in which Chinese films operate globally does not appear to be conducive for China's exercise of soft power. In fact, the success of *Dangal* (dir. Nitesh Tiwari, 2016) – a Bollywood film which raked in USD 186.5 million in its forty-seven-day run in China, 'the first time that the box office for a Bollywood blockbuster in China has outperformed that of its home Indian market' (Hu 2017) – suggests that China might have to eat humble pie from its economically poorer neighbour when it comes to demonstrating the attractive (and affective) dimension of soft power, a gesture shown by President Xi who told the Indian Prime Minister Narendra Modi that he had watched the film and liked it (ibid.). Indeed, it is precisely the affective dimension (or its lack) in contemporary Chinese film that has had an effect on cinema's economic dimension in terms of box-office intakes. As Brian Massumi (1995: 106–7) argues in his reading of US ex-President Bill Clinton's failure to sell his health-care plan to the public because he was perceived to have lost his 'presidential' feel:

The ability of affect to produce an economic effect more swiftly and surely than economics itself means that affect is itself a real condition, an intrinsic variable of the late-capitalist system, as infrastructural as a factory. [. . .] Its ability to come second-hand, to switch domains and produce effects across them all, gives it a metaphorical ubiquity. [. . .]

This fact about affect – this matter-of-factness of affect – needs to be taken seriously into account in cultural and political theory. Don't forget.

The examples of *The Great Wall*, the Wanda Group and the PRC government have shown that the agents may be powerful and some of the effects astonishing, but affect cannot be bought by money alone. The affective environment that China's hard power manœuvres have generated is, from all the evidence I can gather, still rendering the performance of its soft power efforts rather flaccid. These Chinese inflections demonstrate that social science-oriented methodological tools are insufficient to account for the operation of soft power, even on its own empirical, quantitative terms. It is via the humanistic turn to the notion of affect, in all its ontological invisibility, metaphorical complexities and economic imperatives, that we can better appreciate why and how soft power works, precisely because affect is intrinsic in, rather than external to, agent, atmosphere and effect.

Notes

1. Note that Nye first mooted the notion in an earlier book. See Nye (1990).
2. For a critical survey of scholarship on Chinese soft power, see Voci and Luo (2018b: 4–8).
3. For a distinction between affect and affection (following Spinoza), see Massumi (1995), especially pp. 92–3.
4. As Yingjin Zhang notes in his afterword to the edited volume by Voci and Luo, 'Contrary to social scientists, cultural studies scholars prefer close textual analysis to data collection and compilation, and their attention to questions of multiplicity and heterogeneity [. . .] frequently reveal meanings in excess of the intended message in China's soft power projects' (Zhang 2018: 255).
5. The film's co-production companies include Atlas Entertainment, China Film Group, Dentsu, Fuji Television Network, Kava Productions, Le Vision Pictures and Legendary Entertainment. See the Internet Movie Database (IMDb), available at <http://www.imdb.com/title/tt2034800/companycredits?ref_=cons_tt_cocred_tt> (last accessed 4 December 2017).
6. See relevant pages on Box Office Mojo, available at <http://www.boxofficemojo.com/movies/?id=greatwall.htm> (last accessed 27 November 2017). Figures for US 'domestic' box office typically include intakes from Canada, hence my subsequent use of 'North America' in the main text.

7. The film's production history reveals an ironic twist in the cinematic exchange between China and the US. *The Great Wall* was initiated by Hollywood in 2011 by Legendary East, the Hong Kong offshoot of the American media firm Legendary Entertainment, with a story geared for the Chinese market (Hoskin 2017). However, as we now know, because Legendary Entertainment was subsequently bought by China's Wanda Group, the film suddenly transformed from a 'cultural import' to a 'cultural export', with Zhang Yimou brought on board to direct it and Matt Damon added for international appeal (ibid.).
8. For a recent theorisation of the relationship between affect and medium, see Bao (2015), particularly pp. 7–17.
9. It is important to qualify that opinion about China's global influence differs among continents, with countries in North America and Europe and its Asian neighbours tending towards the negative and those in Latin America and Africa viewing it more positively. In a recent Globe Scan (2017) poll conducted for the BBC, negative perception of China's influence is highest in the US (70 per cent), Spain (68 per cent), India and France (both 60 per cent), and positive perception highest in Nigeria (83 per cent), Pakistan and Kenya (both 63 per cent), and Mexico (55 per cent). See <https://www.globescan.com/news-and-analysis/press-releases/press-releases-2017/104-press-releases-2017/420-sharp-drop-in-world-views-of-us-uk-global-poll.html> (last accessed 20 November 2020).
10. I cite the final question from the letter by the Congress members, which is available for download in the report by Tartaglione (2016).
11. There are many theorisations of the notion of affect and they do not always agree with each other. For a summary of affective sources and orientations, see Seigworth and Gregg (2010: 5–9).
12. For one critique of the Confucius Institute, see Sahlins (2015).
13. Lasting 60 seconds in duration, the promotional film was aired fifteen times an hour from 6 a.m. to 2 a.m., clocking up a total of 300 screenings a day and 8,400 showings over a period of four weeks (China News 2011).
14. For an overview of the role of censorship, propaganda and film policy in the PRC and its relationship to the notion of soft power, see Johnson (2020).
15. Even ranked in second place, however, the Chinese box-office intake figure of USD 6.6 billion in 2016 was only slightly more than half of that of the leader, the US, whose figure was USD 11.4 billion (Hoskin 2017).
16. *The Mermaid*'s box-office intake in China is USD 526,848,189, according to Box Office Mojo: available at <http://www.boxofficemojo.com/movies/?page=intl&id=mermaid2016.htm> (last accessed 26 December 2017).
17. *Monster Hunt*'s box-office intake in China is USD 381,860,000 according to Box Office Mojo: available at <http://www.boxofficemojo.com/movies/?page=intl&id=monsterhunt.htm> (last accessed 26 December 2017). *Breakup Buddies*' box-office intake in China is USD 187,970,000, according to Box Office Mojo: available at <http://www.boxofficemojo.com/movies/?page=intl&id=breakupbuddies.htm> (last accessed 26 December 2017).

18. *The Mermaid*'s worldwide box-office intake is USD 553,810,228 (<http://www.boxofficemojo.com/movies/?id=mermaid2016.htm>), making its foreign intake USD 26,962,039. *Monster Hunt*'s worldwide box-office intake is USD 385,284,817 (<http//www.boxofficemojo.com/movies/?page=intl&id=monsterhunt.htm>), making its foreign intake USD 3,424,817; and *Breakup Buddies*' worldwide box-office intake is USD 189,017,596 (<http://www.boxofficemojo.com/movies/?page=intl&id=breakupbuddies.htm>), making its foreign intake USD 1,047,596 (all last accessed dates 26 December 2017). Note that the terms 'domestic' and 'foreign' on Box Office Mojo refer to different geographical regions from my discussion here, as China is regarded as 'domestic' and the rest of the world as 'foreign'.
19. The percentages of foreign box-office intakes to total intakes of top-grossing US films over the same periods are 49.6 for *Rogue One: A Star Wars Story* (2016, dir. Gareth Edwards; <http://www.boxofficemojo.com/movies/?id=starwars2016.htm>), 54.7 for *Star Wars Episode VII: The Force Awakens* (2015, dir. J. J. Abrams; <http://www.boxofficemojo.com/movies/?id=starwars7.htm>) and 36.0 for *American Sniper* (2014, dir. Clint Eastwood; <http://www.boxofficemojo.com/movies/?id=americansniper.htm>) (all last accessed dates 26 December 2017).

Works Cited

Associated Press (2013), 'Premier Li Keqiang Addresses Thai Parliament', *South China Morning Post*, 11 October, <http://www.scmp.com/news/china/article/1329530/premier-li-keqiang-addresses-thai-parliament> (last accessed 20 July 2020).

Bao, Weihong (2015), *Fiery Cinema: The Emergence of an Affective Medium in China, 1915–1945*. Minneapolis and London: University of Minnesota Press.

BBC News (2013), 'China Becomes World's Second-Biggest Movie Market', *BBC News*, 22 March, <http://www.bbc.com/news/business-21891631> (last accessed 20 July 2020).

Beijing qingnian bao (2014), 'Xi Jinping fang Lamei zeng Agenting guanyuan *Shilian sanshisan tian* DVD' (Xi Jinping Gives *Love Is Not Blind* DVD to Argentine Officials in Visit to Latin America), *Renmin wang*, 22 July, <http://politics.people.com.cn/n/2014/0722/c1001-25314547.html> (last accessed 20 November 2020).

Beijing ribao (2016), '*Changcheng* re zhengyi, yingpingren wuquan gantan "Zhang Yimou yi si" ma?' (*The Great Wall* Stirs Controversy, Do Film Critics Not Have a Right to Lament that 'Zhang Yimou is Dead?'), *Renmin wang*, 20 December, <http://sd.people.com.cn/n2/2016/1220/c172851-29486024.html> (last accessed 20 November 2020).

Bloomberg News (2016), 'Wanda's $150 Million "Great Wall" to Test China's Film Boom', *Bloomberg News*, 14 December, <https://www.bloomberg.com/news/articles/2016-12-13/wanda-s-150-million-great-wall-to-test-china-hollywood-films> (last accessed 20 July 2020).

Bloomberg News (2017), 'Wanda Deals in Jeopardy as China Scrutiny Mounts', *Bloomberg News*, 17 July, <https://www.bloomberg.com/news/articles/2017-07-17/china-is-said-to-punish-wanda-for-breaching-investment-rules-j57r4vzy> (last accessed 20 July 2020).

Bradshaw, Peter (2017), 'The Great Wall Review – Zhang Yimou's Damp Squib of a Gunpowder Plot', *The Guardian*, 16 February, <https://www.theguardian.com/film/2017/feb/16/the-great-wall-review-zhang-yimous-damp-squib-of-a-gunpowder-plot> (last accessed 20 July 2020).

Brzeski, Patrick (2016), '"The Great Wall": Why the Stakes Are Sky-High for Matt Damon's $150M China Epic', *The Hollywood Reporter*, 15 December, <http://www.hollywoodreporter.com/heat-vision/great-wall-why-stakes-are-sky-high-matt-damons-150m-chinese-epic-956396> (last accessed 20 July 2020).

Chatin, Mathilde, and Giulio M. Gallarotti (2016), 'The BRICS and Soft Power: An Introduction', *Journal of Political Power*, 9:3, 335–52.

Chief Editor (2017), 'Interpretation of the Film Industry Promotion Law with the Focus on Five Major Highlights', *The Chinese Film Market*, 8 February, <http://mag.chinesefilmmarket.com/en/article/interpretation-of-the-film-industry-promotion-law-with-the-focus-on-five-major-highlights/> (last accessed 20 July 2020).

China News (2011), 'Zhongguo guojia xingxiang xuanchuanpian zai Mei shoubo, chang yin youren zhuzu guanwang' (China National Image Promotional Film Premieres in the US, Frequently Attracting Tourists to Stop and Look), *China News*, 18 January, <http://www.chinanews.com/gn/2011/01-18/2793165.shtml> (last accessed 20 July 2020).

Chitty, Naren (2017), 'Introduction', in N. Chitty, L. Ji, G. D. Rawnsley and C. Hayden (eds), *The Routledge Handbook of Soft Power*. Abingdon and New York: Routledge, pp. 1–6.

Chua Beng Huat (2012), *Structure, Audience and Soft Power in East Asian Pop Culture*. Hong Kong: Hong Kong University Press.

Dean, Jason (2010), 'China's Xinhua to Launch English-language Station', *The Wall Street Journal*, 30 April, <https://www.wsj.com/articles/SB10001424052748703871904575216020649004914> (last accessed 20 July 2020).

Faughnder, Ryan (2016), 'China-owned AMC Seals Deal to Buy Carmike Cinemas, Making it the Largest Theater Chain in U.S.', *Los Angeles Times*, 15 November, <http://www.latimes.com/business/hollywood/la-fi-ct-amc-carmike-20161114-story.html> (last accessed 20 July 2020).

Flatley, Jonathan (2008), *Affective Mapping: Melancholia and the Politics of Modernism*. Cambridge, MA, and London: Harvard University Press.

Frater, Patrick (2016), '"The Mermaid" Reaches $500 Million at Chinese Box Office', *Variety*, 5 March, <https://variety.com/2016/film/asia/the-mermaid-500-million-at-chinese-box-office-1201723721/> (last accessed 20 July 2020).

Fung, Anthony (2016), 'Strategizing for Creative Industries in China: Contradictions and Tension in Nation Building', *International Journal of Communication*, 10, 3004–21.
Hoskin, Peter (2017), 'Hollywood Goes East', *The Spectator*, 1 April, <https://www.spectator.co.uk/article/hollywood-goes-east> (last accessed 20 July 2020).
Hsia, Heidi (2017), '"The Great Wall" Wins China's Razzies New Category', *Yahoo! Lifestyle*, 23 March, <https://sg.style.yahoo.com/great-wall-wins-chinas-razzies-032200261.html> (last accessed 20 July 2020).
Hu, Jianlong (2017), 'Bollywood Offers China Lessons on Soft Power', *South China Morning Post*, 1 July, <http://www.scmp.com/news/china/diplomacy-defence/article/2100682/bollywood-offers-china-lessons-soft-power> (last accessed 24 November 2017).
Huang, Yi-lun (2016), 'Yingpingren eyi fuping tuokua *Changcheng* piaofang? Guanfang jieru huhang xian wangyou lunzhan' (Malicious Bad Reviews by Film Critics Drag Down Box Office of *The Great Wall*? Official Intervention Stirs Debate Among Netizens), *Sanlih E-television News*, 30 December, <https://www.setn.com/News.aspx?NewsID=211916> (last accessed 20 November 2020).
Ji, Li (2017), 'Measuring Soft Power (Section Overview)', in N. Chitty, L. Ji, G. D. Rawnsley and C. Hayden (eds), *The Routledge Handbook of Soft Power*. Abingdon and New York: Routledge, pp. 75–92.
Johnson, Matthew (2020), 'Censorship, Propaganda and Film Policy', in Song Hwee Lim and Julian Ward (eds), *The Chinese Cinema Book*, 2nd edn. London: British Film Institute; New York: Bloomsbury, pp. 246–57.
Kokas, Aynne (2017), *Hollywood Made in China*. Oakland: University of California Press.
Kurlantzick, Joshua (2007), *Charm Offensive: How China's Soft Power Is Transforming the World*. New Haven, CT, and London: Yale University Press.
Lai, Hongyi (2012), 'Introduction: The Soft Power Concept and a Rising China', in H. Lai and Y. Lu (eds), *China's Soft Power and International Relations*. Abingdon: Routledge, pp. 1–20.
Massumi, Brian (1995), 'The Autonomy of Affect', *Cultural Critique*, 31, 83–109.
Nye, Joseph S., Jr (1990), *Bound to Lead: The Changing Nature of American Power*. New York: Basic Books.
Nye, Joseph S., Jr (2004), *Soft Power: The Means to Success in World Politics*. New York: Public Affairs.
Nye, Joseph S., Jr (2012), 'Why China Is Weak on Soft Power', *The New York Times*, 17 January, <http://www.nytimes.com/2012/01/18/opinion/why-china-is-weak-on-soft-power.html> (last accessed 20 July 2020).
People's Daily (2016), 'Renminribao pi Douban, Maoyan: Eping shanghai dianyi chanye' (*People's Daily* Criticizes Douban and Maoyan: Negative Criticism Hurts Film Industry), *Sina Net*, 28 December, <http://www.sina.com.cn/mid/hot/2016-12-28/doc-ifxyxury8902862.shtml> (last accessed 20 July 2020).

Peterson, Rachelle (2017), *Outsourced to China: Confucius Institutes and Soft Power in American Higher Education*. New York: National Association of Scholars.

Phoenix TV (2013), 'Li Keqiang zai Taiguo guohui yanjiang tiji *Tai jiong*' (Li Keqiang Mentions *Lost in Thailand* in Speech in Thai Parliament), *Zhongguo wenming wang*, 11 October, <http://www.wenming.cn/wmzh_pd/jj_wmzh/201312/t20131205_1621147.shtml> (last accessed 20 November 2020).

Reuters (2014), 'Xi Jinping Hails "New Horizons" for China and Argentina on Visit to Buenos Aires', *South China Morning Post*, 20 July, <http://www.scmp.com/news/china/article/1556670/xi-jinping-hails-new-horizons-china-and-argentina-visit-buenos-aires> (last accessed 20 July 2020).

Sahlins, Marshall (2015), *Confucius Institutes: Academic Malware*. Chicago: Prickly Paradigm Press.

Seigworth, Gregory J., and Melissa Gregg (2010), 'An Inventory of Shimmers', in Melissa Gregg and Gregory J. Seigworth (eds), *The Affect Theory Reader*. Durham, NC, and London: Duke University Press, pp. 1–25.

Sharma, Devika, and Frederik Tygstrup (2015), 'Introduction', in D. Sharma and F. Tygstrup (eds), *Structures of Feeling: Affectivity and the Study of Culture*. Berlin: De Gruyter, pp. 1–19.

Shouse, Eric (2005), 'Feeling, Emotion, Affect', *M/C Journal*, 8:6, <http://journal.media-culture.org.au/0512/03-shouse.php> (last accessed 20 July 2020).

Slane, Kevin (2017), '"The Great Wall" is One of the Worst-reviewed Films of Matt Damon's Career', *Boston Globe*, 17 February, <https://www.boston.com/culture/entertainment/2017/02/17/the-great-wall-is-one-of-the-worst-reviewed-films-of-matt-damons-career> (last accessed 20 July 2020).

Stewart, Andrew (2012), 'Wanda Group Acquires AMC Entertainment', *Variety*, 4 September, <http://variety.com/2012/film/news/wanda-group-acquires-amc-entertainment-1118058647/> (last accessed 20 July 2020).

Stewart, Kathleen (2007), *Ordinary Affects*. Durham, NC, and London: Duke University Press.

Tartaglione, Nancy (2016), 'Hollywood & China: U.S. Gov't Agency Agrees to Review Foreign Investment Panel', *Deadline Hollywood*, 4 October, <http://deadline.com/2016/10/china-hollywood-congress-wanda-foreign-ownership-gao-1201830426/> (last accessed 20 July 2020).

Travers, Peter (2017), '"The Great Wall" Review: Matt Damon Battles Monsters, Blockbuster-Audience Boredom', *Rolling Stone*, 17 February, <http://www.rollingstone.com/movies/reviews/peter-travers-the-great-wall-movie-review-w466886> (last accessed 20 July 2020).

Voci, Paola, and Luo Hui (eds) (2018a), *Screening China's Soft Power*. Abingdon: Routledge.

Voci, Paola, and Luo Hui (2018b), 'Screening China's Soft Power: Screen Cultures and Discourses of Power', in P. Voci and H. Luo (eds), *Screening China's Soft Power*. Abingdon: Routledge, pp. 1–18.

Wanda Group (2016), 'Chairman Wang Jianlin Gives a Speech on Globalization of Chinese Culture', *Wanda Group*, 10 December, <http://cms-en.iyunfish.com/2016/latest_1210/1460.html> (last accessed 20 July 2020).

Zhang, Yingjin (2018), 'Afterword: Shifting Perspectives on Soft Power and Chinese Screens', in P. Voci and H. Luo (eds), *Screening China's Soft Power*. Abingdon: Routledge, pp. 252–60.

CHAPTER 2

Building BRICS: Soft Power and Audio-visual Relations in Transnational Context

Stephanie Dennison

This chapter will investigate the relationship between both state and non-state actors in the film industries of BRICS countries (Brazil, Russia, India, China and South Africa), and national and transnational soft power strategies within the grouping. It takes as its main focus a specific case study that has been all but ignored to date by academic scholarship – the BRICS film festivals (2016–19) – and the three BRICS co-productions that have been released at the time of writing – *Where Has the Time Gone?* (2017), *Half the Sky* (2018) and *Neighbors* (2019). It considers the potential significance of the festivals and BRICS-sponsored filmmaking for the soft power kudos of and intercultural relations among these so-called emerging nations.

The 'BRICS', originally an academic term, now has the kind of political purchase the economist Jim O'Neill could never have envisaged when he coined the acronym (then BRIC) in 2001 to describe a group of rapidly emerging economies which he saw as being at a similar stage in their development (Brazil, Russia, India, China and later South Africa) (Cooke 2016: 5). This grouping has become a political entity holding regular international summits, and since 2014 has had its own financial structure, the New Development Bank, aimed at providing an alternative to the US-dominated International Monetary Fund and World Bank. Recently, the BRICS have begun to address the perceived need to build a cultural brand through a focus on film, with a film festival since 2016 forming a kind of cultural companion piece to the annually rotated political/economic summits.

Around the time of the first BRICS conference in 2011 (that is, in its current five-country formation), the more genuinely *emerging* member countries (Brazil, South Africa and India) arguably had more in common, in soft power and public diplomacy terms, and their visibility and image abroad were very different from those in the current scenario. Brazil was heralded in influential international press outlets such as *The Economist* (2009) and *Monocle* (Openshaw 2012) as a rising soft power star, with attention being drawn beyond its then booming economy, if not specifically to its film culture, then at least to the wide variety and international recognition of its popular culture, and to its charismatic Workers' Party president, Luis Inácio Lula da Silva. South Africa was still basking in the dramatic turn away from apartheid, benefiting from the 'Mandela factor' and the socio-political strides made in reinventing the country as a 'rainbow nation'. This 'upworthy' national narrative was lapped up by journalists, by cultural commentators, and by Hollywood studios which took advantage of favourable terms to make movies about South Africa, filmed in the country. In the case of India, Bollywood, as it grew in popularity outside India and the Indian diaspora, was almost singlehandedly held responsible for boosting a positive image of the nation (Thussu 2016).

The soft power ambitions of these countries have more recently been stymied by varying levels of economic and political crisis. As former Brazilian Foreign Minister Celso Amorim has argued (in Dennison 2020), Brazil's soft power cannot be completely divorced from its current socio-political circumstances, a state of affairs also impacting the international image of South Africa and India of late. And the now well-worn criticisms, at least in the Western media, of Chinese and Russian soft power efforts continue unabated.

Just as the BRICS nations do not, in fact, share as many common economic, political and populational characteristics as the success of this transnational grouping might suggest (Cooper 2016: 4), there are a number of features of their individual film cultures that challenge our ability to discuss them usefully as a homogenous group. Their differing relationships with the all-powerful Hollywood is one such feature. While Russia and Brazil constitute two of the largest markets for Hollywood films[1], and while more Hollywood films are screened in South Africa than any other kind, Hollywood has only recently started making inroads into the Indian and Chinese markets.[2] The size, commercial clout and exportability of each national film industry also vary considerably. A remarkable 1,500–2,000 films are made every year in India (ET Bureau 2017), around 900 in China (Anon. 2019) and about 150 each in Russia (EAO 2018) and Brazil (Presidency 2019), while a mere 23 films of South African origin were released in the home territory in 2017 (NFVF 2019).

Cinephiles, and more importantly those in a position to influence what films are screened at festivals and on TV screens, are aware of a 'new wave' legacy in relation to Indian and Brazilian cinema (the films of Satyajit Ray and the Brazilian *cinema novo* movement, for example), but the full breadth and potency of these filmmaking cultures are not always recognised. This is arguably not the case with Russian and Chinese films, whereby Chinese cinema is frequently discussed in terms of successive 'generations', and Russian cinema has rarely been out of the focus of cinephiles, world cinema scholars and festival and art-house theatre programmers since the earliest days of Vertov, via Eisenstein, to Tarkovsky and beyond. South Africa (and the African continent more broadly) is arguably different from the other BRICS in terms of the much less significant volume of film production and the impact it has had on global film culture.

With regard to cultural, and specifically cinematographic, contact zones among the BRICS nations, these are, perhaps unsurprisingly, unevenly spread across the member states. China is once again the focus of the most cited example of film exchange between BRICS countries: the recent remarkable penetration of Indian films in the lucrative Chinese market, spearheaded by Nitesh Tiwari's surprise hit about Indian women wrestlers, *Dangal* (2016). With its USD 10 million budget, *Dangal* made USD 77 million in its home market and USD 193 million in China. Such stories overshadow the other more modest inroads made into film co-operation among BRICS, such as *Bollywood Dream: O Sonho Bollywoodiano* (*Bollywood Dream*, dir. Beatriz Seigner, 2010) and *Vermelho Russo* (*Russian Red*, dir. Charly Braun, 2016), Brazilian co-productions with India and Russia, respectively. In both films a group of Brazilian actresses travel abroad, ostensibly to learn a different acting style (Bollywood in India and the Stanislavsky acting method in Russia). Like these two Brazilian co-productions, Russia and China's first co-produced feature film, *Kak Ya Stal Russkin* (*How I Became Russian*, dir. Xia Hao and Akaki Sakhelashvili, 2019) depicts characters from one country (in this case Russia) attempting to assimilate to another culture (China), to entertaining effect.[3]

While Bollywood cinema is increasingly moving from the margins of the Indian diaspora in South Africa to the mainstream, there is a dearth of programming and screening of South African audio-visual production within the other BRICS countries, and once again there are only isolated examples to quote, such as the China–Africa International Film Festival launched in Cape Town in 2017 (Wu 2018). *A Pair of Golden Wings* (dir. Darrell Roodt), the first South Africa–China feature-length co-production, is currently in development.

The Foreign View of the BRICS

While it may not be sufficiently captured in soft power measurements, Bollywood (as film production centre, genre and industry) provides a good illustration of the extent to which non-state actors in audio-visual culture can play a key role in the promotion of a particular view of people and places: after all, as Rachel Dwyer points out in her chapter in this volume, Bollywood flourished long before it occurred to the Indian government to work together with producers to harness and direct Bollywood's visibility as a soft power asset.[4] It also highlights the challenges of (and rightly warns against) directing or controlling audiovisual culture at a national level: there is, after all, little to be gained from what Joseph Nye (2012) describes as 'brittle propaganda'. But what about images produced beyond the confines of the nation? The BRICS countries are historically united by the significant impact of non-state actors, over whom they have no control, on global understandings of their cultures: namely, foreign filmmakers. By way of example, Hollywood's depiction in the 1930s and 1940s of an exotic, tutti-frutti, technicolour Brazil/South America in so-called Good Neighbour films, starring Brazilian Carmen Miranda, has been widely researched. As Ana Lopez (1993: 68) argues, in such films Hollywood served as 'ethnographer', taking on a key early role in fixing in a global film audience's imagination an idea of different nations and peoples. Consider D. W. Griffith's *The Zulu's Heart* of 1908 and the extent to which it set the tone for a century of representation on screen of black (South) Africans as either murderous savages or loyal servants to white folk. Consider also the extent to which Hollywood contributed to the East Asian 'yellow peril' narrative (Frayling 2014)[5]. More recently, we see that China's strategy of investing in Hollywood in the hope of encouraging more positive views of the Chinese has not been entirely successful. Even when Hollywood filmmakers attempt a sympathetic portrait of China and South Africa, for example, they more often than not fall into the trap of sinological orientalism (Vukovich 2012: see Chapter 5 in this volume), in the case of China, or of South Africa as a playground for white saviours, with black Africans relegated to supporting roles.

Foreign (and particularly Hollywood) representations of emerging nations such as the BRICS countries have, then, rarely been positive, creating a context in which damage limitation and a form of complaint culture have arguably flourished. For example, as early as 1932, the Chinese embassy in the US delivered a formal complaint in relation to the negative portrayal of Chinese culture in the MGM film *The Mask of Fu Manchu*, directed by Charles Brabin (Brook 2014). The Brazilian authorities complained to Fox studios in relation to a now infamous 2002 episode of *The Simpsons* (directed by Steven Dean Moore) and a similar complaint was lodged with the production company behind the feature film *Turistas*, directed by John Stockwell (Dennison 2020: 155–6). The concern in both cases was that stereotypical representations of Brazil as a violent, corrupt country full of confidence tricksters threatened its international tourism industry.

One of the most extreme examples of the potential damage that filmmakers can cause to the international profile of emerging countries can be found outside the BRICS grouping. At a time when so many small nations across Central and Eastern Europe were turning to country branding in an effort to raise their profile and thus become economically competitive within increasingly global markets, the Sacha Baron Cohen-produced *Borat: Cultural Learnings of America for Make Benefit Glorious Nation of Kazakhstan* (dir. Larry Charles, 2006) signalled potential disaster for the small ex-Soviet nation named in the title. A huge success in the US and Western Europe for its critique of American cultural ignorance and nominated for Golden Globes and the Oscar for Best Original Screenplay, it was banned in most Arab countries and widely criticised in both Kazakhstan and Russia. The volume of litigation resulting from the film was considerable. The Kazakh government felt obliged to launch the Heart of Eurasia campaign in order to counter the extremely negative portrayal, through the character of Borat, of Kazakhstan (as backward, incestuous and culturally limited).[6]

Through observations of BRICS and other emerging countries, and how they have been and continue to be portrayed by filmmakers in Hollywood and Europe, what is clear is the lack of level playing field when it comes to the potential impact of circulation of cultural and national stereotypes. As César Jiménez-Martínez (2017: 60) argues, 'Structural asymmetries of visibility mean that the crafting, management and even the contestation of images of the nation very rarely challenge power relations at an international and global level.' Consequently, we would do well to remember, when discussing soft power, cultural diplomacy and/or nation branding, that the issues and tensions facing emerging nations such as Brazil in relation to their image, and the motivating factors for wanting to promote, challenge or increase the presence of that image abroad, will not be the same as the issues facing, say, the UK or Spain. Hence reputation management is quite a large part of the soft power story in Brazil and other emerging nations, where it might not be in the UK, for example (Dennison and Meleiro 2016: 20).

The frequency with which the trope of the evil Brit character appears in Hollywood films, for example, is arguably offset both by the box-office domination of 'positive' high-profile British characters such as Harry Potter and James Bond, and by other 'positive' images of people and institutions that circulate widely of the British and Britishness (the Queen, David Beckham, the BBC, the British Council and so on) . Thus, the evil Brit character is unlikely to impact significantly on broad perceptions of Britishness, given that these are more historically fixed, positive and, importantly, widely disseminated, than those of some of the BRICS countries, for example. As Brazilian filmmaker Lúcia Murat argues in her 2005 documentary *Olhar Estrangeiro* (*Foreign View*), the issue with Hollywood misrepresenting Brazil time and again on screen is that there is not a sufficient global awareness of what Brazil is *really like* to offset such fantasy depictions (Dennison 2020: 154). Nation brander Simon Anholt (2010) has likewise observed: 'Countries with very good, very broad and complex reputations frequently show a remarkable immunity to negative events: this is often a fairly straightforward matter of the degree of knowledge people have about the country in the first place.' Thus, we must recognise that the recurring motifs of Latino drug dealers and trickster lovers, Russian mafiosos, primitive (black) Africans and evil Arabs are more likely to affect the lives of Latinos, Russians, Africans and Arabs as they negotiate global society than, say, the filmic representation of the British as crooks and Germans as mad scientists.

The BRICS Film Festival Phenomenon

It was Indian Prime Minister Narendra Modi who, at the 2015 BRICS summit in Ufa, Russia, suggested organising an annual BRICS film festival, with the first being staged in New Delhi in 2016 to coincide with India's hosting of the annual summit (PIB 2016). The first official festival[7] was relatively low-key and received limited publicity. Taking place alongside a number of other cultural events, such as an international food fair, the festival comprised screenings showcasing recent productions from each of the BRICS countries. The most striking film, in terms of at least nodding to a meaningful dialogue between BRICS countries, was the out-of-competition screening of the documentary *Leo Tolstoy and Mahatma Gandhi: A Double Portrait in the Interior of the Age* (dir. Galina and Anna Yevtushenko, 2016). In contrast, the closing film of the festival, the Jackie Chan vehicle *Skiptrace* (2016), a conventional big-budget Sino-US co-production (with a US director, Renny Harlin) which pits Chan and his US and Hong Kong friends against evil Russian gangsters, will have done little to contribute towards a more nuanced portrayal of BRICS country members.

The following year, a much more ambitious and high-profile event was held in the south-western Chinese city of Chengdu. Here, the opening and closing ceremonies were broadcast live, the event gained its own website, and winning films at the festival, including Best Film, the Brazilian *Nise: O Coração da Loucura* (*Nise: The Heart of Madness*, dir. Roberto Berliner, 2015), were distributed within China's large and potentially very lucrative art-house film circuit.[8] *Nise, The Heart of Madness*, a docu-drama based on the true story of psychiatrist Nise da Silveira and her pioneering approach to treating patients with schizophrenia in Brazil in the 1940s, was the first Brazilian film to secure a commercial release in China: it was screened in a remarkable 600 cinemas in 2018. As discussed below, the festival was notable in that it launched the first of a series of five BRICS-made films, produced by the celebrated Chinese director Jia Zhangke.

The third festival in Durban in July 2018 sought to maintain the momentum established by the previous two editions, but both working within budgetary constraints and a context of political uncertainty seemingly affected the commitment of a number of the BRICS member states to the festival: India failed to send a jury member and their competition entries arrived a day late, forcing organisers to make last-minute changes to the programme, while the Brazilian film delegation was confirmed only twenty-four hours before they were due to travel to South Africa. The festival ran alongside the annual Durban International Film Festival; while this undoubtedly was financially beneficial in terms of the pooling of resources, it meant that the BRICS films were rather lost within the city's festival programming. Some of the competition films, accompanied by Q and As with filmmakers who had travelled halfway across the globe to present their films, screened late at night to almost empty film theatres.

The Best Film award in 2018 went to the Indian feature *Newton*[9] (dir. Amit V. Masurkar, 2017), a quirky, socially conscious film reminiscent, in terms of its whimsy, of the winner of the first festival in 2016, *Thithi* (*Funeral*, dir. Raam Reddy, 2016), also Indian. Like *Thithi*, *Gabriel e a Montanha* (*Gabriel and the Mountain*, dir. Fellipe Gamarana Barbosa 2017), one of the Brazilian entries to the BRICS festival in Durban, made creative use of a predominantly amateur cast, and like *Nise, The Heart of Madness* before it, was based on a true story (that of a young, idealistic Brazilian backpacker and climber who falls to his death in Malawi in 2009). However, far from being an ideal choice for a festival seeking to promote intercultural communication, *Gabriel and the Mountain* failed to excite the festival jury, arguably as a result of its problematic portrayal of a (white and privileged) Brazilian tourist in Africa.[10]

It is unlikely that the Chinese selection committee ever expected the 'intercultural communication' of the Jackie Chan vehicle *Kung Fu Yoga* (dir. Stanley Tong, 2017) to translate into the Best Film prize at the festival in Durban in 2018. Originally pitched as a Sino-Indian co-production, the Chinese entry went on to be one of the highest-grossing films in China, and its action set-pieces certainly went down well, if not with the judges, then at least with its packed South African audience when it screened at the Playhouse in downtown Durban. In the film, Jackie Chan plays an archaeologist who, together with his Chinese colleagues, 'saves' ancient Indian culture. It memorably ends with a high-octane Bollywood dance number performed by Chan and a number of well-known Chinese and Indian actors. While *Kung Fu Yoga* was arguably too commercial to stand a serious chance of winning top prize at the film festival, the choice was none the less inspired, given that it potentially spoke to a local popular audience and specifically to the very large Indian diaspora in the city of Durban.

The Chinese delegation and presence at the fourth festival in Niterói, Brazil was considerably smaller than the one in Durban, despite the strong economic ties between the two countries. This can, in part, be explained by the troubled relationship between Brazil and China at a state level in 2019, triggered by the criticisms aimed at the latter country by the politically naïve and profoundly unstatesmanlike new Brazilian president, Jair Bolsonaro. After some uncertainty as a result of the victory at the polls of Bolsonaro, who, together with key members of his kakistocratic cabinet, has been openly critical of South–South diplomacy,[11] the eleventh BRICS annual summit, scheduled to be hosted by Brazil in 2019, took place in November 2019 in Brasilia. And despite the disbanding by Bolsonaro of the Ministry of Culture, cuts to film funding and criticisms of film culture more broadly, Brazil honoured the remit to host the fourth BRICS film festival.

Funding for the fourth BRICS festival had been guaranteed before the presidential elections of 2018 in Brazil, with administrative responsibility being granted to a federal university (UFF, in Niterói), working with the city council and the freshly downgraded Special Culture Secretariat, now being overseen by the newly formed Ministry of Citizenship.[12] The programme devised by the festival organisers, as well as the regular competitive strand (two recent films per member state competing for a range of prizes), included a classic film series, a seminar on film preservation, a week-long film school for budding filmmakers from BRICS nations, and a film market.

The only representative of Bolsonaro's government present at the festival, Ricardo Rihan, Audiovisual Secretary in the Ministry of Citizenship, appeared and spoke briefly at the opening ceremony, to a chorus of boos from students in the audience.[13] But like the festival as a whole, the incident received barely any media attention. Senior BRICS government representatives stayed away from the event, as they had done in relation to the Durban festival, where even the Brazilian Film Institute Ancine failed to acknowledge their own presence at the festival on their social media calendar. Unlike the previous festivals, the Brazil-hosted one was first and foremost an academic event, with thematic emphasis on film history and film preservation, two significant focal points of research carried out at the Federal Fluminense University.

The BRICS Compilation Films

The second, and by far the most notable, BRICS film festival (Chengdu) premiered the first of a proposed five BRICS co-productions: *Where Has Time Gone?* (2017), executive-produced (and partly directed) by award-winning Chinese filmmaker Jia Zhangke and involving contributions from established names in world cinema from BRICS countries, such as the Brazilian Walter Salles. The second BRICS co-production, *Half the Sky* (2018), premiered in Durban. In this portmanteau movie, five women directors from the BRICS nations each made a short film focusing on women's experiences in their countries of origin. The third film, *Neighbors*, premiered at Jia Zhangke's Crouching Tiger Hidden Dragon Film Festival in Pengyao, China, in October 2019.

Described in the press kit as anthology features, the films consist of five short segments set in each of the BRICS countries which tackle a common theme. The first of these, *Where Has Time Gone?*, deals with the relationship between time and the contemporary world, and more specifically, the impact that the kind of aggressive development associated with BRICS countries has on individuals' experience of the passing of time. The second, *Half the Sky*, takes its inspiration from Mao Tse Dong's famous aphorism which points to the fact that women make up half the population and thus symbolically hold up half of the sky. In this compilation, five women filmmakers present short features around female characters facing different kinds of challenges in their daily lives. The third BRICS film takes as its title *Neighbors*, pointing to discussions of interpersonal and intercultural relations. It is directed by a mix of male and female filmmakers.

All the films to date have been executive-produced and distributed by Chinese concerns, and most recently (October 2019), the third feature, *Neighbors*, premiered in Pengyao, rather than at the fourth BRICS film festival staged shortly before in Brazil. The previous year, after its rather downbeat premiere in Durban, *Half the Sky* opened the Pingyao festival: there, a number of the directors involved in the production launched the film, together with executive producer Zhangke.

One can see evidence of the influence of Jia Zhangke and his own preferences and connections in the choice of participants in the films.

For example, the Brazilian segment of the first film was directed by Walter Salles, one of Brazil's most high-profile filmmakers, a close friend of Zhangke and responsible for *Jia Zhangke, A Guy from Fenyang* (2016), an intimate film essay on the life and work of the filmmaker. The Brazilian baton was then passed in film two to Daniela Thomas, Salles's long-standing collaborator.[14] The Russian segment of the second BRICS film was directed by Elizaveta Stishova, recipient of the Roberto Rossellini prize at Jia's Pengyao film festival in 2017 for her first feature film, *Suleiman Mountain* (2017). Beatriz Seigner's *Los Silencios* (2018) screened at the 2018 Pengyao festival: Seigner was then invited to make the Brazilian segment of the 2019 *Neighbors*.

Jia's own segment of the first film, entitled 'Revive China', sets the tone and demonstrates the communicative potential of the BRICS films in a striking way. It opens with a colourful feast of sword-wielding combat familiar to audiences of Wuxia period dramas. Our expectations are quickly debunked, however, when the combat is abruptly interrupted by the appearance of mobile phones on selfie sticks and it is revealed that the protagonists of 'Revive China' are actors in period dress, paid to bring to life the ancient cityscape of Pingyao for tourists (Fig. 2.1).

This blending of traditional culture and modernity re-emerges and is given a striking twist in the Russian segment of the second BRICS film, *Half the Sky*. In 'Catfishing', Elizaveta Stishova continues the quirky approach taken by fellow Russian Alexey Fedorchenko in *Where Has the*

Figure 2.1 Tradition and modernity meet in Jia Zhangke's 'Revive China'.

Figure 2.2 Elizaveta Stishova's 'imagined' Russian village in 'Catfishing'.

Time Gone? and here invents a regional culture frozen in time (Fig. 2.2). According the film's press notes (Fabula Entertainment, n.d.), Stishova imagines what a Russian village would be like if Russians

> treated our traditions as Asian people do. That's why together with production designer and costume designer we created a world that could have been Russia in the 21st century, where everything is mixed – horse cart and contemporary bike, stove and notebook, Russian dress from 19 century [sic] and modern fancy Keds.

The South African segment of *Where Has the Time Gone?* likewise combines images associated with premodern African culture (and, in particular, tribal face and body paint) and the iconography of science fiction, in a nod to Afrofuturism of the kind widely discussed in light of the success of films such as the South African *District 9* (Neill Blomkamp, 2009).[15]

In *Half the Sky* both the Indian and Chinese segments focus on city life, generational issues and the place of modern technology in urban society, and in both *Where Has the Time Gone?* and *Half the Sky* potential audience expectations regarding markers of Chinese and Indian traditions (dress and local colour, cultural history and religious practices) are interwoven into modern cityscapes and intimate personal stories.

The Brazilian segments of the first two BRICS films eschew a discussion of the well-worn cityscapes and traditions that have featured widely in films made by both Brazilian and foreign filmmakers, turning instead to depictions of the rural landscape of the much less familiar interior region of Minas Gerais. In 'When the Earth Trembles', Walter Salles took advantage of the opportunity to work on the BRICS project to denounce in the fictional mode the ecological disaster of the Mariana dam explosion of 2015, making use of the real landscape of landslides and the ongoing temporary housing schemes to striking effect, having them serve as a reminder of a darker side to capitalist development and its impact on communities far removed from the centre of economic decision-making (Fig. 2.3).

In her segment in *Half the Sky*, entitled 'Back', Daniela Thomas returned to Minas Gerais to tell the story of Maria Helena Dias, a black woman who lives in a poor squatter community in São Paulo and begrudgingly goes back to her village when she receives news that her mother is dying. Thomas's tale is noteworthy for the extent to which it can be seen to serve within her own œuvre as a corrective to her 2017 feature film *Vazante*, a tale of nineteenth-century slavery which was roundly criticised on its release for presenting a white-centred story of suffering. 'Back' is based on the true story of a woman Thomas met while location-shooting *Vazante*. Both 'When the Earth Trembles' and 'Back' also highlight the commitment of the Brazilian filmmakers to expose in their film segments the flipside to the otherwise positive narrative of the rising South, to reveal the truth of the 'deeply precarious nature of work and livelihoods' across the BRICS (Nilsen and Von Holdt 2020).

As the main institutional focus of cultural exchange between countries of the bourgeoning BRICS trade bloc, and thus companion pieces to the

Figure 2.3 Real-life landslide wreckage as backdrop to Walter Salles's 'When the Earth Trembles'.

summits, the BRICS film festivals have demonstrated that, among BRICS nations, there is currently considerable curiosity, but concrete cultural relations remain at best tentative and risk being overshadowed by political tension. All editions thus far of the BRICS film festival have focused in large part on the individual film production of the BRICS nations, with discussions involving cultural exchange tending to be limited to presentations by film institutes and national funders on potential production and marketing strategies, or to ad hoc side-bar events.[16] To be sure, concrete results of these discussions have emerged over the last three years, including the signing of co-production agreements where these did not already exist (for example, between South Africa and Brazil, and between South Africa and China, both signed in 2018). The existence of formal co-production agreements is, however, no guarantee of an increased cultural exchange (consider, for instance, Brazil's long-established but woefully underused film treaty with India).

Furthermore, there is no denying that, overall, China has been the main driving force for cultural interaction as part of the festivals, which reflects China's geo-political leadership ambitions and risks the creation of dialogue that is skewed to respond to its specific business interests. What is worth bearing in mind, however, and particularly in a context of China being constantly berated for its heavy-handedness when it comes to attempts to use the film sphere to generate soft power outcomes, is that not all the Chinese gestures in this regard have been state-driven. While it is hard to read the overbearing presence of the local Confucius Institute at the 'Chinese night' of the third BRICS film festival in Durban as anything other than statecraft,[17] it was local business interests (a Chinese-owned vineyard in South Africa) that took advantage of an approach from the Durban festival organisers to sponsor the festival, resulting in a tangible Chinese presence throughout, and a Chinese business presence on stage throughout the closing ceremony. And likewise, it was a private production company that signed a co-production deal with the South African Film and Video Foundation in a private ceremony as part of the same 'Chinese night'.

In the current political climate it is difficult to say what, if any, impact the fourth BRICS film festival will have had on relations between Brazil and the other BRICS nations.[18] However, on a small but still important level, the festival offered a much-needed fillip to the currently maligned Brazilian film community of directors, university staff and students, and film audiences. That meaningful conversations took place between the key participants and the Russian contingent with a view to providing continuity of effort in the next festival (due to be staged in Moscow in 2020 but postponed as a result of the coronavirus pandemic) bodes well for the ambition to increase the prestige of the annual festival on the film festival circuit.[19] But with the administrative and logistical challenges of working among the BRICS film industries and no common budget to draw on, the success of the festival looks likely in the short term to depend entirely on the investment of individual countries, with their focus perhaps understandably being on what each individual country can gain from the hosting of the event.

The BRICS compilation films constitute a high point in BRICS cultural collaboration to date. The fifteen short films of which they are comprised thus far are largely made by politically committed filmmakers who would be unlikely to be drawn to a filmmaking project that offered nothing but the opportunity to make 'brittle propaganda'. The films can thus be understood to offer filmmakers something that exists beyond BRICS cultural and public diplomacy: an interesting creative and collaborative space for both established and, crucially, emerging filmmakers and writers from the BRICS countries to showcase their work on an international stage. While these are fascinating, well-made and visually striking films, their reach has been relatively limited. With China-based sales agents Fabula Entertainment charging premium rates for screenings, it is hardly surprising that they have not been seen outside China beyond a very small number of festivals.

Conclusion

As Stone et al. (2017: 7) have argued, 'we require of filmmakers that they operate as the bearers of a national identity. The implication is that by doing so we risk ghettoising or maintaining the invisibility of certain types of film production, such as transnational co-productions.' And how might we unpick soft power kudos from a transnational co-production? It is also the case that complex co-productions and multi-authored films often struggle to find an audience: one only needs to recall the dismissal in the 1990s of European Union-funded co-productions as 'europuddings', and of the fact that the much-hyped, multidirected *Cities of Love* film series practically disappeared without a trace after their release.

It is also worth reflecting on the significance of the Chinese segment of *Neighbors*, directed by Han Yan and entitled 'Old Neighborhood', opening the Pingyao festival in 2019, rather than the compilation film in its entirety.[20] And elsewhere (the international film festival in São Paulo, for example, which has screened all three BRICS films in the year of their release) the BRICS films circulate as Chinese product.[21] The fact that the third film, *Neighbors*, premiered at Pingyao rather than at the fourth BRICS film festival, which took place only one week before, reminds us to regard neither the festivals nor the BRICS films as part of any intergovernmental strategy to promote cultural interaction among the BRICS. It points instead to an unstructured approach to supporting the festival, whereby, for countries not involved in hosting, it is rather far down the list of film promotional priorities. Gustavo Rolla (2017), representative of Brazil's film institute Ancine to the third festival in Durban, admitted that the choice of films to represent Brazil in the festival competition had more to do with opting for what was available, than a strategy either to maximise the chances of commercialisation of Brazilian films, as was clearly the case with the Chinese choice of *Kung Fu Yoga* that year, or to select films likely to win the competition, as is arguably the case with all of the Indian entries to date. This explains why there appeared to be no concerted attempt to build on the commercial success of *Nise: Heart of Madness* in terms of choice of film. Nor was there any move to promote dialogue and exchange on race with South African filmmakers and audiences by screening Afro-Brazilian films, in the year when a record number of films directed by black Brazilian filmmakers screened at the Brazilian film festival in Brasilia.

There are a number of recent examples of films being made with the express purpose of promoting a particular film festival. Consider, for example, the compilation film series *Asian Three-Fold Mirror*, produced by the Tokyo International Film Festival, ostensibly to increase intercultural dialogue among East and South-East Asian film cultures in the run-up to Tokyo's (postponed) hosting of the Summer Olympics in 2020, or one-off film collections sponsored by festivals to celebrate festival and filmmaking anniversaries, such as the seventy short films made as part of the Venice Film Festival's film history project *Venice 70 Future Reloaded*. But rather than promoting the BRICS film festival, the links between the BRICS compilation films and the Crouching Tiger Hidden Dragon Film Festival in Pingyao discussed above suggest that, if anything, the BRICS films serve to promote the Pingyao festival. As we have discussed, the films and their filmmakers have been given a privileged platform at the festival.

One might also argue that the Pingyao film festival has, to date, done more to promote BRICS filmmaking than any other festival, but it is perhaps more accurate to suggest that the promotion of BRICS filmmaking has taken place within the wider context of the Belt and Road Initiative.[22] One of the ongoing themes of the festival is, after all, cultural exchange between East and West. At the Pingyao festival in 2019, for example, discussions that clearly matter the most for China in relation to the BRICS, such as Indian films and the Indian film market, were made central: the programme included a lavish series on New Indian Cinema. Brazil's profile was raised by the presence of World Cinema darling Kleber Mendonça Filho, who delivered a masterclass and screened his award-winning *Bacurau* (2019). A Brazilian film, *A Febre* (*Fever*, dir. Maya da-Rin, 2019), won the important Roberto Rossellini prize. India, Russia and China were represented on the jury of the first Pingyao festival in 2017, as were the important film cultures of France and Italy. Meanwhile, there has been no engagement with South African film thus far at the festival.

China is not alone among the BRICS in having competing cultural and audio-visual priorities in geo-political terms, which explains to an extent the lack of investment in BRICS cultural projects. In fact, in recent years Brazil, Russia, India and South Africa have all sought to increase their share of audio-visual markets within their immediate geographical regions. And the significance of the major European film festivals for visibility and soft power kudos means that when domestic funding is scarce, that tends to be where investment in film festivals is made.

Within the BRICS, China serves as facilitator, promoting a wide range of cultures as well as its own.[23] By assuming the role of facilitator in this regard, China's approach to cultural diplomacy is similar to that of nations with long-established cultural institutions, such as the British Council and Germany's Goethe Institute, and therefore quite different from the rather heavy-handed activities associated with the much-maligned Chinese Confucius Institutes. It is from this role that China, performing as a super-BRICS member (Cooper 2016: 4), stands to acquire soft power kudos in the transnational audio-visual sphere.

Notes

1. More European films are screened in Russia than US films, but it is the US films that dominate the Russian box office (Macnab 2019).
2. With 70–80 releases per year, Hollywood contributes 10–15 per cent to box-office revenues. Thus, while the percentage of Hollywood films is relatively small, their exposure and rentability are very significant (Wernau 2019).
3. The film is based on a popular Russian TV series of the same name from 2015, which screened in China, and which featured an American rather than a Chinese character at large in Russia.
4. See also the work of Daya Thussu, such as 2016.
5. In contrast, Griffith made one of his finest films about a Chinese man in *Broken Blossoms* (1919), in what is widely accepted to be a sympathetic portrayal of Chinese immigration to the US.
6. It is worth noting that implied in the film's subtitle is a playful critique of the very notion of nation branding. For a fascinating account of the impact of *Borat*, see Saunders (2008). As we go to press, Baron Cohen has released

a follow-up to *Borat* entitled *Borat Subsequent Moviefilm: Delivery of Prodigious Bribe to American Regime for Make Benefit Once Glorious Nation of Kazakhstan* (dir. Jason Woliner, 2020). It is interesting to see that, rather than attempting to counter the potential bad publicity from the film, Borat's catchphrase, 'Very nice!', has been embraced and adopted as a slogan by the Kasakh tourist board; see Sullivan (2020).

7. Other minor and ad hoc festivals that use the BRICS moniker can be found, such as the Echo BRICS Film Festival in Russia (since 2017) and the BRICS Film Festival at the Indo Cine Appreciation Foundation in Chennai, India, in 2019, run with support from the local Russian Cultural Centre.
8. Distribution was officially contingent on the signing in 2017 of a co-production agreement between Brazil and China.
9. It is interesting to note that both *Newton* and the second Brazilian competition film, *Arabia* (*Araby*, dir. Affonso Uchoa and Joao Dumans, 2017) featured as part of the Emirates inflight entertainment on planes to Durban at the same time that the festival took place.
10. See Clayton Dillard's crushing review in *Slant* (2018).
11. Brazilian Vice-president Hamilton Mourão visited China in May 2019 and reportedly smoothed the way for continued dialogue between the two countries.
12. On 7 November 2019, the Special Cultural Secretariat (SECULT) was transferred to the Ministry of Tourism.
13. The context here is a sense of the Federal Fluminense University (UFF) being under attack from the Bolsonaro government as a result of both massive cuts to the funding of public universities and the high-profile criticisms of Bolsonaro by both staff and students of UFF that pre-date his election to the presidency.
14. Walter Salles's contribution to the first BRICS compilation film was written by Gabriela Amaral, an important emerging filmmaker and very much Salles's 'protégée'.
15. See Womack (2013).
16. Consider, for example, the workshop on BRICS, cultural diplomacy and film that Chris Homewood and I ran as part of the festival in Durban and Niterói in 2018 and 2019, respectively.
17. China set up its Confucius Institutes in 2004, ostensibly along a similar model to language teaching and cultural exchange organisations such as the British Council and the Instituto Cervantes (Spain). Many of the controversies associated with them, including their presence on university campuses and the potential threat they pose to academic freedom, are discussed in Marshall Sahlins's *Confucius Institutes: Academic Malware* (2015).
18. As highlighted in the Introduction to this volume, film preservation, one of the key themes of the fourth festival, took a major hit in the Brazilian context with the dismantling of the Cinemateca Brasileira (Brazilian national film archive) in 2020. The Cinemateca has, in fact, been at the centre of Brazil's

'culture wars' since at least January 2019 and the start of the presidency of Jair Bolsonaro.
19. A scaled-down online version of the festival took place in October 2020.
20. The full film did screen as part of the festival. Han Yan's 'Old Neighborhood' was reportedly a last-minute replacement when the opening film, Li Shaohong and Chang Xiaoyang's *Liberations* (2019), was pulled at the last minute (Scott 2019).
21. FIAPF, the International Federation of Film Producers Association, took six Chinese films to Paris in May 2019, including *Where Has Time Gone?*
22. The Belt and Road Initiative (BRI) was conceived in 2013 and launched in 2017. It is comprised of more than 900 infrastructure projects and will form an economic 'belt' across the Eurasian continent and a maritime 'silk road' through South-East and South Asia to the Middle East, with the goal of deepening economic integration and connectivity (Thussu 2018: 117). The first BRI-sponsored film, the Chinese documentary feature *Common Destiny*, was released in 2019 to lukewarm reaction at home and disdain from the international news media (*Economist* 2019).
23. We must acknowledge that China took on this facilitator role in the audio-visual sphere with the global expansion of its news media, and in particular CCTV (now CGTN). Observers are already treating such expansion with suspicion: see, for example, Lim and Bergin (2018).

Works Cited

Anholt, Simon (2010), 'Editorial: What Makes a Good Story?', *Place Branding and Public Diplomacy*, 5, 263–7.
Anon. (2019), 'Number of Films Produced in China from 2014 to 2019', *Statista*, <https://www.statista.com/statistics/1060823/china-film-production-volume/> (last accessed 22 November 2020).
Brook, Tom (2014), 'Why Are Russians Always the Bad Guys?', *BBC*, 5 November, <http://www.bbc.co.uk/culture/story/20141106-why-are-russians-always-bad-guys> (last accessed 12 November 2020).
Cooke, Paul (2016), 'Soft Power, Film Culture and the BRICS', *New Cinemas*, 14: 1, 3–15.
Cooper, Andrew F. (2016), *The BRICS: A Very Short Introduction*. Oxford: Oxford University Press.
Dennison, Stephanie (2020), *Remapping Brazilian Cinema in the Twenty-first Century*. London: Routledge.
Dennison, Stephanie, and Alessandra Meleiro (2016), 'Brazil, Soft Power and Film Culture', *New Cinemas*, 14:1, 17–30.
Dillard, Clayton (2018), 'Review: *Gabriel and the Mountain*', *Slant*, 12 June, <https://www.slantmagazine.com/film/gabriel-and-the-mountain/> (last accessed 12 November 2020).

EAO (2018), '30% Rise in the Number of Films Released in Russia Since the Arrival of the Digital Age', *European Audiovisual Observatory*, <https://www.obs.coe.int/en/web/observatoire/home/-/asset_publisher/9iKCxBYgiO6S/content/30-rise-in-the-number-of-films-released-in-russia-since-the-arrival-of-the-digital-age-> (last accessed 12 November 2020).

Economist (2019), 'From the Party, With Love', *Economist Online*, 5 September, <https://www.economist.com/china/2019/09/05/china-releases-a-movie-drama-featuring-its-belt-and-road-project> (last accessed 12 November 2020).

ET Bureau (2017), 'Film Industry in India to Hit $3.7 billion by 2020, Says Report', *Economic Times*, 9 October, <https://economictimes.indiatimes.com/industry/media/entertainment/media/film-industry-in-india-to-hit-3-7-billion-by-2020-says-report/articleshow/60998458.cms?from=mdr> (last accessed 12 November 2020).

Fraying, Christopher (2014), *The Yellow Peril: Dr Fu Manchu & The Rise of Chinaphobia*. London: Thames and Hudson.

Jiménez-Martínez, César (2017), 'Which Image? Of Which Country? Under Which Spotlight? Power, Visibility and the Image of Brazil', *Revista Trama Interdisciplinar* 8:3, 52–70.

Lim, Louisa, and Julia Bergin (2018), 'Inside China's Audacious Global Propaganda Campaign', *The Guardian*, 7 December, <https://www.theguardian.com/news/2018/dec/07/china-plan-for-global-media-dominance-propaganda-xi-jinping> (last accessed 12 November 2020).

Lopez, Ana (1993), 'Are All Latins From Manhattan? Hollywood, Ethnography and Cultural Colonialism', in John King, Ana Lopez and Manuel Alvarado (eds), *Mediating Two Worlds: Cinematic Encounters in the Americas*. London: BFI, pp. 67–80.

Macnab, Geoffrey (2019), 'Russian 2019 Box Office Report: Territory Bounces Back After World Cup Struggles', *Screen Daily*, 23 December, <https://www.screendaily.com/features/russian-2019-box-office-report-territory-bounces-back-after-world-cup-struggles-/5145749.article> (last accessed 12 November 2020).

NFVF (2019) 'FAQs About the South African Film Industry', *National Film and Video Foundation*, <http://www.nfvf.co.za/home/index.php?ipkContentID=255&ipkMenuID=61> (last accessed 12 November 2020).

Nilsen, Alf Gunvald, and Karl Von Holdt (2020), 'BRICS and COVID: Rising Powers in a Time of Pandemic', *The Wire*, 24 July, <https://thewire.in/world/brics-and-covid-rising-powers-in-a-time-of-pandemic> (last accessed 12 November 2020).

Nye, Joseph S., Jr (2012), 'China's Soft Power Deficit', *Wall Street Journal*, 8 May, <http://www.wsj.com/articles/SB10001424052702304451104577389923098678842> (last accessed 12 November 2020).

Openshaw, Jonathan (2012), 'The Sun's Shining on Brand Brazil', *Monocle*, 20 July, <https://monocle.com/monocolumn/business/the-sun-s-shining-on-brand-brazil/> (last accessed 24 November 2020).

PIB (2016), 'BRICS Film Festival – A New Hope for BRICS Nations'. *Indian Press Information Bureau*, 10 September, <https://pibindia.wordpress.com/2016/09/12/brics-film-festival-a-new-hope-for-brics-nations/> (last accessed 12 November 2020).
Presidency of the Republic of Brazil (2019), 'Number of Cinemas in Brazil Grows Again After 43 Years', <http://www.brazil.gov.br/arts-culture/film-and-theatre/number-of-cinemas-in-brazil-grows-again-after-43-years> (last accessed 12 November 2020).
Rolla, Gustavo (2017), Personal Conversation with the Author.
Sahlins, Marshall (2015), *Confucius Institutes: Academic Malware*. Chicago: Prickly Paradigm Press.
Saunders, Robert (2008), *The Many Faces of Sacha Baron Cohen: Politics, Parody, and the Battle over Borat*. Lanham, MD: Lexington Books.
Scott, Matthew (2019), 'Pingyao Film Festival: China's Indie Darling Kicks Off With Han Yan's "Old Neighborhood"', 10 October, *Hollywood Reporter*, <https://www.hollywoodreporter.com/news/chinas-pingyao-festival-kicks-han-yans-old-neighborhood-1246749> (last accessed 12 November 2020).
Stone, Rob, Paul Cooke, Stephanie Dennison and Alex Marlow-Mann (2017), 'The Latitude and Longitude of World Cinema', in Rob Stone, Paul Cooke, Stephanie Dennison and Alex Marlow-Mann, *The Routledge Companion to World Cinema*. London and New York: Routledge.
Sullivan, Helen (2020), '"Very nice!": Kazakhstan adopts Borat's catchphrase in new tourism campaign', *Guardian*, 27 October, <https://www.theguardian.com/world/2020/oct/27/very-nice-kazakhstan-adopts-borats-catchphrase-in-new-tourism-campaign-sacha-baron-cohen> (last accessed 25 November 2020).
Thussu, Daya (2016), 'The Soft Power of Popular Cinema – The Case of India', *Journal of Political Power*, 9:3, 415–29.
Thussu, Daya (2018), 'BRI: Bridging or Breaking BRICS?', *Global Media and China*, 3:2, 117–22.
Vukovich, Daniel (2012). *China and Orientalism: Western Knowledge Production and the PRC*. London and New York: Routledge.
Wernau, Julie (2019), 'Hollywood Takes a Back Seat to China's Own Domestic Filmmakers at Box Office', *Wall Street Journal*, 18 December, <https://www.wsj.com/articles/hollywood-takes-a-back-seat-to-chinas-own-domestic-filmmakers-at-box-office-11576674000> (last accessed 12 November 2020).
Womack, Ytasha L. (2013), *Afrofuturism: The World of Black Sci Fi and Fantasy Culture*. New York: Lawrence Hill.
Wu, Yu-Shan (2018), 'How Media and Film Can Help China Grow its Soft Power in Africa', *The Conversation*, 7 June, <https://theconversation.com/how-media-and-film-can-help-china-grow-its-soft power-in-africa-97401> (last accessed 12 November 2020).

CHAPTER 3

The Global Animation Market: Opportunities for Developing Countries
Alessandra Meleiro

The purpose of this chapter is to discuss how an emerging nation with a strong domestic audio-visual industry, but no sense of 'national film and audio-visual brand' in the international arena, has been working to increase its visibility. Case studies of internationalisation of Brazilian animation products and services will show that soft power can undeniably be used as an instrument of government foreign policy, as it is connected to standards of behaviour and consumption.

The presentation in this chapter of a set of indicators capable of describing the reality of the animation production chain in a country may become an important analysis and planning resource for development policies in the animation sector, within planned intervention. The chapter also points to the potential of using animation for foreign policy purposes, along the lines of the theoretical model of soft power as developed by Joseph Nye.

Soft Power, Cultural Diplomacy and Nation Branding

Research carried out in 2010 by the Brazilian Trade and Investment Promotion Agency (Apex-Brazil) in partnership with GFK Roper Public Affairs, in twenty countries and over the course of 20,000 interviews, gathered information about how Brazil's image was perceived compared with that of other countries. The methodology was based on seven elements for the construction of this country image: *exportation, governance, culture, people, tourism, investment and immigration* (GFK 2010). The report concluded that Brazil is in twentieth place on a list of fifty countries on the Nation Brand Index (NBI), with the *culture* dimension having most relevance (tenth place). The words most commonly associated with the perception of Brazil's image were *corruption, carnival, sport, receptivity, vibrant, fascinating* and *development*. Brazil's performance on the Anholt–GFK Roper Nation Brand Index[SM1] between 2004 and 2010 was also notable, as it was one of the few countries to show continuous, gradual improvement in its global scores year on year, and is still the only developing country to break into the top twenty overall most admired nations on the NBI (Ipsos 2019).

In comparison with the year 2000, the above result suggests a positive evolution of the perception of Brazil's image. In the year 2000, the Ministry of Development, Industry and Foreign Trade commissioned a similar study from the McCann Erickson agency,[2] which, at the time, concluded that Brazil was directly associated with five words: *sun, sand, song, sexiness* and *soccer* (the five 'Ses'). Thus, Brazil has appeal for 'soft factors' such as tourism, cuisine, culture and people, but struggles to position itself as a responsible player in international affairs, as a desirable destination for foreign direct investment or as a significant economic actor (Ipsos 2019). Achieving this is an enormous task.

There is acute awareness in Brazil, both at state level and within the culture industry itself, of the extent to which the nation has been a victim of negative stereotyping, a feature arguably shared with other BRICS nations. Consequently, we would do well to remember, when discussing soft power, cultural diplomacy and/or nation branding, that the issues and tensions facing emerging nations such as Brazil in relation to their image abroad, and the motivating factors for promoting, challenging or increasing the presence of that image overseas, will not be the same as the issues facing, say, the UK or Spain. Hence reputation management is quite a large part of the soft power story in Brazil and other emerging nations, where that might not be the case in the UK, for example (Dennison and Meleiro 2016: 20).

The Brazilian Creative Industry in a Time of Crisis

The COVID-19 pandemic has profoundly affected the creative sector. In Europe, several countries have acted promptly to provide assistance and mitigate the effects that the suspension of on-site creative activities has caused. In Brazil, interruption of these activities has given rise to a series of urgent situations that reveal not only the weaknesses of Brazilian cultural policies but, above all, the government's inability to articulate any reaction to the crisis, even within the framework of existing policies and instruments.

Even before COVID-19 hit, Brazil's reputation had been undermined by immense administrative ineptitude, especially on an economic level, and governments were characterised relentlessly within the Brazilian news media as massively corrupt. And they definitively reached their lowest level after the October 2018 election results, when the controversial far-right politician Jair Bolsonaro won the presidential ballot; he quickly appointed an equally controversial 'anti-globalist' and flat-Earthist Foreign Secretary, Ernesto Araújo. An editorial in a major Brazilian newspaper captured the concern felt by many about the potential damage to Brazil's perception abroad:

> The gloomy set of ideas that until now seemed to herald a setback in Brazilian foreign policy began to materialise in the administration of President Jair Bolsonaro. Unless there is profound reflection from the government about its terrible effects, the apparent 'turn' led by Chancellor Ernesto Araújo – which might well be called a 'crusade' – has the potential to end what still remains of Brazil's good reputation in the civilized world. (O Estado de S. Paulo 2019)

Since then, the world has been receiving rather confusing signals about the effective direction taken by Brazilian general government, foreign or cultural policies, initiated during the campaign and in the immediate follow-up to the elections. What was expected at the beginning of the government's term was a clear statement regarding the main guidelines to be followed by Brazilian diplomacy at the time of inauguration of the President and his Chancellor (Almeida 2019: 81).

The cultural sphere, and specifically that of cinema, concerning foreign policy as a potential soft power asset, has never figured explicitly on the agenda of the Brazilian right, which understands it as a commercially unpopular and expensive art form that relies heavily on state funding for its survival, and that has close associations with left-wing politics (Dennison and Meleiro 2016: 28). Bolsonaro's government does not readily recognise cinema as part of 'Brand Brazil', and worked systematically in 2019–20 to transform the National Film Agency (Ancine, which regulates, oversees and fosters the sector) and the Audiovisual Sector Fund (which finances the sector in reflection of its political vision and economic premise). This transformation includes the non-renewal of the screen quota for films produced nationally, and the detachment of Ancine from the Ministry of Culture and its transferral to the Ministry of Tourism, to name but two examples.

In soft power terms, this appears to have brought us back to a set of damage limitation exercises, within the context of reputation management, rather than encouraging the presence of any ambitious programme involving the galvanising of soft power assets, such as the major awards won by Brazilian films at international festivals in 2019 (*Bacurau* by Kleber Mendonça Filho and Juliano Dornelles at the Cannes Film Festival, *A Vida Invisível de Eurídice Gusmão* (*The Invisible Life of Eurídice Gusmão*) by Karim Aïnouz at the Cannes Film Festival, *Pacified* by Paxton Winters at the San Sebastian Festival, and *A Febre* (*Fever*) by Maya da-Rin at Locarno Film Festival, among others).

Soft Power and the Misery of Diplomacy

Regarding the major items on the international agenda, in terms of regional commitments and bilateral opportunities, the fact is that the current government has not yet offered a comprehensive and systematic presentation of Brazil's international strategy, specifying what the regional and multilateral priorities are, how it intends to organise economic openness and trade liberalisation, what it will do with the Mercosur trading bloc, and how it proposes to resolve the challenges of the country's global insertion in the great circuits of the world economy (Almeida 2019: 19) or its relations with the BRICS – an important strand of the 'active and assertive foreign policy' of the diplomacy of the Lula–Workers' Party years (2003–10).

Since the turn of the millennium, the very few guidelines we have seen include the notion of 'ideology-free foreign policy' and what appears to be a misguided view of what the role of foreign trade in a notoriously closed country like Brazil means to the development process. As Paulo Roberto Almeida states in 'Miséria da Diplomacia: A Destruição da Inteligência no Itamaraty':

> As the coefficient of Brazil's external openness is less than half of the world average, to aspire for the external partners to act in favour of more robust growth rates would be to have the commercial tail wagging the dog of development, without delving into the quality of these interactions. (Almeida 2019: 90)

Thus, judging by the lack of tangible results to be presented by the government of President Jair Bolsonaro and by the Ministry of Foreign Affairs – in all areas, including that of culture, and given the context of the decommissioning of previous policies, of condemnation, refusal and reversal of what had been done so far – added to the huge loss of Brazil's image and soft power due to its current environmental policy (Mello 2019), the analysis of the animation industry in Brazil that follows is limited to the reality experienced up to December 2018

The Animation Industry in Brazil in the Context of Creative Economy

The creative industries, situated in what is called the creative economy, are known for their use of creativity and talent as their main input and by their potential to generate income and jobs through their employment of intellectual capital. They constitute a heterogeneous group of activities centred on knowledge (Meleiro and Fonseca 2012: 50). The dual 'cultural' and 'economic' nature of the products of the creative industries – that is, the fact that this is a sector of great economic importance and, at the same time, a tool via which cultural expressions manifest themselves transnationally – demands analyses that can balance these two dimensions.

Culture is not only an energising factor in economic growth throughout the contemporary world (generating income and skilled employment opportunities in developed and developing economies), but also a great challenge for the different theoretical frameworks of the economy. To move towards an 'information economy' or a 'creative economy' means abandoning the old industrial world of tangible assets to turn to the production of intangible resources (Meleiro and Fonseca 2012: 39).

While certain economic elements in this group have always been incorporated into the most traditional economic activities, only recently has the group been recognised as a distinct economic sector. Despite the global recession, world exports of creative goods and services practically doubled between 2002 and 2015, according to the latest survey by the United Nations Conference on Trade and Development (UNCTAD 2016). The most significant players are still China and the US, although emerging countries such as Brazil, Turkey and India are increasingly expanding their export of creative services. Data indicate that the majority of commercial transactions take place between a developed country and a developing country (North–South); however, there is room to undo this paradigm in exploring new partnerships between emerging economies (South–South), as is the case, for example, with audio-visual co-productions and negotiations within Mercosur and between Brazil and China (MinC/UNESCO 2018: 13–14).

Representing 25 per cent of the audio-visual market, the value of global animation industry total revenues amounted to USD 100 billion in 2006, 222 billion in 2013, and 259 billion in 2018, projected to reach 270 billion by 2020. Animation is one of the global creative industry sectors with the highest growth potential. Furthermore, in 2013, the digital animation industry handled about USD 500 billion in brand and character licensing, more than double the figure in 2006 (200 billion) (Gama 2014: 95; Research and Markets 2019).

Within this panorama, we can state that the animation industry has become a sector of relevant economic dimensions for some countries and an important mechanism of economic growth for others: in the US, animation has become the country's sixth largest industry; Canada is the world's biggest animation producer, with 400 hours a year; in Europe, a total of 2 billion euros has been earmarked to finance 500 animations on the continent via the European Union; in Japan, the entertainment industry is the third largest in the country; and lastly, animation production in South Korea is so significant that it currently accounts for one-third of all animation production in the world (Gama 2014: 95).

The strong overall performance of the digital animation market in recent years suggests an economic opportunity for companies not tied to the US majors, including those in developing countries, and the penetration of companies from developing countries of the global animation market permeates international division of labour and the new specialisation of production between developed and developing countries.

The Film and Animation Industry in Brazil

Even though certain aspects of the creative industry occupy an increasingly central role in global economic discussions, such as regulations relating to intellectual property, the creative industries are still insufficiently studied in their economic aspects in developing countries. This is the case in Brazil. The need for information about the animation sector becomes so much more urgent when we consider that we have not solved the problem of sustainability of our industry in relation to the national space, local or regional, and we do not have consistent information systems.

In this respect, the market study and sector diagnostics for animation in 2018/19, carried out by Anima Mundi/JLeiva, with the author of this chapter acting as consultant, aimed to meet this demand for information; if the animation sector has economic significance, this significance must consequently be measured (Meleiro 2019). Anima Mundi is responsible for the International Anima Mundi Festival, the second largest animation festival in the world after the Annecy festival, which has been held in France for over fifty years.

The growth of Anima Mundi's initiatives was fostered by a series of partners, among whom are Brazil's state oil enterprise Petrobras; BNDES (Brazilian Development Bank); SEBRAE (Brazilian Small Enterprise Assistance Service); Firjan (Industry Federation of the State of Rio de Janeiro); Rio de Janeiro city council via RioFilme and the Municipal Department of Education; São Paulo city council through SPCine (an office for the development, financing and implementation of programmes and policies for the film and audio-visual sectors in the city of São Paulo); and several private businesses and investors. During its trajectory, partnerships were established with several animation schools and professionals around the world, who attended the festival and conducted masterclasses and workshops, in exchanges held with the aim of strengthening co-production ties between participating countries. Among the schools, the following may be cited: the French Les Gobelins, l'École Supinfocom Valenciennes (Rubika) and La Poudrière; and the American CalArts (California Institute of Arts) and USC (University of Southern California); the Vancouver Film School from Canada; and the Danish Animation Workshop (Anima Mundi 2016).

Several renowned international animation festivals also maintain a relationship of partnership with Anima Mundi, among which are the International Festival of Annecy and Carrefour du Cinéma d'Animation in France; Ottawa Animation Festival in Canada; the Festival of Hiroshima in Japan; and Animateka, from Slovenia. In addition, several production companies and institutions participated in the Anima Mundi Festival and maintain a partnership relationship, as well as interchange and exchange of information (Anima Mundi 2016).

In marketing terms, the Mapping of Animation in Brazil used three tools. The first of these was an online questionnaire with forty-five questions sent to producers, freelancers and individual authors, as well as being distributed by partners and industry associations. This stage reached more than 1,700 producers, of whom 455 responded to the survey (179 companies and 276 freelance professionals from twenty-four Brazilian states). The second tool, aimed at widening understanding of the context of development of the sector and its bottlenecks, consisted of in-depth interviews with eighteen representatives from the animation chain: public departments, sponsors/motivators, educational institutions, distributors, exhibitors, festivals, associations and software developers. The third tool, used to understand details of the activity from the perspective of workers in the sector, was a focus group held in April in São Paulo, and attended by ten people, including producers, 2D animators, stop motion animators, screenwriters and sound editors.

Thus, it was revealed who and how big the animation studios in Brazil are; the number of professionals acting in the formal market; professional profiles; identification of the main demands for workforce training and where there is a lack of training in certain specialisations within production; and types of products involved, among other information, as can be verified in Chart 3.1.

Despite animation being the top service provided by the mapped companies, only 44 per cent of professionals working in the area have some training in animation: that is, many are trained by the market itself

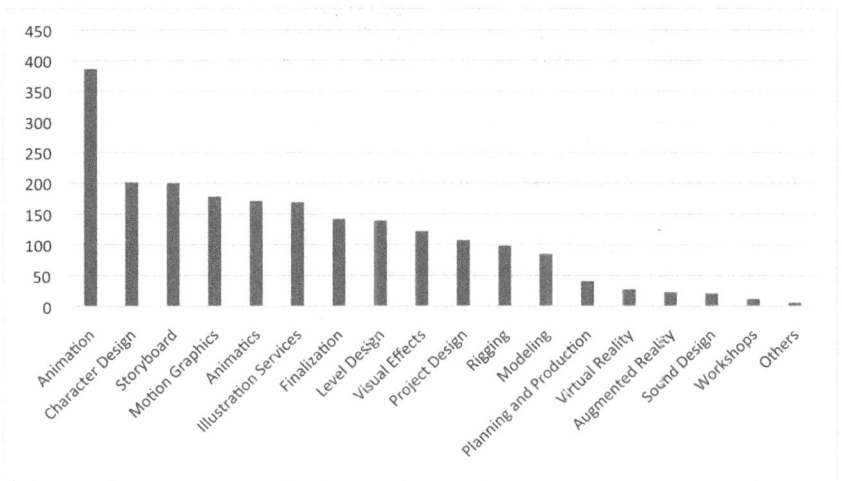

Chart 3.1 More common services/jobs.
Source: Mapping of Animation in Brazil, 2019.

(Anima Mundi 2016). Professional training appears as the limiting factor (72 per cent of companies stated that it is limiting) for development of the sector – be it in the technical area (animators) or higher qualifications (in the areas of management and script) – demanding qualification initiatives to guarantee the quality of products able to compete in the global market.

Origin of Resources and Intellectual Property Ownership

The audio-visual work involved in new and innovative animation is immaterial, intangible content and the fruit of human creativity, and can therefore be classified as intellectual property, in relation to copyright and trademark registration and patents, assuring its creator the right to protection and exploitation of the brand and characters created. Intellectual property generates revenue for a company and gives visibility to the brand and the characters, feeding a reputation that is key to the survival of businesses working in creative industry markets (Caves 2000; Gama 2014: 105). In the case of series or feature-length animated films for television, direct-to-video and cinema, the advantage for the studio in content production is the possibility of intellectual property ownership and, consequently, the generation of complementary distribution incomes and licensing (Gama 2014: 101).

Despite the sale of products/services and public funds/tax incentives being the main origins of resources for Brazilian animation works, as

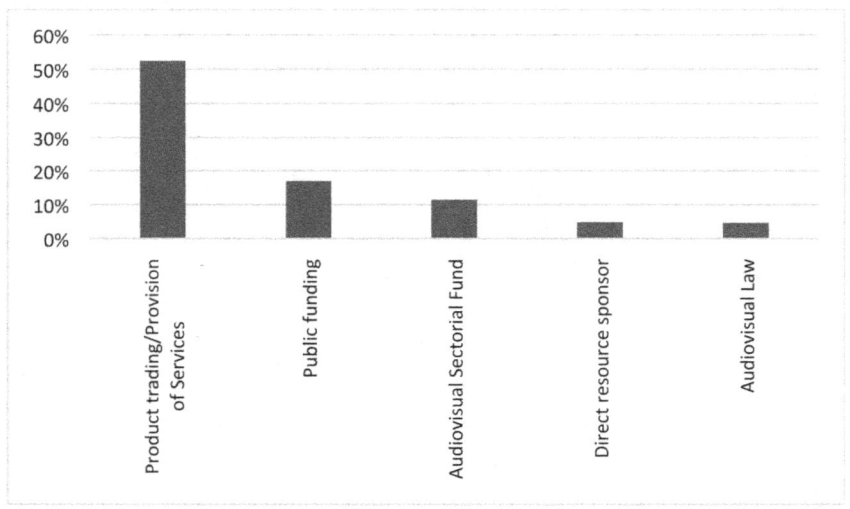

Chart 3.2 Origins of resources and intellectual property ownership.
Source: Mapping of Animation in Brazil, 2019.

shown in Chart 3.2, the Brazilian animation industry has managed significant achievements in the generation of intellectual property over the past few years. Television production began to appear on TV screens with the release of series such as *Peixonauta* (TV Pinguim 2009), shown in more than twenty countries; *Escola pra Cachorro* (Dog School, Mixer, 2009–10), which increased the viewing figures for Argentina's Nickelodeon channel by 138 per cent; and *Meu Amigão Zão* (My Big, Big Friend, 2DLab, 2011), which took third place in the Discovery Kids listings in Latin America. These were followed by the series *Tromba Trem* (Bouncing Train) and *Carrapatos e Catapults* (Ticks and Catapults) (both Anima Tv and Copa Studio, 2010).

Distribution Platforms of the Animation Segment

From a demand point of view, the main markets for digital animation are those in which the products consumed are feature films and animated short-duration series for television (famous cartoons such as *SpongeBob* and *Peppa Pig*); animation series made to be viewed in a non-linear form by the consumer, such as DVDs (for example, the *Baby Einstein* series); and digital services, which include video on demand (VOD), such as Now da Net, subscription video on demand (SVOD), Netflix, and over-the-top services such as iTunes and YouTube-like internet channels (Gama 2014: 102) (Chart 3.3).

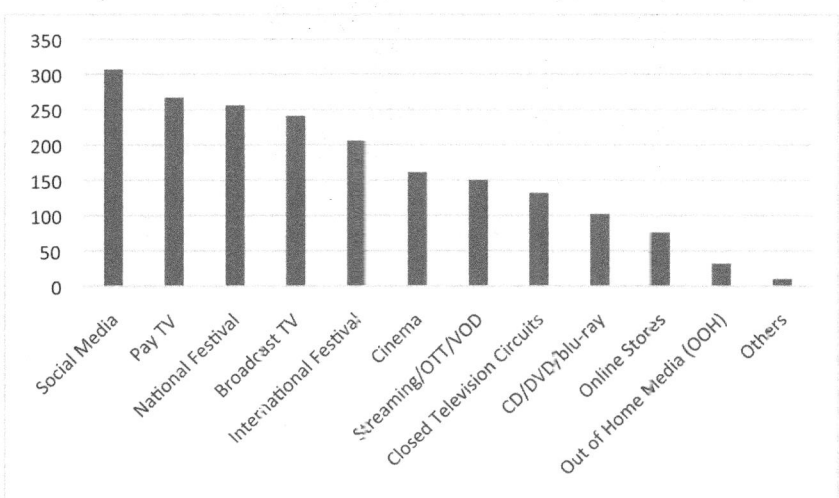

Chart 3.3 Distribution platforms in the animation segment.
Source: Mapping of Animation in Brazil, 2019.

In the case of the Brazilian animation industry, it is noticeable that, although it is a very new segment of the audio-visual sector, it nevertheless presents significant upward growth. In just ten years, the demand for animation content for the various communication platforms has increased considerably, which has enabled the emergence of Brazilian producers and studios specialised in this area.

There are currently twenty-five animated series on air on Brazil's television channels, and several more in production. Some 15 per cent of the programming of Cartoon Network in Brazil is made up of productions made in Brazil, including those on prime time. These are: *Irmão do Jorel* (Jorel's Brother, Copa Studio, 2014), *Turma da Mônica* (Monica's Gang, Cartoon Network Studios, Maurício de Sousa Produções and Split Studio, 2018–19), *Historietas Assombradas para Crianças Malcriadas* (Haunted Cartoons for Spoiled Children, Copa Studio, 2013), *Sítio do Picapau Amarelo* (Yellow Woodpecker Farm, Mixer Films and Rede Globo de Televisão, 2012), *Carrapatos e Catapultas* (Anima Tv and Copa Studio, 2010), *Tromba Trem* and *Gui & Estopa* (Mariana Caltabiano Criações, 2004) The main highlight is that these national series are audience leaders on their respective channels in Brazil and throughout Latin America.

So, in Brazil, animation has achieved strategic status in the production chain of the creative industry. Talented animators, formerly absorbed by international studios, are now the producers and exporters of Brazilian animation content in a wide variety of formats (web content, games, applications, series, movies, VOD, licensed products). Studios have been established, government grants have been developed and lines of credit have become available (Anima Mundi 2016: 18).

Export of Content and Service Provision of Animation to Overseas Companies

The internationalisation of production and division of animation work take place through two parallel movements: outsourcing and co-production.

The fact that animation is a labour-intensive activity requiring a specialised workforce has generated a cost structure that forces the outsourcing of animation production by large, globally competing firms located in developed countries to smaller studios based in developing countries, where wage costs are lower. In the case of Brazil, 43 per cent of Brazilian animation producers have exported animation content or services (Gama 2014: 117).

Part of the animation production of major studios in the main countries of production – the US, Europe, Japan and Canada – is outsourced to small studios in developing nations, such as those located in Asia, especially South Korea, Taiwan, India and China, but also to Brazil, a country which, in addition to guaranteeing low production costs, offers a workforce skilled in computer graphics. North America is where Brazilian producers mostly export content or animation services to, as can be seen in Chart 3.4.

In this process, the studios in developed countries are still responsible for the creative core, which develops the concept, preproduction, postproduction and distribution of the audio-visual work, with greater added value, while the studios in developing countries retain the production itself, of lesser value and technical complexity – and, without the property rights (Gama 2014: 117 and 135). Nevertheless, the advantage of possible outsourcing is the opportunity for studios in developing countries to gain expertise in higher-quality animation production, as well as acquiring knowledge of the best artistic and computational techniques, reducing costs, and increasing global animation output (Lee 2011: 16).

Co-production in the animation sector is also strategic for entering the global market competitively, with the creation of property rights and as a possible source of soft power. Here, a question arises regarding 'recognisable identity' or symbolic charge associated with an origin and with the sector, as Nye (2004) has pointed out when discussing the great potential of anime and manga as a source of soft power. The recognition

THE GLOBAL ANIMATION MARKET 69

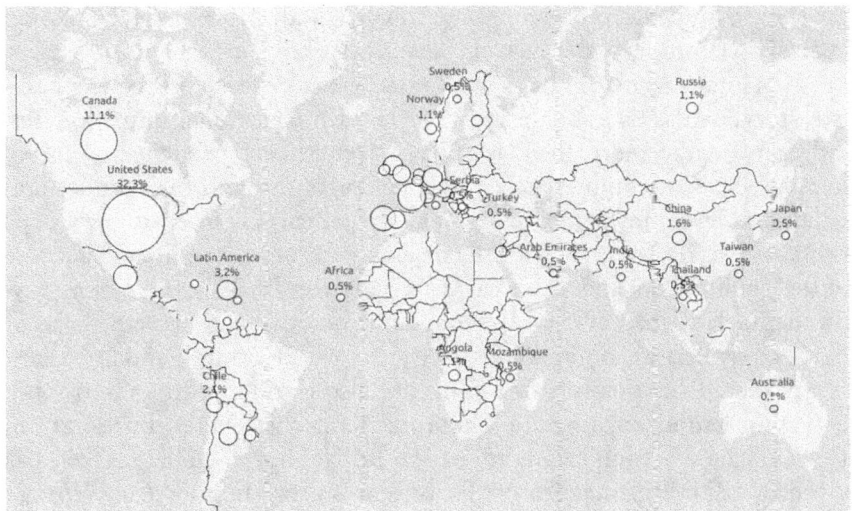

Chart 3.4 Export of content and animation service provision to overseas companies.
Source: Mapping of Animation in Brazil, 2019.

of an 'identity' (associated with a geographical origin) is a fundamental factor for the adoption of a cultural product as a soft power resource of a certain locality, group or nation. This association is what will ensure that the benefits generated in symbolic, affective and political terms are linked to the promoter of soft power actions. However, the process of deterritorialisation will influence perception of the origin of manifestations and products, like the various animations produced outside Japan with the same aesthetics and visual gags of animes. Added to this is the fact that, in the process of deterritorialisation, regardless of the existence of similar competitors, what assurance can be given that, in the overall consumption processes, there is a proper association of cultural expressions and products with their geographical origin? These points certainly pose risks around the question of recognition of an identity and perception of origin of animations.

In this sense, the SEA (South America–Europe–Asia) Project (Anima Mundi 2016: 30), which involved Brazilian, European and Japanese producers and creatives, well illustrates the trend towards deterritorialisation and strengthening of connections between the international animation industry and young artist development across the three territories. SEA, supported by the European Union's Media Mundus programme, was a two-week intensive concept development master class based on cooperation between the three continents, represented by Anima Mundi (Brazil), the Animation Workshop (Europe) and Office H (Japan), respectively.

This intensive master class was for early-career directors, concept artists, storyboard artists and designers from the international animation film industry. Furthermore, the master class strengthened participants' ability to create strong, commercially viable concepts through case studies and hands-on development processes. The main goal was to create new concepts and make them ready for the market – with export potential because of the dubbing tool and universal visual language, making them more easily adaptable to markets in different countries – that can form the basis of new deterritorialised animation-based story worlds, brands and universes.

Animated Brazilian feature films are also beginning to gain ground, nationally and internationally. The Annecy International Animation Film Festival, the most important animation festival in the global market, has given awards to Brazilian feature films for two years running. *Uma História de Amor e Fúria* (A Story of Love and Fury), by Luiz Bolognesi, was the winner of the Cristal Award in 2013 and *O Menino e o Mundo* (The Boy and the World), directed and produced by Alê Abreu, received the Cristal Award for Best Film selected by the Jury and the Public Prize, in 2014.

In January 2016, *O Menino e o Mundo* was nominated for the 2016 Oscars in the Best Animation category. Oscar-winning Best Foreign Films tend to be those that have, or will have, played on the festival circuit and have garnered prizes along the way, thus increasing their chances of playing as widely as possible in the US. They often have their own provocative back story and have usually received both critical and public support (Dennison and Meleiro 2016: 27). *O menino e o mundo* did not win the Oscar but has demonstrated its appeal to international popular taste, having functioned very effectively as a soft power resource.

The mobilisation involved in getting that far was huge. Weeks before the production team set foot in Los Angeles, 300,000 Brazilian reals (£75,000) had already been invested in the film's international publicity campaign by SPCine. SPCine took advantage of the animation for a soft power action, seeking to generate cultural, political and economic benefits for the city of São Paolo, in an alternative approach to public development and management.

With the SPCine resources, the distributor was able to announce the feature in the main publications that revolve around the event. As a consequence, the film was distributed in more than ninety countries, and won forty-five international awards (including the Annie Awards of 2016, considered the American Oscar for animation, as Best Independent Animated Film). The consumption mobilised through these festivals and prizes can be understood in a broader sense: it refers not only to their materiality or related products, but also to a whole set of symbols and ideas that collaborate in the construction of the images people have of Brazil. Leaving Brazil to reach consumers all over the world, the feature created movements of financial resources, people, ideas and ideals that involve and affect individuals, economies and policies (especially in Brazil itself).

SPCine then created a government programme to promote the city as a creative hub for animation, with the slogan 'São Paulo – An Animation City', the first and only measure of the use of animation as a soft power resource in Brazil. However, the slogan had no take-up in the national press or international media, and was completely forgotten after a change of administration at the city council.

A new opportunity for the opening of visibility flows occurred in 2018. Brazil was selected as the country to be honoured at the Annecy Festival, which features a retrospective of films, a panorama of contemporary artists, an exhibition and the presence of a special delegation and presentation at the International Animation Film Market (MIFA). The choice clearly demonstrated the potential and attractiveness of Brazilian animation in the eyes of the festival curators and the French public, and their likely effect both on the nation as a powerhouse of soft power, and on film production in the country, more broadly speaking.

Nevertheless, the initiatives promoted by the Brazilian government (through the Brazilian Cinema Programme, Apex/Ministry of Foreign Affairs) did not consider the condition imposed on a potential soft power resource: the ability to create actions of self-promotion. Thus, a potential reserve of soft power was systematically squandered.

The initiatives outlined above describe a scenario in which, with varying degrees of success, an emerging nation with a strong domestic audio-visual industry, but no sense of 'national film and audio-visual brand' in the international arena, has been working to increase its visibility. However, within this effort, soft power kudos is a bonus, rather than the prize, which ultimately continues to be increased sales (Dennison and Meleiro 2016: 25).

In discussing culture in the context of public diplomacy, or rather, as an instrument of foreign policy, Joseph Nye's soft power concept draws attention to the fundamental role of legitimisation played by culture in a country's international actions. However, in order to use audio-visual culture – and specifically animation – as an instrument of soft power, effective methods of internationalisation must be explored (Dennison and Meleiro 2016: 20). As this chapter has sought to highlight, the animation sector offers the potential to raise the international profile of Brazilian audio-visual production, with its attendant soft power rewards, but this is unlikely to be achieved without planned intervention.

Notes

1. In 1996, Simon Anholt coined the term 'nation brand' and originated an important field of research and practice. Since then, he has advised heads of state and heads of government in fifty-six countries to help them plan the policies, strategies, investments and innovations to lead their respective countries towards an improved profile and reputation. In addition to his advisory work, Professor Anholt developed the measurement systems: the Nation Brands Index^{SM} (NBI) and City Brands Index^{SM} (CBI), to assess how global citizens view the nations, cities and regions of the world (Anholt 2005; Ipsos 2019).
2. The research was carried out with foreign businesspeople in nine different countries.

Works Cited

Almeida, Paulo Roberto (2019), 'Miséria da Diplomacia: A Destruição da Inteligência no Itamaraty', *Coleção Comunicação e Políticas Públicas*, vol. 42. Boa Vista: Editora da Universidade Federal de Roraima.

Anholt, Simon (2005), *Brand New Justice: How Branding Places and Products Can Help the Developing World*. Oxford: Elsevier Butterworth–Heinemann.

Anima Mundi (2016), 'Centro Virtual de Animação: Apoio a Projetos Estruturante das Cadeias Produtivas da Economia da Cultura', February. Rio de Janeiro: BNDES.

Caves, R. (2000), *Creative Industries: Contracts Between Art and Commerce*. Cambridge, MA: Harvard University Press.

Dennison, S., and A. Meleiro (2016), 'Brazil, Soft Power and Film Culture', *New Cinemas*, 14:1, 17–30.

Gama, M. (2014), 'A Inserção dos Países em Desenvolvimento no Mercado Global de Animação', *Revista do BNDES* (Banco Nacional de Desenvolvimento Econômico e Social), 1:1, 42.

GFK Roper Public Affairs (2010), *Percepção da Imagem Brasil*. Brasília: GFK Roper Public Affairs/Apex-Brasil.

Ipsos (2019), 'Ipsos Public Affairs: Anholt Ipsos Nation Brands Index (NBI)', <https://www.ipsos.com/sites/default/files/19-05-50_Anholt_v2.pdf> (last accessed 2 August 2019).

Lee, J. (2011), *Animating Globalization and Development: The South Korean Animation Industry in Historical–Comparative Perspective*. Durham, NC: Duke University Press.

Meleiro, A., and J. Fonseca (2012), 'Economia Criativa: Análise Setorial', *Pragmatizes: Revista Latino Americana de Estudos em Cultura*, March, 2:2.

Meleiro, Alessandra, Reynaldo Marchesini and JLeiva Cultura & Esporte (2019), 'Mapeamento da Animação no Brasil', *JLeiva/Anima Mundi*, <http://mapeamentoanimacao.com.br/> (last accessed 27 October 2019).

Mello, Patrícia Campos (2019), 'Brasil e França Vivem Crise Diplomática mais Severa em Décadas', *Folha de S. Paulo*, <https://www1.folha.uol.com.br/mundo/2019/08/brasil-e-franca-vivem-crise-diplomatica-mais-severa-em-decadas.shtml> (last accessed 24 August 2019).

MinC/UNESCO (2018), *Manual de Exportação de Bens e Serviços Culturais*. Brasília: Secretaria de Economia Criativa.

Nye, Joseph S., Jr (2004), *Soft Power: The Means to Success in World Politics*. New York: Public Affairs.

O Estado de S. Paulo (2019), 'Editorial', 10 January.

Research and Markets (2019), 'Global Animation, VFX & Games Industry Strategies, Trends & Opportunities', *Cision PR Newswire*, <https://www.prnewswire.com/news-releases/global-animation-vfx--games-markets-2018-2020-total-value-of-global-animation-industry-is-projected-to-reach-us-270-billion-300773718.html> (last accessed 27 October 2019),

UNCTAD (2016), *Creative Economy Outlook: Trends in International Trade in Creative Industries (2002–2015)*. Geneva: UNCTAD.

CHAPTER 4

(Masha and) the Bear Diplomacy: Soft Power as World-building and Russian Non-governmental Agency

Vlad Strukov

Introduction

In his study of soft power, Joseph Nye identifies three areas of public diplomacy understood as a form of government-led agency. The areas are determined using two criteria: firstly, the frequency and duration of communication; and secondly, its strategic goal. The first area, then, includes 'daily communications', or social, economic and cultural information which is released on a day-by-day basis by government agents. The second area encompasses strategic communication: that is, 'branding the central theme and advancing a particular government policy'. Finally, forming the third area of activity, public diplomacy focuses on 'the development of lasting relationships with key individuals over many years through scholarship, exchanges, training, seminars, conferences, and access to media channels' (Nye 2004: 108–9). According to Nye, through successful deployment and management of all three areas of public diplomacy, nation-states gradually build the capacity to possess significant soft power in a region and globally. In this regard, how successful has Russian public diplomacy been in recent years?

The Russian government's daily communications, such as those released by Maria Zakharova, Director of the Information and Press Department of the Ministry of Foreign Affairs, are mistrusted by the international community, especially by Anglophone media. When reporting political events, they tend to avoid references to Zakharova and other spokespersons of President Putin, reducing the effect of Russian daily communication. Russian strategic communication has misfired on many occasions. For example, in spite of the attempts in 2013–17 to brand the Russian military as peacekeepers in the Middle East, the Russian government has been held responsible for President Bashar al-Assad's actions against the Syrian people.[1] Similarly, in terms of global concerns, Russia is seen to be cultivating, not combating, climate change (Smeets 2014), and Russian strategic communication on this subject is geared toward aggressive promotion of its own economic interests, especially in the Arctic. As for the development of lasting relationships, the Russian leadership has developed contacts with the autocratic regimes of China and Turkey, whilst minimising or even severing links with Western democracies.[2] Overall, in spite of the country's recent efforts to stage global soft power events such as the Sochi Olympics and the football World Cup, Russian government-led public diplomacy has produced either negative or mixed results.

In this context, is it possible to speak of Russian soft power? Is there Russian non-governmental soft power? How does it affect, if at all, the image of the country? Do these non-governmental, grassroots agents advance a different image of the country on the global stage? Which channels of communication do they use? And from a theoretical point of view, how relevant is government-led public diplomacy in the era of grassroots-led digital communication and global media events such as memes, flash mobs and user-driven online campaigns? How does a consideration of these channels extend Nye's notion of soft power, public diplomacy and agency? In this chapter, I answer these questions by assessing the effectiveness of Russian soft power in the era of digital communication networks controlled by Western powers, especially the US. I also consider whether soft power depends exclusively on positive branding of a country, or if it can also make use of some negative connotations. Ultimately, I conceptualise the interconnections of negative and positive flows, effectively expanding and fine-tuning the notion of soft power.

The Rise of the Bear, or a Theoretical Recap

Elsewhere (Strukov 2017), taking the discourse around the release of Andrei Zviagintsev's *Leviathan* as a case study, I analysed Russian soft power, arguing that, on the one hand, it includes positive aspects which are similar to those employed by other countries, such as, for example, the promotion of Russian films at festivals in Europe and elsewhere. On the other hand, Russian soft power includes negative aspects, such as deliberate construction of the image of a hostile, powerful country These negative strategies are employed by the Russian government as a securitisation[3] tool at times of crisis and at times when 'positive' strategies have been exhausted. To paraphrase Nye's definition of soft and hard power, this kind of 'negative soft power' has been used to achieve hard power objectives, such as securing Russian sovereignty and protecting Russian business from exposure to global competition and global scrutiny.

Whilst analysing the discourse around Zviagintsev's *Leviathan*, I also showed that Russian soft power has both an international and a domestic dimension. This means that the Russian government has the purpose and the mandate to use external soft power tools to maintain the integrity of the Russian Federation. This is an increasingly difficult task in a country which is 'a federation of nations', with some autonomous republics taking charge of their political and economic development.[4] Moreover, Russian soft power is transnational in so far as it targets communities and policymakers in the country and abroad, and it is produced by agents within and outside of the Federation. For example, the popular liberally biased media outlet Meduza targets Russophone users from Riga, Latvia, whilst being officially registered in a British offshore territory. Equally, in the UK, Russian media magnate Lebedev, a former KGB officer, has manœuvred the British political establishment in order to receive a nomination from the Prime Minister for a peerage (Steerpike 2020). Russian soft power is no longer tethered to the realm of the 'Soviet empire' as it was conceived by Nye a decade after the dissolution of the USSR, but instead exists as a transnational, multi-agent realm which continues to evolve into a world, not just a series, of interconnected activities.

'Russian manipulative soft power' encompasses external and internal dimensions of public diplomacy and its relationship to non-governmental agency. It allows the Russian government to retool and repurpose negative communication to its advantage, for example, by transforming negative external perceptions of the country into positive publicity at home, aiming to advance Russian nationalism domestically. At the same time, the government employs transnational flows of Russian soft power to construct the notion of Russianness as a transborder phenomenon: that is, one stretching beyond the state borders of the Russian Federation and including communities in Georgia, Ukraine and elsewhere. This fluid notion of Russianness, the state and the country, whose borders continue to change externally and internally,[5] in combination with the transnational aspect of Russian soft power agency and a developed global telecommunication infrastructure, presents a difficult case for conceptualisation in so far as it cannot be determined using a binary system of values proposed by Nye.

In the West, Russian 'manipulative soft power' has been perceived as a series of threats to Western security, democracy and economy.[6] These have been framed as conventional threats and digital threats. The following examples illustrate this point. In the first instance, in the aftermath of the annexation of Crimea, a threat of Russian occupation of the Baltic States (RFE/RL 2018) has been used as a means to promote the security agenda of these countries in the European Union. In the second instance, a threat of Russian hackers attacking servers of foreign governments and transnational corporations[7] has been identified as a major concern.[8] Also, in the digital realm, Russian manipulative power has been identified as an attempt to influence elections in Western democracies such as during the 2016 US elections.

The striking feature of the discourse around Russian influence is an attempt to safeguard from it not only Western political institutions but Western values, too. For example, Facebook has implemented tools that block Russian malign communication. Facebook has also been compelled to present a strategic vision for the company and its capacity to protect values such as privacy and freedom of expression. To confirm, Russian influence had revealed Facebook's vulnerabilities in terms of infrastructure and in terms of the company's policies and practices concerning data collection, sharing and protection of privacy, leading to a mass exodus of users from the platform. Thus, Russian soft power is imbricated in the very fabric of Western discourse and, I would argue of Western democracies per se, as a threat and a symbolic counter-agent.

Western interpretation of Russian influence is rooted in the perceptions of Russia and the Russian state which have a long-standing history. In his study of regimes of (re)branding post-Soviet states, Robert A. Saunders writes that 'through popular culture and other forms of national image projection, Britain and the US engaged in the ideological Othering of Russia to reinforce their own credos and reify their "mutable self-images"' (Saunders 2017: 29.) Strategies of othering Russia – and other entities, indeed – take different forms, including the production and repetitive use of specific metaphors and visuals. These processes were critiqued and theorised by Edward Said in his *Orientalism* and, since then, in the expanding field of postcolonial studies. In recent years, postcolonial theory and the emerging discipline of popular geo-politics (Saunders and Strukov 2018) have turned their attention to popular culture. For example, in an article, tellingly titled 'Jungle Politics: Animal Metaphors in International Relations', Ioana Lung (2018) discusses the ways in which symbols and stereotypes derived from the animal world are used to account for international relations and domestic policies. The researcher notes that the Russian bear, 'originally used by the British and other Westerners as early as the sixteenth century to ridicule the big, brutal clumsy Russia, was later adopted and embraced by Russia itself as a symbol that projected power (and instilled fear)' (ibid. 236).

This is a historical example of how negative connotations can be adopted to achieve a strategic advantage. The image of the bear as a symbol of Russian public diplomacy allows me to theorise the ways in which

Russian public diplomacy aims to project power and, when necessary, to instil fear. The first part of the chapter title – 'bear diplomacy' – makes a reference to Russian public diplomacy and its perception in the West, effectively sustaining the discourse about the weaknesses of Russian soft power, or reframing it conceptually as a kind of soft power which is inseparable from hard power. Another element of the chapter title – '*Masha and the Bear*' – alludes to a different kind of power. It originates in the agency of private capital: namely, artists, performers and creative directors whose main objective is to advance their audio-visual product to new markets, and who, in that process, strengthen Russian soft power. Indeed, *Masha and the Bear* is the name of an animated television series which has gained global popularity, thanks to its producers using the internet, especially YouTube, as their principal distribution platform. Masha (also known as Maria) is the name of a little girl who is one of the characters in the series and whose image can be interpreted as that of Russia itself (Fig. 4.1).

Therefore, the full title of the chapter – '(*Masha and*) *the Bear* diplomacy' – is not meant to pivot government-led agency against non-governmental agency, and top-down diplomacy against grassroots diplomacy. To confirm, I do not wish to reiterate the binary approach to soft power advocated by Nye. Instead, my purpose is to propose a new understanding of soft power which relies on the convergence of multiple flows. In this framework, different forms of soft power, negative soft power and manipulated soft power bleed one into another with the effect

Figure 4.1 The Bear enjoying afternoon tea. *Masha and the Bear*, episode 1.

of supplying an image of the country which, in terms of its origins, formation, distribution and consumption, is not binary but rather multiple. I develop these concerns in the third section of the chapter, where I conceptualise soft power in relation to transmedia storytelling and symbolic capital. In the second section, I provide an in-depth critique of Nye's conceptualisation of Russian soft power from the perspective of poststructuralist theory.

Masha and the Bear was created by Oleg Kuzovkov in collaboration with a US-based creative collective and produced by Animaccord Animation Studio (Moscow). It shows the adventures of a mischievous little girl named Masha and a bear that keeps her company. The first instalment was released in 2009. With each episode lasting on average 6 minutes, over seventy episodes have been released so far. *Masha and the Bear* has been translated into twenty-five languages. Some episodes of the series have over one billion views on YouTube. One of the episodes, entitled *Recipe for Disaster* (Masha plus kasha) (Fig. 4.2), has more than 3.3 billion views, making it the fifth most viewed video of all time, and the most viewed video on YouTube which is not a music video (Stolworthy 2016). The popular success of Masha and the Bear remains unaccounted for in literature, including the fields of Russian studies, film studies, politics and popular geo-politics.

My case demonstrates how Russian soft power straddles national borders and the boundaries between online and offline worlds, thus producing soft power in the form of network. It relies on instantaneity of

Figure 4.2 Masha making 'kasha' (porridge). *Masha and the Bear*, episode 17.

communication, multiple vectors of communication (many to many, not one to many), and non-linear forms of production and dissemination of content. It also includes new makers of soft power – users of the internet and social media – who participate in the production of a country's soft power through their activity on different platforms and gadgets such as mobile phones and tablets. My understanding of agency as ongoing, networked and cross-platform allows me to theorise (Russian) soft power in the twenty-first century as that of world-building.

I define world-building as a way to create and sustain long-term engagement of users with a fictional universe which extends beyond existing notions and forms of cultural exchange. World-building relies on horizontal forms of exchange and participation, not on top-down management of audiences. In this regard, power is soft not because it differs from hard power of the state, but because it enables fluid associations and collaborative participation of imaging and creating a world.

To account for local and global concerns, in my discussion below I use the acronym 'the RF' to refer to the Russian Federation, a country that emerged on the world scene after the dissolution of the USSR in 1991. Its purpose is to emphasise the multicultural, multiconfessional, multiethnic and multilingual construction of the new state. I use the term 'Russian' to refer to a cultural tradition which has been sustained over centuries on the territory, or some parts of it, currently occupied by the RF and previously by the USSR and Russian Empire.[9] The latter term designates overlapping but incongruent spaces of cultural production and political influence which have been created with the help of cultural producers whose origins and belongings have always been multiple. As a result, in my understanding, the term 'Russian' exceeds any specific form of governance or national construction.[10] Where necessary, I provide original Cyrillic titles and terms in a transliterated form in brackets: for example, 'the bear' (medved').

Masha and the Bear: The Soft Power of a Fluid State

Russia has an ambiguous country image. On the one hand, according to Saunders (2017), Russia has one of the most powerful brands in the world; on the other, this brand has negative connotations due to the Soviet past. To complicate the situation, the RF is a new state that is in the process of examining its relationship with the (Soviet) past. The brand of Russia is being reimagined and reinvented using multiple and contradictory elements. The relationship between the Soviet era and the contemporary period is not straightforward. Indeed, in 1991, the leadership of the newly formed RF assumed legal responsibility over Soviet institutions, including the nuclear arsenal, international debt and so on. However, it has been argued[11] that the RF is not a political, social and cultural extension of the USSR (not just 'a successor state') but rather a new entity with a global outlook ('a post-state'). In fact, due to the constant change of borders and spaces, of organisation and governance, and of economic models, Russia is a fluid state challenging classical models of the nation-state. Thus, a critical review of Nye's conceptualisation of Russian soft power is required.

Approaching Russian Soft Power from the Poststructuralist Perspective

Although Nye's book was originally published in 2004 – that is, over a decade since the dissolution of the USSR – it makes no distinction between the Soviet Union and the RF. To be precise, Nye discusses Russian soft power through the framework of Soviet soft power. This is a conceptual moniker of the so-called 'transition studies', or transitology. In this paradigm, the RF is investigated using a binary approach (for example, 'Is Russia pro-Western or anti-Western?'). In fact, Nye uses Russia to define other entities: according to him, what makes American soft power is what Soviet power was not. For instance, he (2004) claims that the USSR had no popular culture, and as a result could not supply values or cultural products that it could champion worldwide. By contrast, the US had both a cultural industry and appealing cultural products. Nye celebrates the popularity of US cultural products and equates their popularity with their impact without considering whether responses to these products were always positive in the short term (how the audiences constructed their responses to the experience) and in the long term (how the ideology of these products influenced the evolution of democratic societies in specific local contexts).[12]

Ultimately, by reading Russian as Soviet, Nye supplies a US-centric conceptualisation of soft power. To paraphrase Said, Nye orientalises Russia by assigning it one kind of agency, one that is dependent on the state and informed by communist ideology. Contrary to Nye, my understanding of soft power is polycentric. My analysis of *Masha and the Bear* reveals the role of non-government agency in exercising soft power. Moreover, I argue that this agency and soft power are informed by neoliberal logic, according to which cultural capital in the form of the symbolic economy and transmedia story-building is manipulated to advance free trade and free exchange of information, the primary purpose of which is to generate capital, not to advance progressive social reforms. Ultimately, to resist self-neoliberalisation of research, I do not wish to investigate whether Russian soft power is pro- or anti-Western; instead I wish to investigate what objectives Russian participation in the multisited project of globalisation aims to achieve. To reiterate, the difference in research questions connotes the orientation of research vis-à-vis the economic and cultural project of neoliberalism.

The neoliberal orientation of *Masha and the Bear* is evident in the themes it explores. For example, the series places a lot of emphasis on a person's individuality and the process of individualisation itself. In the majority of episodes, Masha is portrayed as living on her own; indeed, the bear is her friend but arguably an imaginary one. The disinterest in a fair society is hardly a problem that can be explained by poor storytelling and characterisation. Rather, it manifests social and cultural changes that have occurred in the RF and elsewhere in the world, including the breakup of traditional communities and discontinuation of previous modes of socialisation. By comparison, Soviet animation celebrated the relationship of an individual to society; in fact, a Soviet individual was to emerge, thanks to a symbolic entry into the Soviet ideological system embodied in the family and community (Kaganovsky 2008). Similarly, the transition to a neoliberal system is evident in the ways in which the series addresses the issue of social responsibility, such as education and the duties of a parent vis-à-vis the state. To explicate, since the dissolution of the USSR, the RF leadership has reversed many social practices, including the Soviet principle of collective responsibility for the education of children. In the twenty-first century, the privatisation of education has manifested itself in a proliferation of private institutions such as schools and universities, as well as in a shift of parents' duties from the public arena (that is, various social groups, clubs and so on) to that which is private (that is, the family, consumption-oriented spaces and so on). Thus, *Masha and the Bear* celebrates the neoliberal ideology of consumption, austerity and decreased role of the state, thus rejecting Nye's allegation of Russian soft power being linked to communism.

Approaching Russian Soft Power from the Transnational Perspective

Because Nye disregards the concerns of other global agents, his conceptualisation of soft power, its nature and scope, remains one-sided and therefore vague. For example, he uses an example derived from the 9/11 attacks and the ensuing war on terror to discuss Polish soft power. Nye notes that 'the Polish government decided to send troops to post-war Iraq not only to curry favour with the United States but also to create a broader positive image in world affairs' (2004: 10). For Nye, the Polish government managed to extract soft power from the application of hard power. This contradicts his view on Russian soft power whereby all Russian power is always a type of hard power, never leading to the creation of soft power. Nye explains that this is because it serves the interests of the Russian state. However, I argue that this is due to Nye defining soft power on the basis of the political and economic interests of the US alone. Hence, his reading of the Russian case is ideological/orientalist.

To continue with the Polish example, Nye is not invested in examining whether those people who support the war on terrorism objected to tactical decisions such as the invasion of Iraq. I argue that, for some, Poland did not gain, but rather lost, some of its soft power. For example, writing in *Al Jazeera English*, Tallha Abdulrazaq, a researcher at the University of Exeter's Strategy and Security Institute, describes the invasion of Iraq as 'the original sin of the 21st century' (2018). From this perspective, Polish involvement in the war in Iraq is questionable in terms of the country's execution of soft power. From the perspective of the US government, this involvement was useful in so far as it validated the US actions. This is a case which shows how Nye uses soft power to legitimate hard power.

With the RF, Nye's refusal to consider non-government agency sustains the dominant reading of Russian soft power. It is regularly attributed to the government alone and described using the terms 'propaganda', 'disinformation', 'information war' and so on. My contention is that the Russian government has, indeed, used propaganda and disinformation to advance its agenda (see Strukov 2018). However, Russian soft power is not locked to the government alone. Instead, there are multiple actors responsible for Russian soft power globally. In some cases, their role in advancing the positive image of the country has been more powerful than that of the state. Hence, the constellation of Russian soft power requires a critique of Russian government-backed and independent agents, as well as a critique of the Western discourse around Russia and its soft power.

The Cold War era division of contemporary Russian actors into pro- and anti-government – the so-called 'supporters of the regime' and 'dissidents' – has been challenged on many occasions. In fact, elsewhere (2017), I argued that the Russian government has been in a response mode to non-government agents of soft power. The government has attempted to co-opt and exploit, not to initiate or stimulate, the work of independent cultural producers. These actors are used to 'distract public attention away from pressing concerns at home such as the deteriorating economic situation (including capital flight and the devaluation of the rouble), the escalation of class antagonisms, migration, and so on' (Strukov 2017: 43). Different kinds of soft power create 'zones of mediation and dispute' (Strukov 2016: 43). *Masha and the Bear* is one of such zones which overlaps with others, creating a complex, world-like system of distribution and influence.

This consideration allows me to theorise Russian soft power in a new way. I propose a conceptualisation that is not binary (for example, 'the individual versus the government'), but multicentric ('the government is one of many actors on the global stage'). In this conceptualisation, Russian soft power reveals not only the concerns of Russian people and the Russian state but those of globalisation itself. To paraphrase the title of the animated series, 'bear diplomacy' represents not only the hard power of the Russian government, but hard power per se. Therefore, the key area of impact of *Masha and the Bear* is the project's capacity to enquire about global concerns such as the use of power and the role of grassroots cultural producers.

The choice of this tale is based on the familiarity and popularity of the characters, on the one hand, and on the tale's soft power potential, on the other, thus making it a perfect case for popular geo-politics. For many centuries, in Western discourse, an image of a young woman has been used as a symbol of the Russian nation, whilst the bear is synonymous with the Russian state (Saunders 2017). Domestically, then, the series offers audiences an interpretation of a familiar narrative, and internationally, it makes use of existing stereotypes in order to draw audiences into a new world. The series employs a familiar language – read, the brand of Russia – in a humorous setting to create and advance a new language – and a new brand – hence promoting a new perception of the country.

With *Masha and the Bear*, soft power is realised through the process of world-building, not through a public relations campaign, advertising, or a similar tactic which has been described in literature on nation branding (see, for example, Dinnie 2015; Surowiec 2016). In comparison with previous government-led branding projects, such as that of the former Soviet republics of Estonia and Georgia (Kaneva 2011), *Masha and the Bear* brands Russia using bottom-up, cross-platform, transnational methods. To confirm, the series helps brand Russia and, conversely, uses the brand of Russia to achieve its economic goals, not the brand of the RF. The latter is the domain of the government, wherein a dichotomy between different branding strategies and different notions of the state are maintained. Literature on Russian culture and history of the Russian Empire (see, for example, Condee 2009) identifies a rift between what constitutes Russia, on the one hand, and the RF, on the other. I contend, firstly, that this dichotomy, or rather difference, is evident in diverging strategies of branding, not in the ideological positioning vis-à-vis the West (pro- or anti-Western), and secondly, that the opening gap provides opportunities for political and economic manœuvring by different agents of power, including independent cultural producers.

I also argue that, whilst exercising soft power in a transnational setting, *Masha and the Bear* has impacted the national context, too. By supplying a globally successful product, the makers of the project have redefined the relationship between cultural producers and other agents of power such as the government. These new configurations of power, capital and creativity deserve a focused examination in a separate publication. However, in the subsequent section I focus on how soft power is constructed across different platforms as a transmedial phenomenon.

Masha and the Bear: The Soft Power of Post-celluloid Cinema

Until recently, in film theory, animation had been treated as a 'less important medium'. In present-day scholarship, animation occupies a more central position due to the perceived 'death of cinema'. Lev Manovich (2001) has pointed out that animation has greater capacity in terms of production of abstract and mimetic imagery. For Manovich, film is a sub-medium of animation, or to be precise, is a particular mode of creating an animated image of real and imaginary worlds. In other words, animation is a more general term encompassing different kinds of the still and the moving image, such as photography and video. With the emergence of digital imaging, animation has become a more widespread and prominent medium.

In addition, animation has emerged as a site for experimentation in terms of production and distribution, such as distribution of audio-visual content on social media sites and content streaming services such as YouTube. Animation produced with the help of digital tools such as Macromedia Flash naturally allows for serialisation and customisation in terms of content and channels of distribution, for example, by email (for further discussion see Strukov 2007). These characteristics enable me to label contemporary digital animation a type of 'post-celluloid cinema', or cinema that advances new modes of production, distribution and reception. It belongs to the post-broadcast era of media and cultural circulation characterised by horizontal, multivector and multispeed exchanges.

These new modes employ novel methods of storytelling, including transmedia storytelling. They also produce new forms of symbolic capital, which was not accounted for in Nye's original conception of soft power due to its location within the context of the broadcast era, not in the post-broadcast era. In the two sub-sections below, I explore the ways in which soft power is produced by non-state actors in the new context of global cultural exchange. I start by analysing the transmedia storytelling of *Masha and the Bear*, and I conclude with an account of the serial's symbolic capital, which, I argue, translates into Russian soft power. In both instances, I consider *Masha and the Bear* not only as a text but also as a world which is to be encountered and explored by the user.

Masha and the Bear's Transmedia Storytelling

Masha and the Bear's world-building capacity is accounted for by transmedia storytelling. Employed by Henry Jenkins to describe the work of Hollywood producers (2007), transmedia storytelling is about conveying and building a single story or an experience across multiple platforms and formats. Transmedia storytelling invites contributions from audiences so that they become prosumers (producers + consumers) of content and active members in world-building. Structurally, the world of *Masha and the Bear* encompasses a broad range of elements such as:

(a) original films produced by the animation studio, which are made available for free on television (for example, Russian Channel One and British Sky), on the official website (https://mashabear.ru/), on mobile applications, on YouTube and social media, both Russian and Western (Vkontakte and Facebook, respectively), and in online cinemas such as Netflix
(b) all kinds of merchandise providing a multisensory experience of the *Masha and the Bear* world[13]
(c) sites and blogs where parents share their views on the series[14]
(d) fan art[15]
(e) storyboards on Pinterest and similar user-generated platforms
(f) collaborations with transnational food producers such as Burger King and Danone; and so on.

The use of transmedia helps construct meaning across many platforms, create an effect of interactivity and immersion, provide a multisensory experience and build a user-oriented world. *Masha and the Bear* is dependent on non-linear extensions of the world, using several genres and styles. Serialisation plays an important role in the proliferation of the world. On one level, each episode makes a new contribution to the existing world; on another, each addition rehearses an existing narrative, thus making meaning through multiplication. Transfer of content from one platform to another creates new contexts and associations, through which meaning is conveyed. The recursive nature of the constructed work is experienced as its duration. For example, on YouTube, several episodes of the series are combined into a single video, lasting over an hour, thus providing continuous but serialised entertainment. With the addition of algorithmic catalogues used by Netflix and other streaming services, the world of *Masha and the Bear* transpires as circular (it develops in a loop) and serial (it consists of self-referential iterations). The effect of this form of organisation of the world is that it is navigable and explorable, thus enabling a different kind of agency which is different from the linear agency of government-led public diplomacy identified by Nye. Serialisation provides *Masha and the Bear* with additional visibility, which, I argue, translates into a more effective tool of soft power.

Masha and the Bear transmedia storytelling is intermedial in so far it encompasses different media, as well as online and offline worlds. For example, a Georgian puppet company called Mul'ti-Pul'ti has been commissioned to stage live performances. And in 2015, a Slovak company, Comunique, created an ice show based on the series, while in Budapest, Hungary, *Masha and the Bear* live events became extremely popular. The space of the series is international: the series is currently available in twenty-four languages. Whilst the animation studio responsible for the production of *Masha and the Bear* is registered in the RF, the company that owns the brand of the series is registered in the USA, thus sustaining a transnational network of agency and soft power.

Masha and the Bear has received a number of prestigious awards for its innovative design, including a 2018 Best Animation Kidscreen Award, which is the equivalent of an Oscar for animation films. The series is produced using 3D rendering software (Autodesk Maya and Pixar Renderman), some of which was created by Russian developers specifically for the series. Although the technology is different, *Masha and the Bear* exploits the stylistics and distribution systems of its predecessors, such as the British series *Salad Fingers*, created by David Firth in 2004, and the Russian *Masiania*, created by Oleg Kuvaev in 2002. The last two became international hits in the 2000s when the increased speed of data exchange on the internet allowed for downloads and streaming of short clips. In my previous analysis (2005: 12), I noted that flash animation

> employs assemblage syntax to images and sound to advance technology-animated animism, expressed as an interactive aesthetic of negotiation and computer agency. The visual element belongs to the realm of improvisation, re-enactment: the sound dominates the compositional plane, the visual – the improvisational.

Masha and the Bear maintains the two planes – compositional and improvisational – except for the fact that, nowadays, these planes are spread over multiple media and platforms in the transmedia world.

Masha and the Bear's symbolic capital

The case of *Masha and the Bear* reveals that, in the era of digital technologies, it is the availability of a cultural product for free consumption across multiple platforms that guarantees its success in terms of symbolic capital. Revenue is generated through sales of merchandise, copyright permissions and advertising. In addition to direct economic benefit, the studio invests in the increase of its symbolic capital. Pierre Bourdieu (1990: 122) explains that

> the existence of symbolic capital, that is, of 'material' capital misrecognized and thus recognized, though it does not invalidate the analogy between capital and energy, does remind us that social science is not a social physics; that the acts of cognition that are implied in misrecognition and recognition are part of social reality and that the socially constituted subjectivity that produces them belongs to objective reality.

To paraphrase, the shift from materiality to immateriality of capital and vice versa signifies transfers between ideas and values and between symbolic capital and soft power. As a result, an assessment of cultural capital must reveal the potentiality of soft power.

In the case of *Masha and the Bear*, its symbolic capital is manifested in online statistics – the number of views, shares, likes and so on – which indicate the activity of prosumers sustaining the development of the world. It is also manifested in the power to negotiate new contracts, such as that with Netflix, and to secure funding from private investors for future projects. Finally, the symbolic capital of *Masha and the Bear* is in interconnectedness: the visual style of the series is recognised globally and therefore what the makers of the series have supplied is not only a particular story, or a character, but a visual identity of a whole world.

Masha and the Bear is one of the first Russian transmedia projects with an international outreach. In the 2000s, Timur Bekmambetov, a Kazakhstani–Russian–US film director and producer, attempted to create a transmedia world on the basis of Sergei Luk'ianenko's fiction series called *Night Watch* (Nochnoi dozor), about vampires roaming the streets of Moscow.[16] Whilst the films were critically acclaimed and were released in mainstream cinemas in the West, *Night Watch* did not have a global resonance. I argue that it was due to the weakness of Russian cultural industry of the time, not the creative potential of *Night Watch*.[17]

Following the economic crisis of 2008 and readjustment of economy in ensuing years, the RF, and especially its capitals, Moscow and St Petersburg, developed a robust cultural industry with a range of government-backed and independent initiatives attracting global attention. In terms of cinema, it is the work of Andrei Zviagintsev and Vitalii Manskii; in fashion, Gosha Rubchinskiy for Comme des Garçons and Maria Jahnkoy for Puma; in visual arts, the Ural Biennale of Contemporary Arts, directed by Alisa Prudnikova, and Garage Museum of Contemporary Art, directed by Anton Belova, and so on. Russian cultural producers have extended their economic, social and aesthetic capital through a range of projects, including, for example, the opening of educational centres in countries like Brazil, where lecturers from Russia teach local students art, design and digital culture. These projects are often independent – that is, not affiliated or supported by the Russian state – and are often transnational. For example, the Design School that opened in São Paolo is a branch of the British School of Design (Moscow), which uses the brand of a British university and the expertise of Russian lecturers in the multicultural context of Brazil's largest city.

As the Russian cultural industry matures, it enters into competition with Western cultural producers, including Hollywood. With the last, as Stephen Norris (2012) has noted, rather than restricting access to Hollywood productions, or advancing a different aesthetic informed by an anti-hegemonic ideology, Russian cinema has employed the strategy of adopting and adapting cinematic narratives and styles, producing what Norris has labelled 'the patriotic blockbuster'. It is an amalgamation of characters, story lines, mise-en-scène and so on, all borrowed as a language of contemporary cinema and repurposed to express Russian domestic concerns.

Like the patriotic blockbuster produced with the support from the Russian state, *Masha and the Bear* is an example of the hybridisation of aesthetic forms, media and storytelling. Indeed, the pairing of two characters resembles that of classical Hollywood, whilst the emphasis on a female character and gender fluidity makes a reference to the issues of the #MeToo era. However, unlike the patriotic blockbuster, *Masha and the Bear* does not advance the ideological concerns of the Russian state. To reiterate, *Masha and the Bear* is not concerned with the Russian geo-political, social and economic problems which are evident in cinematic blockbusters such as *Legend 17* (Legenda 17, Nikolai Lebedev, 2013). Moreover, unlike, these movies, the serial is consistent in its multiculturalist agenda. Indeed, the patriotic blockbuster should be seen as a form of cultural hybridisation with nationalist undertones, which is characteristic of the contemporary RF. By contrast, *Masha and the Bear* attempts to speak about global citizenship from the Russian perspective:

that is, through the lens of a character and within a world that features elements of Russian culture alongside markers of difference. *Masha and the Bear* is responsible for marketing Russian culture to a global audience with the view of monetising shared values and increasing its own symbolic capital.

Conclusion: World-building and Soft Power

Russian soft power agents make use of Western distribution platforms such as YouTube. In this regard, they contribute to Western-led globalisation whilst broadening the notion of the West to include the RF. Another way to read this use of media technologies is as an attempt to reconfigure globalisation so that it emanates from multiple centres. Cultural products available for free enjoyment on the internet advance this sense of multiplicity, whereby attribution of soft power to a particular agent is nowadays a complex procedure. My discussion above has showcased how, in terms of its orientation, as is evident in its aesthetic and circumstances of production, *Masha and the Bear* is an element of Russian soft power, yet in terms of circulation, it is trans- and multinational, advancing a sense of multipolar and multidirectional globalisation.[18]

The latter is possible, thanks to the serial's world-building capacity, whereby all consumers engage in the construction of the world of *Masha and the Bear* through different forms of participation. These interactions and the very structure of the world exceed Nye's understanding of soft power, which relies on 'daily communications' and strategic communication. The world of *Masha and the Bear* overlaps to an extent with Nye's third category, that of 'the development of lasting relationships with key individuals over many years'; however, for Nye, these relationships are elite-oriented – 'key individuals' – and built around top-down activities such as 'exchanges, training, seminars, conferences, and access to media channels', whilst *Masha and the Bear* realises horizontal, user-oriented and user-generated activities and contributions, thus advancing a completely different sense of (Russian) soft power.

Masha and the Bear's involvement in the production of horizontal connections means that there is a new relationship between popularity and visibility, which, in its turn, foregrounds new forms of symbolic capital. In this regard, grassroots agents and independent actors have greater power than the Russian state to advance a new image of the country and its culture on a global scale. It is no longer a choice between 'bear diplomacy' and 'Masha diplomacy': that is, negative and positive elements of soft power. Instead, it is a choice between different forms of public – global, mobile and interconnected – that requires new forms of daily, strategic and long-lasting communication. Along with global media events such as memes, flash mobs and user-driven online campaigns, *Masha and the Bear* has the capacity to develop and advance these forms through its world-building potential.

This analysis has also revealed that the convergence of media, forms of governance and modes of entertainment in the age of digital communication produces a complex system of exchanges that rehearse, subvert and circumvent existing images of a country, its culture and its people. The speed with which these exchanges occur means that an estimation of their outreach and impact requires new methodologies and new conceptualisations. This chapter has proposed a new form of assessing and conceptualising these phenomena, that of world-building.

Implications and uses of soft power as world-building are broad. For example, for international relations, to consider soft power as world-building means allowing for the development of soft power of states – or, in my terms, worlds – that are fictional, not rooted in the project of the nation-state building and legacy of imperialism and postcolonialism. For political science, such worlds can be more effective in exercising soft power than public diplomacy and corporate-driven advocacy, thus posing more questions about the realms of the political in the twenty-first century. For cultural studies, worlds exemplified by *Masha and the Bear* articulate new areas of dominance and new modes of resistance which are to be considered in future research on the global circulation of transmedial projects, symbolic capital and horizontal modes of exchange.

Notes

1. See, for example, the following article on the BBC website: 'Syrian President Bashar al-Assad: Facing Down Rebellion', *BBC*, 31 August 2020, available at <https://www.bbc.co.uk/news/10338256> (last accessed 12 December 2018).
2. For example, the expulsion of US diplomats in 2018, the refusal to participate in international agreements, and so on.
3. The concept of securitisation is associated with the Copenhagen school of security studies, which suggests that security should instead be seen as a speech act, where the central concern is not whether threats are real or not, but the ways in which a certain issue is constructed as a threat. See Balzacq 2010.
4. For example, Nancy Condee has revealed how this 'imperial trace' (2009) impacts Russian cinema as an institution and aesthetic.
5. I refer to the annexation of Crimea in 2014, and territorial disputes with Japan and Lithuania, as well as attempts to redraw borders of the nationality republics within the Russian Federation.

6. Recent research has focused on different manifestations of conventional and digital threats, leading to the publication of literature on Russian 'disinformation' and 'information war' (for example, the government-backed multilingual international media (RT and Sputnik). See, for example, Helmus et al. 2018; McCauley 2016; Singer and Brooking 2018.
7. See, for example, Brattberg and Maurer 2018.
8. Metaphorically speaking, the Russian hacker stands for the deterritorialised, transnational, fluid and manipulative agent of influence.
9. The space designated 'Russian' is fluid: for example, in Russian populist discourse, the annexation of Crimea in 2014 and subsequent enlargement of the RF only formalised the actual dimensions of 'Russian space'.
10. For an analysis of national and imperial discourses and the applicability of the term 'Russian', see Condee 2009.
11. See, for example, Sakwa 2017.
12. The relevance of Nye's approach has been challenged recently during the Black Lives Matter campaign, as a result of which a lot of US cultural products have been questioned due to their promotion of racism.
13. This is a sample description of a product 'Get ready for adventures in Dreamland with this adorable Masha and the Bear Nightie! Featuring Masha and her protective friend, Bear, with their woodland pals Panda and Hedgehog against a forest background. The show's colourful logo is on the top of the night gown. Complete with frilled sleeves and edge, and a bow detail on the neck, this pyjama is a perfect choice for fans of mischievous Masha!' Available at <https://www.character.com/products/masha-and-the-bear-nightdress?utm_medium=cpc&utm_source=googleshopping&variant=13570404483134> (last accessed 12 December 2018).
14. For example, <https://www.commonsensemedia.org/tv-reviews/masha-and-the-bear/user-reviews/adult> (last accessed 12 December 2018).
15. For example, <https://www.deviantart.com/rnj-nj/favourites/72849714/Masha-and-the-Bear-Fanart> (last accessed 12 December 2018).
16. See Strukov 2010 for a detailed analysis of the franchise.
17. See Strukov 2018 for a discussion of the evolution of the Russian cultural industry.
18. For more on polycentric globalisation, see Strukov 2018.

Works Cited

Abdulrazaq, Tallha (2018), 'Invasion of Iraq: The Original Sin of the 21st Century', *Al Jazeera*, 20 March, <https://www.aljazeera.com/indepth/opinion/invasion-iraq-original-sin-21st-century-180320095532244.html> (last accessed 12 December 2018).

Balzacq, Thierry (2010), 'Constructivism and Securitization Studies', in Myriam Cavelty and Victor Mauer (eds), *The Routledge Handbook of Security Studies*. London: Routledge, pp. 56–72.

Bourdieu, Pierre (1990), *The Logic of Practice*. Stanford: Stanford University Press.

Brattberg, Erik, and Tim Maurer (2018), 'Russian Election Interference: Europe's Counter to Fake News and Cyber Attacks', *Carnegie Endowment for International Peace*, <https://carnegieendowment.org/2018/05/23/russian-election-interference-europe-s-counter-to-fake-news-and-cyber-attacks-pub-76435> (last accessed 12 December 2018).

Condee, Nancy (2009), *The Imperial Trace: Recent Russian Cinema*. Oxford: Oxford University Press.

Dinnie, Keith (2015), *Nation Branding: Concepts, Issues, Practice*. London: Routledge.

Helmus, Todd C., Elizabeth Baron-Bodine, Andrew Radin, Madeline Magnuson, Joshua Mendelsohn, William Marcellino, Andriy Bega and Zev Winkelman (2018), *Russian Social Media Influence: Understanding Russian Propaganda in Eastern Europe*. Santa Monica, CA: Rand Corporation, <https://www.rand.org/pubs/research_reports/RR2237.html> (last accessed 16 November 2020).

Jenkins, Henry (2007), 'Transmedia Storytelling 101', blog post, <http://henryjenkins.org/blog/2007/03/transmedia_storytelling_101.html> (last accessed 12 December 2018)

Kaganovsky, Lilya (2008), *How the Soviet Man was Unmade: Cultural Fantasy and Male Subjectivity Under Stalin*. Pittsburgh: Pittsburgh University Press.

Kaneva, Nadia (ed.) (2011), *Branding Post-Communist Nations: Marketizing National Identities in the 'New' Europe*. London: Routledge.

McCauley, Kevin (2016), *Russian Influence Campaigns Against the West: From the Cold War to Putin*. CreateSpace Independent Publishing Platform.

Lung, Ioana (2018), 'Jungle Politics: Animal Metaphors in International Relations', *European View*, 17:2, 235–7.

Manovich, Lev (2001), *The Language of New Media*. Cambridge, MA: MIT Press.

Norris, Stephen (2012), *Blockbuster History in the New Russia: Movies, Memory, and Patriotism*. Bloomington: Indiana University Press.

Nye, Joseph S., Jr (2004), *Soft Power: The Means to Success in World Politics*. New York: Public Affairs.

RFE/RL (2018), 'U.S., Baltic States Discuss Russian "Threat" to European Security', 6 March, <https://www.rferl.org/a/us-an-baltic-states-discuss-russian-threat/29083467.html> (last accessed 12 December 2018).

Sakwa, Richard (2017), *Russia Against the Rest: The Post-Cold War Crisis of World Order*. Cambridge: Cambridge University Press.

Saunders, Robert A. (2017), *Popular Geopolitics and Nation Branding in the Post-Soviet Realm*. London: Routledge.

Saunders, Robert, and Vlad Strukov (eds) (2018), *Popular Geopolitics: Plotting an Evolving Interdiscipline*. London: Routledge.

Singer, P. W., and Emerson Brooking (2018), *LikeWar: The Weaponization of Social Media*. Boston: Houghton Mifflin Harcourt.

Smeets, Neil (2014), 'Combating or Cultivating Climate Change? Russia's Approach to Global Warming as an Obstacle to EU Environmental Pioneering', conference paper, UACES 44th Annual Conference Cork, 1, <https://www.uaces.org/archive/papers/abstract.php?paper_id=834> (last accessed 12 December 2018).

Steerpike (2020), 'Evgeny Lebedev's Unlikely Peerage', *The Spectator*, 31 July, <https://www.spectator.co.uk/article/evgeny-lebedev-s-unlikely-peerage> (last accessed 5 August 2020).

Stolworthy, Jacob (2016), 'Russian Cartoon Masha and the Bear Has Been Watched More Than a Billion Times on YouTube', *The Independent*, 4 February, <https://www.independent.co.uk/arts-entertainment/tv/news/russian-cartoon-masha-and-the-bear-has-been-watched-more-than-a-billion-times-on-youtube-a6853461.html> (last accessed 12 December 2018).

Strukov, Vlad (2005), 'Masiania, or Reimagining the Self in the Cyberspace of Rusnet', *The Slavic and East European Journal*, 48:3, 438–61.

Strukov, V. (2007), 'Video Anekdot: Auteurs and Voyeurs of Russian Flash Animation', *animation: an interdisciplinary journal*, 2, 129–51.

Strukov, Vlad (2010), 'The Forces of Kinship: Timur Bekmambetov's Night Watch Cinematic Trilogy', in Anindita Banerjee (ed.), *Russian Science Fiction Literature and Cinema*. New York: Academic Studies Press.

Strukov, Vlad (2016), 'Russian "Manipulative Smart Power": Zviagintsev's Oscar Nomination, (Non-)Government Agency and Contradictions of the Globalized World', *New Cinemas: Journal of Contemporary Film*, 14:1, 31–49.

Strukov, Vlad (2017), 'Introduction', in Vlad Strukov and Victor Apryshchenko (eds), *Memory and Securitization in Contemporary Europe*. London: Palgrave.

Strukov, Vlad (2018), 'Introduction', in Vlad Strukov and Sarah Hudspith (eds), *Russian Culture in the Age of Globalisation*. London: Routledge.

Surowiec, Pawel (2016), *Nation Branding, Public Relations and Soft Power: Corporatising Poland*. London: Routledge.

CHAPTER 5

The Limits of Hollywood as an Instrument of Chinese Public Diplomacy and Soft Power

Chris Homewood

At the turn of the millennium, the People's Republic of China (PRC, hereafter China) expanded its international outlook through 'Zou Chu Qu', the so-called 'Going Out Policy', which started life as an attempt to expand exports and increase foreign exchange earnings but was quickly expanded to include a diplomacy remit. As Yanling Yang writes:

> The 'Going Out Policy' was then further emphasised in the eleventh (2006–10) and twelfth Five Years Plans (2011–15) as an important way to 'improve the image of China abroad and build up its soft power; to present and disseminate Chinese culture around the world'. (2016: 84–5)

China's film industry was, and remains, central to this ambition. For China's State Administration of Radio, Film and Television (SARFT), 'the primary objective of film "going out" was to "disseminate China's voice to the world, especially North America and West European [sic], to show the real China, and China's attitudes, views and opinions on key international issues"' (ibid.: 85).

Aptly enough, this determination to use film as a vehicle for attracting foreign publics to China's side coincided with the nation's entry into the World Trade Organisation and a boom in domestic film production. None the less, China still struggles to make its presence felt in the mainstream global cinema market.[1] While traditional Chinese culture can be a source of attraction, the 'soft' potential of Chinese cinema as a vehicle of cultural dissemination is hindered by a potent mixture of what the Western(ised) world already knows and what it believes it already knows about the 'real China'. Moulded by modern authoritarianism, China's political values and the role these play in its foreign policies often shackle the nation's attractiveness amongst the publics and political elites of Western democracies that are active and vocal in promoting liberal values. At the same time, there has existed an enduring positional bias against China, and its customs, peoples and Western diasporas. Echoing longstanding US–Western apprehensions about China's place in the established world order, popular geo-political discourses have long encouraged Western publics to think and feel negatively about all things Chinese. Indeed, Western cultural production has exhibited a persistent tendency to imagine China and 'Chineseness' through the narrow cultural lens of orientalism, Edward Said's (1978) term to describe a fearful and contemptuous regime of invented binaries and knowledge production that propose, preserve and perpetuate assumptions about Western superiority.

Hollywood has been chief in this regard. Unless otherwise motivated, the major studios tend to do what is easy, relying on stereotypes about foreign peoples and polities that nourish a US–Western perspective. From MGM's *The Mask of Fu Manchu* (1932) to the 'moody orientalism' of film noir (Naremore 1998: 227) and the Chinese (American) villains that proliferate in the action cinema of the 1990s, at regular historical junctures Hollywood has employed the pejorative and denigrating representational practices of orientalism to reflect, disseminate and deal with greater practical and formal anxieties about China as belonging to a geo-political region the US–West considers dangerously different and threatening to its global authority (see, for example, Bernstein and Studlar 1997; Park 2010).

However, recent shifts in the flow of global market forces have seemingly provided Hollywood with the stimulus it needed to change. The astonishing rise of China's film market – which surged from a total box office of USD 630 million in 2009 to 8.86 billion in 2018 (Shackleton 2019) – is prompting the major studios to make amends for their long-standing perpetuation of anti-Chinese prejudice and to adopt a more ecumenical understanding of global political space that transcends the dominant paradigm of patriotism/enemy othering. Keen to deepen their penetration of China's now highly lucrative yet still tightly regulated market, the majors today appear to be in the business of helping China with its public diplomacy efforts, creating a transformed framework in which many of the popular ideas about China as belonging to the 'Orient' can be contested rather than reinforced, and specific aspects of Chinese foreign policy discourse can be promoted. In other words, Hollywood's financially motivated decision to alter long-standing norms when it comes to popular–geo-political representation appears to have allowed the Chinese government to co-opt Hollywood as an adjunct tool of Chinese statecraft, especially public diplomacy and, it hopes, soft power.

Building on previous work (Homewood 2018), in this chapter I explore the twists and turns that characterise China's recent attempts to utilise the soft potential of Hollywood. The discussion is divided into two sections. The first examines Hollywood as an important tool in China's public diplomacy, leveraged by the Chinese government to communicate a favourable image to foreign publics and, in so doing, build soft power, especially in the West. Central to this goal is the transmission of Chinese strategic narratives. As a common feature of international affairs, strategic narratives are the stories a nation must tell the world, and itself, to build and maintain a competitive edge in the international system. Put another way, they are a key tool for political actors who seek to influence others; so much so that, for Laura Roselle et al., 'Strategic narrative *is* soft power in the 21st century' (2015: 71). However, as they also note, while Joseph Nye certainly emphasises the role of narratives in international affairs, which he argues has become a matter of 'whose story wins', 'he does not explore the nature of narratives or attempt to explain how a narrative becomes persuasive to target audiences' (ibid.: 71). This is certainly the case where China's leverage of Hollywood to tell what it hopes will be a winning story is concerned, albeit less with Nye (who has little to say on the matter) and more amongst the political and cultural commentators who casually identify Hollywood as a Chinese soft power asset yet fail to pause and question what this means in practice (Albert 2018; Ge 2017).

The devil is in the detail, and in the first section I therefore aim to demonstrate how Hollywood's apparent change of heart regarding China is far from being cut and dried. Although Hollywood is willing to accommodate and even endorse Chinese strategic narratives, the geopolitical influence and ambition that these narratives underpin (such as the proliferation of Chinese norms and rising sentiment towards Chinese global leadership) are attenuated by an encompassing image of China that, while it appears favourable, relies on updated orientalist knowledge to preserve the status quo of US–Western positional superiority. In the second section, I move to a discussion of the factors that limit Hollywood's ability to make China attractive to Western audiences. Positioned against the respective responses of US administrations in the twenty-first century, it becomes clear that, at the elite level, Hollywood's recent attempt to bring foreign publics to China's side is showing little sign of success. Similarly, whereas Hollywood may now seek to position Chinese characters alongside – although by no means equal to – their American counterparts, it faces tough competition from other Western media, which still tend to emphasise China's difference and foster mistrust. The chapter concludes with germane analysis of a recent episode of *South Park* that extends this mistrust to Hollywood's messaging, challenging the new Sino-Hollywood status quo by shining a light not only on China's censorship, but also on the strategic opportunism of the major studios.

The Formation and Projection of Chinese Strategic Narratives in Hollywood Movies

As Andreas Antoniades et al. explain, strategic narratives are a 'tool through which great powers can articulate their interests, values and aspirations for the international system in ways that offer the opportunity for power transitions that avoid violent struggle between status quo and challenger states' (2010). In the case of China, the first of these, Falk Hartig observes, is actually:

> a narrative used by other states: a narrative *about* China, exemplifying how other states such as the US think China may behave in the future, how they wish it would behave and how other states aim to deal with such a rising China. In this narrative, China is described and perceived 'alternatively as an aspiring normal great power to balance others or as a rising hegemon'. (2015: 49)

However, as Hartig also notes, this 'international system narrative about China' has, at the same time, been largely internalised by China; it is closely related to the self-understanding and the principal narrative communicated by China, which 'is based on the idea of peaceful Rise/Development' (ibid.: 49). Herein, China projects a point of view that 'is primarily about reassuring the rest of the world that the rise of China will not pose a threat to peace and stability and that other nations will actually benefit from China's growing power and influence' (ibid.: 2015: 49). Despite China's emergence as a primary challenger to US pre-eminence in the international system, recent US blockbusters have tended to foster this merged point of view, endorsing the (self-)perception of China as a rising hegemon in depictions that are simultaneously intended to allay formal and practical fears about a China threat.

Science fiction has emerged as a one of the principal genre vehicles for Hollywood's communication of China's 'peaceful rise' and 'win–win' tropes to the global mainstream. A prism for geo-political trends (see Weldes 2003; Dittmer and Gray 2010; Dittmer and Dodds 2013), science fiction is, as Robert Saunders reminds us, 'a genre of *space* (terrain, topography, "zones", etc), as well as *outer space*' that, since the Cold War, has 'steadily morphed into a medium for global ideological contestation and identity negotiation' (2015). Space capability and the technological prowess it represents have long been attributes of great power and indications of global leadership status, as Kennedy made clear in his 1962 'moon speech' to Congress:

> Now is the time to take longer strides – time for a great new American enterprise – time for this nation to take a clearly leading role in space achievement which, in many ways, may hold the key to our future on earth. (Kennedy 1962)

In the twenty-first century, Beijing is determined to make space achievement a Chinese enterprise. Although China only sent its first astronaut into orbit in 2003, it is already pushing ahead with plans to build a new space station, establish a moon base and conduct a mission to Mars. A clear demonstration of China's ambition to become a space power and scientific force can be seen in the fact that, in 2019, it became the first country to land an automated spacecraft on the far side of the moon. For commentators, this was 'a clear statement about the level of maturity that China's technology has reached' and provided an indication that 'Beijing's long-term goal to match US capabilities could now become a reality within two decades' (Kaplan et al. 2019).

In accord with Kennedy's comments, American popular–geo-political discourse has often located outer space as the new American frontier, as the next chapter in the project of American exceptionalism and manifest destiny. But rather than reproducing and elucidating practical and formal geo-political anxieties about the (symbolic) threat posed to US dominance in the international system by China's rapid advances in space capability, Hollywood appears to be countersigning the notion of China's 'heavenly rise'. In *Gravity* (dir. Alfonso Cuarón, 2013), salvation for stranded American astronaut Ryan Stone (Sandra Bullock) is underwritten by Chinese technological provision: Stone saves herself from disaster by first utilising the fictional Chinese space station Tiangong, or 'heavenly palace', and then riding the existing Chinese space capsule Shenzhou ('divine craft') back to the Earth. Along similar lines, in Ridley Scott's *The Martian* (2015), NASA is able to rescue another stranded American astronaut only with help from China's space agency. Meanwhile, in the more fantastical *Independence Day: Resurgence* (dir. Roland Emmerich, 2016), the fictional Earth Space Defence (ESD) moon base – the world's first line of defence against alien threats – is commanded by China's Jiang Lao (played by Singapore-born actor Chin Han) (Fig. 5.1). Viewed through Hollywood's adjusted lens, China no longer challenges global peace and security but instead helps America to preserve it.

The same goes for Earth-bound science fiction, action and fantasy films, such as *Transformers: Age of Extinction* (dir. Michael Bay, 2014), *Pacific Rim: Uprising* (Steven S. DeKnight, 2018) and *The Meg* (Jon Turteltaub, 2018), all

Figure 5.1 Film grab from Roland Emmerich's *Independence Day: Resurgence* (2016). China's Commander Jiang (Chin Han) watches over the Earth from the Earth Space Defence Moon Base.

of which communicate the notion of China's world beneficial role to the global order. In these and other films, an assortment of virtuous, physically powerful and/or technologically skilled Chinese characters embody 'peaceful rise' and 'win–win' tropes by working alongside American allies to vanquish imaginative threats to global security. A sign of Hollywood's growing hesitancy to promulgate depictions that might run the risk of offending not only Chinese but also audiences in other foreign markets, these threats are increasingly triggered by the actions of morally compromised or outright corrupt Americans (often tech billionaires, such as Joshua Joyce (Stanley Tucci) in *Transformers: Age of Extinction* and Morris (Rainn Wilson) in *The Meg*) who believe that their 'hard' power protects them and entitles them to do as they please in the world. The menacing surfeit of oppressive state power that once served as a chief signifier of China's dangerous Otherness to the West is refigured in these films not as a Chinese but as an American problem. In so doing, these films implicitly endorse a view of China as benign, and to some extent even weaken the positional superiority of the US vis-à-vis China, which, more than just being a passive victim of American folly, assumes an active role in helping to right American-led wrongs. In *Transformers: Age of Extinction*, moral authority is divested from a delinquent representative of US–Western power,

Joyce, and reinvested in a Chinese woman, Su Yueming (depicted by Chinese star Li Bingbing), who provides co-stimulus – alongside the film's principal hero, Yeager (Mark Wahlberg) – for Joyce's eventual ethical rehabilitation (see Homewood 2018).

At this juncture, however, it should be noted that Hollywood's reassuring image of China comes with a caveat. Despite formal fears that the major studios' apparent change of heart regarding China is handing Beijing the upper hand in global affairs,[2] Hollywood still functions to safeguard prevailing structures of global power, which privilege the US. Big-budget films may accommodate and even endorse Chinese strategic narratives but they renege on the idea of a major reorganisation of global political space, ultimately operating to contain China in a dependent role vis-à-vis the US. China is accepted and promoted as a responsible stakeholder in global affairs but *under* US leadership, which these films work to persuade audiences is still needed most to advance global security and prevent international system chaos. What is more, Hollywood's move to an affirmatively framed yet safely contained understanding of China's place in the established world order relies on a bespoke arrangement of elements of 'old' orientalism and a 'new' China-specific form of orientalism identified by Daniel Vukovich.

In *China and Orientalism: Western Knowledge Production and the PRC*, Vukovich reworks the postcolonial concept of mimicry to argue that since the programme of Chinese economic reform and 'opening up' initiated in 1978, Western knowledge about China has been dominated and defined by what he terms 'Sinological-orientalism'. Formerly the irreducible Other and thus the location of absolute difference to the West, China is now regarded as a place of 'becoming sameness' to the West (2012: 2). China remains the Other, but is placed within a scale of hierarchical difference in which it 'is seen as in a process of haltingly but inevitably becoming-the-same as "us": open, liberal, modern, free. Put another way, China is understood as becoming generally equivalent to the West' (ibid.: 1). However, China therefore finds itself always stuck in the realm of the 'not yet': it is perceived by Western observers as wanting to become the same as the West but always lagging behind or lacking (ibid.: 3). As such, a paradox emerges in which discourses suggesting that China is 'becoming democratic, normal, civil, creative artistic (avantgarde), liberal, and so on' simultaneously aver that China 'still lacks something (often the same items)' (ibid.: 9).

The adjusted entity that Hollywood today frames as China is suggestive of aspects of sinological orientalism. I provide a caveat here because, stemming from China's candid appeal for 'positive Chinese images' (Pulver 2013), the ordinarily attendant notion of Chinese lack is itself lacking. Keen to avoid the kind of perceptible offence that could jeopardise market access, the Hollywood majors are not only curtailing imaginative old (and often nakedly racist) orientalist markers of ontological Chinese difference and lack but also decoupling China from the real and existing variance in norms and values that drive Western perceptions of its shortcomings. Evidence of China's authoritarian model of domestic social order, its repressive effects and the tensions this can create vis-à-vis the US–West's declared observance of liberal–democratic values (as well as the barriers this can pose to real-world examples of the co-operation imagined by Hollywood movies), are nowhere to be found. Under these circumstances, movies dissolve the hierarchical scale of difference that underpins the idea of China's tentative march to equivalence, and instead of being held in a perpetual, stumbling state of *becoming* generally equivalent to the US–West, Hollywood tends to present China as already having *become* 'normal', as already being generally equivalent to or the same as 'us'.

In its remaking of China as a territory now separate from the geographies of danger and threat that confront the US–West, it appears that Hollywood is attempting to make Chinese strategic narratives persuasive to their target audiences by embedding them in a larger filmic discourse of sameness and its inferred corollaries – like-mindedness and compatibility. However, this attempt at persuasion comes at a cost for Chinese identity: Hollywood discourses that suggest China is already equivalent to the West still illustrate the problems of positionality that are associated with Western cultural production. Although China has been successful in its economic leverage of Hollywood to transmit a story it wants the world to receive, the voice we hear is not China's own (even if it does reflect aspects of a strategic Chinese self-understanding) but rather the continued product of an authoritative American lens whose willingness to interpret all things Chinese in a favourable light is contingent on the innately 'denigrating and condescending faith that they are, after all, becoming the same as us (or should be made to do so)' (Vukovich 2012: 3). Despite Beijing's alleged influence on the major studios, Hollywood is no more inclined to cede legislative rights to China today than it was during the last century.

Enacting the 'should be made to do so' of Vukovich's statement, Hollywood places China in rigid conformity with Western expectations of what it 'must' become – that is, just like 'us'. In the absence of traces of China's political variance to the US–West, Hollywood's Chinese characters inevitably recognise, and thus implicitly mimic, the Western political ideas, norms and outlook of their American and/or European colleagues. In effect, we are presented with a Chinese version of a Western cultural model, and while characters like Blink in *X-Men: Days of Future Past* (dir. Bryan Singer, 2014) and Su in *Transformers: Age of Extinction* embody specific Chinese narratives, they ultimately reflect the attitude of the dominant foreign culture. This imposed process of acculturation extends beyond political ideas. Where social constructions of Chinese identity are concerned, sport becomes a prime ground for the overwriting of Chinese with Western cultural characteristics. Although a wide variety of sporting activities, both Western and traditional Chinese, have become popular in China, films tend to stress the former: in *Looper* (dir. Rian Johnson, 2012), young Joe plays soccer with a group of children in Shanghai, and the sport of American football features prominently in *Transformers: Age of Extinction*. Close to the film's climax, Yeager uses a Chinese teenager's American football to triumph against a wanton CIA agent. The victory of the film's principal American hero is underwritten by Chinese 'provision' that is, in turn, made possible by (what the film presents as) China's cultural equivalence to, and resulting compatibility with, the US–West.

At the same time, this ardent move to a logic of sameness still relies in part on an organisational motif of old orientalism. Moreover, the intersection of older and more recent orientalist epistemes permits Hollywood access to new – at least where China is concerned – strategies of containment that obscure the geo-political anxieties they are intended to assuage. While a great many of the hoary orientalist stereotypes that encourage negative Western regard for China as a (geo-)political and social entity (such as primitivism, perilous exoticism, irrationality) are being held in abeyance, recent portrayals are still apt to a lingering and, in the words of Karen Leong, 'especially powerful trope of old orientalism' – namely, the 'feminisation of East Asian nations' (2005: 2). In other words, orientalism is gendered. As Jane Chi Hyun Park elaborates: 'the East is figured as the eroticised, feminised other that exists to be known, penetrated, and subordinated by the masculinized West' (2010: 3).

Figure 5.2 Grab from Steven S. DeKnight's *Pacific Rim: Uprising* (2018). Tech expert Liwen Shao (Tian Jing) battles world-threatening monsters.

The sheer preponderance of Chinese women in Hollywood's modified accounts of China's place in global political space points to the perpetuation of this trope. To date, Chinese capability has been embodied by physically powerful Chinese women: Li Bingbing, Fan Bingbing (*X-Men: Days of Future Past*), model-turned-actor Angelababy (*Independence Day: Resurgence*) and Tian Jing (*Pacific Rim: Uprising*), to name but a few examples (Fig. 5.2). However, while the feminisation of Chinese power and prowess persists, the most palpably denigrating properties of this trope are dissolved by the homologising lens of sameness, in which race remains an unnamed or hidden signifier. The application of this second lens creates a distance from the perilously enigmatic Otherness proposed by the first, giving rise to a largely de-exoticised space in which Chinese women, although still sexualised/eroticised, are permitted to confound racialised expectations of gendered behaviour. As I have emphasised in previous writing (Homewood 2018), although a feminised China is still subordinated by the masculinised West, subjugation is no longer achieved by recourse to old orientalist binaries or ontologically distinctive tropes such as 'racist love' (see Park 2010: 89). Instead, assembled according to the imaginative fruition of Western expectations of what China should become, movies are turning to the conservative yet ostensibly non-racialised gender politics that govern Hollywood action cinema as pretence to quietly disadvantage Chinese women like Su in *Transformers: Age of Extinction* and Suyin in *The Meg*, recuperating the 'sameness structured by hierarchical difference' that safeguards the positional hegemony of the US–West (Vukovich 2012: 126).

As Lisa Purse argues, Hollywood action cinema deploys tropes designed to contain or compensate for the threat posed by the presence of powerful women to the genre's structuring fantasy of male hegemony. One such trope is the 'credibility continuum', along which 'the relationship of the hero's feats to real-world laws of physics and physiology run' (Purse 2011: 79). While the action man tends to occupy the more realistic end of this spectrum (he is 'permitted to sweat, strain and be bloodied as he engages in combat'), the feats of the action woman are often positioned towards the less plausible end of the range: films 'downplay significantly the physical consequences of [female] action, such as pain and injury' (ibid.: 81). The investment, Purse explains, seems to be in diminishing the credibility of the action woman's feats in relation to those of her male counterpart, upon whom the gender-biased 'privilege of ultimate empowerment' can then be conferred (ibid.: 14).

Viewed through the lens of sameness, physically potent Chinese action women are treated equivalently, which is to say as equals amongst their already unequal Western female counterparts. In *Transformers: Age of Extinction*, the loss of American positional superiority that was brought about by Su's upper hand in her relationship with the morally compromised Joyce is eventually restored by Yeager, alongside whom Su is permitted to coexist as a largely autonomous and capable but, crucially, never quite as credible action body. The intersection of gender and race to manage US–Western geo-political anxiety is still in operation but obscured by the films' observance of seemingly non-culturally specific tropes that operate to contain the threat posed to masculine dominance by formidable women *in the main*.

In sum, then, shifts in the flow of global market forces have opened Hollywood's geo-political culture regarding China to change. Motivated by the promise of financial gain, the major studios appear to have retired China from the network of invented binaries that describes old orientalism and adjusted the country's position in the Western hierarchy of the familiar and the Other that orders the world. This development has allowed Beijing to co-opt Hollywood as an adjunct tool of China's public diplomacy, the aim of which is to increase China's soft power in the Western(ised) world. Hollywood's changed perception of China as no longer antithetical to the US–West has created a space in which specific Chinese strategic narratives can be communicated to foreign publics. However, this does not signal an end to the problems of positionality associated with Western cultural production in Hollywood. The major studios' revised perspective of China as a place of familiarity, equivalence and thus compatibility with 'us' still amounts to a projection of US–Western discursive power, albeit a less discernible one: Hollywood's willingness to transmit a favourable image not only of China's place in global affairs but also of its culture and ethnic identities is dependent upon the overwriting of Chinese with Western cultural characteristics. The homologising lens of sameness grants the majors access to new, yet (where Chinese state media officials are concerned) less perceptibly offensive, containment strategies. Their movies are able to preserve and perpetuate the notion of US–Western supremacy whilst honouring their de facto commissioned aim of promoting Chinese national interests.

Curious in this regard, the logic of sameness and its attendant containment of China does not necessarily work at cross-purposes to China's soft power ambitions. If, as Nye insists, 'popular culture is more likely to attract people and produce soft power in the sense of preferred outcomes in situations where cultures are somewhat similar rather than widely dissimilar' (2004: 16), then Hollywood movies that – however perversely – employ updated orientalist knowledge to insist upon China's cultural familiarity and compatibility with the West do not necessarily disaccord with the Chinese government's ambition to cultivate a friendlier international environment. Western(ised) moviegoers are now routinely hailed by a transformed popular–geo-political imaginary that positions China not as inexorably dissimilar foe but as inevitably similar friend. But despite China's successful leverage of Hollywood to transmit a favourable image of China to Western publics, the question of whether Hollywood can succeed in creating favourable public opinion is another matter, to which we now turn.

Hollywood's China Information and the 'Contest of Competitive Credibility'

In 'Public Diplomacy and Soft Power', Nye stresses the extent to which 'Politics has become a contest of competitive credibility.' He elaborates thus:

> Among editors and cue-givers, credibility is the crucial resource and an important source of soft power. Reputation becomes even more important than in the past, and political struggles occur over the creation and destruction of credibility. Governments compete for credibility not only with other governments but with a broad range of alternatives including news media, corporations, nongovernmental organisations (NGOs), intergovernmental organizations, and networks of specific communities. (2008: 100)

As we have seen, China has found one such editor or cue-giver in Hollywood, even if the willingness of the major studios to engage with and reinterpret China for their spheres of influence is predicated on hard (economic) leverage. However, while Hollywood's dominance of the global mainstream makes it a valuable resource for reaching foreign publics with the narrative China wants them to hear, its ability to persuade the target audience of the credibility of this narrative and elicit a positive response is less straightforward. Far from being the only producer of geo-political knowledge in Western circuits of information exchange, Hollywood and its ability to reshape our common-sense understanding of China for the better faces stiff competition from practical, formal and other popular cue-givers, few of which seem to share Hollywood's affirmative stance.

That said, for a time at least, there was a degree of congruence between Hollywood's popular geo-political China information and the practical discourse of the US government. Hollywood's remaking of China as a responsible stakeholder in the maintenance of a peaceful international environment coincided with the presidency of Barack Obama (2009–17) and was in large part consistent with (yet not contingent on) the changes made by his administration to US practical geo-politics.[3] Keen to restore global public confidence in US leadership, which had been undermined by the gung-ho militarism of the Bush administration's foreign policy approach (see Steinberg 2008), the Obama administration observed a global mind-set and evinced a renewed emphasis on bi- and multilateral agreements. In this regard, an economically resurgent China was placed at the top of the list, and while tensions between Washington and Beijing still occurred, they did so within more convivial patterns of recognition. Concomitant with the sentiment of a 2009 US Center for Strategic and International Studies (CSIS) report which insisted that 'Virtually no major global challenge can be met without US–China co-operation', in a 2009 speech Obama maintained that: 'The relationship between the United States and China will shape the 21st century, which will make it as important as any bilateral relationship in the world' (Anon.: 2009).

More recently, however, his optimistic prediction has been disturbed. In their assessment of US–China relations two years into the Trump presidency, David Dollar et al. noted how:

> U.S. policy towards China now appears to be animated by a judgement that the past trajectory of the bilateral relationship favoured China and disadvantaged the United States in a long-run competition for global leadership. To try to break this trajectory, the Trump administration over the past two years has adopted an increasingly zero-sum, unilateralist, protectionist and nativist 'America first' approach to the relationship. (2019)

From the long-standing trade dispute to Washington's solicitation of a global ban of Huawei's 5G equipment, characterised both as an example of intellectual property theft and a security risk, US practical geo-political logic has swiftly repositioned China as a looming threat to US(–Western) stability, security and global hegemony. Drawing on the Huawei dispute, in 2019 the academic and Assistant Secretary of State for International Security and Nonproliferation, Christopher A. Ford, addressed his 'anger and distress over China's behaviour' to the US–China Economic and Security Review Commission, insisting that 'despite the "win–win" rhetoric', China does not envision a 'peaceable, benevolent live-and-let-live vision of 21st-Century international engagement' (2019: 2). Instead, he avers that 'China is working to export its model of authoritarianism through its "Community of Common Destiny" to reshape global governance'; that 'China expects eventually to dictate the rules of the world system' (ibid.: 3). At the elite level, then, Hollywood's now ten-year attempt to persuade foreign publics of China's peaceable intent and foster a favourable environment for China's geo-political ambition shows little sign of success.

The emergence of the global pandemic in late 2019 served only to intensify Washington's enmity towards China, even if initially – and despite evidence of a Chinese cover-up and repression of whistle-blowers (Belluz 2020) – President Trump had heaped praise on Beijing's response to COVID-19. Admiration quickly turned to admonishment and the reinstatement of a hawkish attitude towards Chinese leadership when, in March (against the backdrop of a sharp rise in infection rates in the US), a Chinese official spread a conspiracy theory that the US military had, in fact, brought the virus to Wuhan (Molter and Webster 2020). Angered by this groundless accusation, the Trump administration would link COVID-19 directly to China. The President began referring to it as the 'Chinese virus' or 'Wuhan virus' (Fig. 5.3); so, too, did US Secretary of State Mike Pompeo, who also accused China of putting the world at risk by not revealing more details about the outbreak (Pamuk and Brunnstrom 2020) – a far cry from the responsible global stakeholder of Hollywood's imagination.

At the mass level, it also seems increasingly doubtful that Hollywood's affirmative remaking of China for Western audiences will be able to gain the desired traction. While it is unlikely that revivified and rapidly rising US practical and formal geo-political anxieties will leak their way back into Hollywood so long as China's film market remains durable, the recursive link between censorious practical, formal and the extensive popular geo-political reasoning that occurs outside the direct scope of Hollywood's influence poses a considerable impediment to the soft potential of large-scale movies. In simple terms, Hollywood is outnumbered by critical discourses and censorious images which encourage the kind of negative regard for China that, with no

Donald J. Trump
@realDonaldTrump

I always treated the Chinese Virus very seriously, and have done a very good job from the beginning, including my very early decision to close the "borders" from China - against the wishes of almost all. Many lives were saved. The Fake News new narrative is disgraceful & false!

11:46 · 18/03/2020 · Twitter for iPhone

82.5K Retweets and comments **295K** Likes

Figure 5.3 President Trump tweets about what he terms the 'Chinese Virus'.

loss of irony, the major studios once helped to propagate but now seek to challenge.⁴ But even when relations between Washington and Beijing were more cordial, numerous implicit challenges to the credibility of Hollywood's China rhetoric could (and still can) be found elsewhere in US–Western popular culture, especially the mainstream news media.

On the one hand, Western news organisations can be an undeniably important resource in the global narrative of a rising superpower that practises an authoritarian system of governance and tightly controls its own media – for instance, by holding China to account for human rights violations, such as its treatment of Uighur Muslims, and Western leaders for failing to take meaningful action. On the other hand, scholarship suggests that their analysis tends to be weighted towards a negative depiction that blends justified criticism (what the West already knows) with ideological assumptions (what the West thinks it already knows) and reveals little about how most Chinese live or see themselves and the(ir) world (see, for example, Hewitt 2011; Huang and Leung 2006; Sparks 2010). Put another way, analysis is still apt to emphasise China's difference and alert audiences to what it still lacks vis-à-vis Western values (democracy, freedom and so on) – even if they often ignore the West's own shortcomings in the same areas.⁵ The enduring plethora of attention-grabbing accounts that frame China not only as dangerously oppressed but also as downright weird – this, we are told, is a place where escalators are deadly (Morley 2016) and it is normal for parents to sell their children for the latest iPhone (Horton 2016) – preserve and perpetuate the kind of hoary orientalist knowledge of an unbridgeable distinction between 'them and us' which Hollywood is, by and large, holding in abeyance.⁶

Although the mainstream news media's China analysis illustrates many of the problems associated with Western positionality, it nevertheless stands as a powerful and highly prevalent counterproposal to Hollywood's favourable image of China and its intentions. Crucially, the willingness of news outlets to criticise the Chinese polity also implicitly discloses the structuring absence in – and arguably the greatest impediment to the authority of – Hollywood's own China information. As Nye emphasises, (self-)'criticism is often the most effective way of establishing credibility' (2008: 106), but while few would lament the decline of singularly negative and often nakedly racist assumptions about China in Hollywood movies, the complete elimination of any and all material that could be perceived as painting the Chinese government in a critical yet fair light threatens to serve the inverse of its intended function. By sidestepping difficult questions around China's domestic affairs and international behaviour, a co-opted Hollywood faces similar credibility problems as other Chinese public diplomacy instruments, such as Confucius Institutes (CIs). Writing about CIs, Hartig notes how their:

> tendency to omit delicate issues demonstrates that the institutes are generally not introducing the 'real China.' Such an introduction would mean presenting a comprehensive picture of China, rather than a 'correct version' of China. This is further complicated by the fact that it is precisely those sensitive topics which are probably most familiar to the CI target audience as they regularly appear in the media. This causes a potential perception gap which hampers the credibility of CIs and their attempts to communicate China's narratives to the world and to enhance China's soft power. (2015: 254)

Part of Hollywood's success as an instrument of American public diplomacy and soft power is predicated on its separateness from the US government (Nye 2004: 15–17). If so inclined, the majors are free to be critical of US policies, actors and instruments, thereby creating the impression that their movies offer a comprehensive or credible picture of America. However, as an instrument of Chinese public diplomacy, the absence of criticism in Hollywood movies – a necessary corollary of continued market access – raises the presence of Chinese governmental intrusion, in turn opening the messages that these movies communicate to the same accusations of propaganda that beset CIs. And if information is considered to be propaganda, then its credibility, along with its ability to attract and generate influence, is lost.

For a time, popular talk of Hollywood's relationship with China tended to be framed around studios' efforts to court Chinese audiences by adding Chinese faces and places to their largest-scale movies and no longer gravitating to Chinese (Americans) as their go-to 'bad guys'. In his 2014 review of *Transformers: Age of Extinction*, Robbie Collin of British broadsheet *The Telegraph* makes cursory mention of how, 'In the film's third act, the story relocates to China – aka, Hollywood's largest emerging market – where the Autobots and Decepticons do battle in Hong Kong', while Clarence Tsui of trade magazine *The Hollywood Reporter* noted that, 'For a change, there are no Chinese villains' (2014). However, as the Sino-Hollywood quid pro quo has developed, so too have the parameters and tone of the discussion that surrounds it, with talk moving away from big-budget efforts to ingratiate the studios with Chinese audiences and towards the political concessions and consequences that the major studios are willing to accept in the first place in order to gain access to the world's second-largest market. Direct accusations of kowtowing, (self-)censorship and outsourcing of Chinese government propaganda are not only becoming more common, but they are also becoming more visible, working their way into mainstream, new and social media spaces.[7]

With reference to challenges to the credibility of Hollywood's picture of China, a possible watershed moment occurred in October of 2019, when the famously controversial American adult animated show *South Park* (1997–) began its twenty-third season, the second episode of which, 'Band in China', explores the convergence of the free market and Chinese censorship in the American entertainment industry by focusing on Hollywood, specifically Disney. In the no-holds-barred episode, Randy Marsh tries to expand his Tegridy Farms marijuana business to China. On the flight, he encounters Disney-owned movie characters, all of whom are travelling at the behest of Mickey Mouse, who has the same expansion model in mind. Upon arrival, Randy is arrested and then imprisoned for carrying a large quantity of drugs in his luggage. Placed in an unsanitary prison, he witnesses summary execution and is subject to re-education through forced labour, torture and Communist Party propaganda. He also meets fellow prisoners Winnie the Pooh and Piglet, whose inclusion in the episode (and incarceration in the plot) is a thinly veiled reference to the decision to ban the A. A. Milne characters after internet memes comparing Xi Jingping to Disney's version of Pooh Bear became popular in China (see Haas 2018).

Randy is eventually brought before a Chinese court, where he criticises the government's treatment of prisoners. When Mickey Mouse learns of Randy's criticism, he angrily confronts him over the business Disney stands to lose as a result. Randy, who is determined to maintain his 'tegridy' (his word for integrity), persuades Mickey to join him in making a case to Chinese officials that business should not be conducted on the basis of intimidation and that they should support his marijuana import idea. Both pleas are rejected, which Mickey attributes to 'the Pooh matter'. Randy responds by using honey to lure Pooh to a secluded alley and strangling him to death. At the end of the episode, Randy returns to South Park and we discover that his marijuana business is now a huge success in China. Still covered in blood and honey, Randy watches as dumper trucks full of money unload at his farmhouse.

As this synopsis suggests, the episode takes direct aim at Hollywood's apparent decision to place profits above principles, exposing and elucidating what it sees as the majors' willingness to sacrifice their (artistic) freedom – the cornerstone of American identity – and their 'tegridy' to appease a government that infringes the rights and freedoms of its citizens. Had viewers been left in any doubt about the message, it is rendered explicit by the sub-plot, which lends the episode its title. Back in South

Figure 5.4 A Chinese censor amends Stan's film script in the *South Park* episode 'Band in China'.

Park, Randy's son, Stan, and his friends have formed a metal band. While Randy is in China, the band and its members catch the attention of a manager, who wants to make a film about them. Stan writes the screenplay himself but is told that it needs to change so that the final product can be distributed in China. 'Now I know how Hollywood writers feel,' Stan opines, while a uniformed Chinese censor stands over his shoulder and erases passages he disagrees with (Fig. 5.4). Stan eventually abandons the film, stating that he cannot bring himself to compromise for China and that whoever can is worthless.

Significantly, the episode – which garnered a 1.3 million audience amongst adults aged 18–49, making it 'the top cable comedy telecast of the year' in America (Baysinger 2019) – would quickly become an international viral sensation when the double meaning of its title turned into a self-fulfilling prophecy: for criticising China's censorship standards and human rights record and mocking the sensitivities of its president, 'Band in China' caused *South Park* to be banned in China. This turn of events was probably anticipated and even welcomed by *South Park*'s agent provocateur creators Trey Parker and Matt Stone, who were quick to issue a faux apology on the show's official Twitter account:

> we welcome the Chinese censors into our homes and into our hearts. We too love money more than freedom and democracy. Xi doesn't look just like Winnie the Pooh at all. Tune into our 300th episode this Wednesday at 10! Long live the Great Communist Party of China! May this autumn's sorghum festival be bountiful! We good now China? (7 October 2019)

Members of the Hong Kong protests, also known as the Anti-Extradition Law Amendment Bill movement, certainly did tune in. They screened the controversial episode on the streets of Hong Kong as a symbol of mainland resistance, and, according to *The Hollywood Reporter* at least, Parker and Stone were praised as 'rare Western media figures willing to show "strong backbone" in response to the Chinese government's efforts to stifle international free speech' (Parker and Chu 2019).

'Band in China' stands as an especially potent challenge to the credibility of Hollywood's China information: a challenge whose reach and visibility were boosted significantly by the media attention that China's decision to ban *South Park* would inspire. Almost overnight, the episode's spotlighting of the majors' self-interest and the Chinese influence that undergird Hollywood's 'correct version' of China was brought to a hitherto unseen level of mainstream awareness, with social media posts and news articles on the matter trending throughout the Western(ised) world. Had there been any uncertainty about the Hollywood–China quid pro quo, the genie, it would seem, is now irrevocably out of the bottle.

*****

Moving forward, then, while Hollywood remains an effective vehicle for reaching foreign publics with the messages that China wants them to hear, its ability to build trust in those messages appears ever more uncertain when confronted by the numerous cue-givers that are not only quick to offer contradictory proposals but also increasingly inclined to present Hollywood as a vehicle of 'silent Chinese propaganda' in the West (Hendricks 2018). However, we still need to be careful about the conclusions we draw here. While it is certainly true that, since around 2010, Hollywood, undoubtedly driven by economic expedience over narrative integrity, has sidestepped sensitive issues and repositioned China as a necessary ally and friend to the US, this does not equate to an outright corrective to the foreboding political and media framings that can be found elsewhere. As I have argued in the first part of this chapter, accusations that Hollywood is a vehicle of unproblematically positive or 'correct' images of China overlook the persistent presence of orientalist diminishment and the untiring preservation of American positional superiority. It is imperative that we do not overlook the specific and very particular framing of Chinese characters within Hollywood movies and alongside American characters, for when we do so, we find that while the major studios may be less inclined to deploy plainly racist epistemes and may not share a view of China as a danger to global stability, their representations none the less uphold the notion of US pre-eminence. It is in this regard that overly simplistic binaries that position Hollywood's seemingly new-found Sinophilia against an increasingly hostile US–Western political and media landscape begin to dissolve. Limits to the efficacy of Hollywood as a tool of Chinese public diplomacy and soft power stem not just from without but also from within.

Notes

1. Although this situation could be changing, at least where online platforms like Netflix are concerned. Keen to expand its Mandarin-language content, Netflix has recently acquired the rights to Chinese blockbuster films *Wolf Warrior II* / 战狼 2 (Wu Jin, 2017), *Operation Red Sea* / 红海行动 (Dante Lam, 2018) and *The Wandering Earth* / 流浪地球 (Frant Gwo, 2019), to name but a few examples.
2. Robert Daly, Director of the Kissinger Institute on China, suggested that a remiss Hollywood is no longer promoting foremost the global interests of the US but rather those of its 'most formidable strategic, economic and ideological competitor' (2016).
3. Practical geo-politics describes actions and reasoning that underpin the actual practice of geo-political strategy.
4. Most recently, the Trump administration's determination to tie the pandemic directly to China not only prompted #ChinaVirus and #WuhanVirus to trend on Twitter in the US, but it also led to 'a spike in discrimination and xenophobic attacks' (Vazquez 2020; see also Escobar 2020).
5. For example, the Human Rights Watch *World Report 2019: Events of 2018* noted how 'The United States continued to move backward on human rights at home and abroad in the second year of Donald Trump's administration' (Anon. 2019).
6. In addition, the once widely accepted theory that COVID-19 originated at a so-called Chinese 'wet market' has revivified 'racist stereotypes about "dirty" Chinese eating habits' in formal and popular geo-political discourse (Cho 2020; see also Zhang 2020).
7. Since 2017, there has been a steady yet significant increase across a range of media in reports that suggest a perilous dimension to Hollywood's courtship of China's film market. Examples include the US conservative think tank the Heritage Foundation ('How China is Taking Control of Hollywood'), the multimedia web portal Big Think ('The Silent Chinese Propaganda in Hollywood Films', Hendricks 2018) and dedicated news website *Axios* (Hollywood's Cave to China on Censorship', Savitsky 2019), as well as video reports from NBC ('How China is changing Hollywood') and Vox (also 'How China is changing Hollywood'), to name but a few.

Works Cited

Albert, Eleanor (2018), 'China's Big Bet on Soft Power', *Council on Foreign Relations*, 9 February, <https://www.cfr.org/backgrounder/chinas-big-bet-soft-power> (last accessed 9 May 2019).

Anon. (2009), 'Obama: U.S.–China Ties Shape 21st Century', *CBS News*, 27 July, <https://www.cbsnews.com/news/obama-us-china-ties-shape-21st-century/> (last accessed 23 October 2019).

Anon. (2019), *World Report 2019: Events of 2018*, Human Rights Watch, <https://www.hrw.org/world-report/2019> (last accessed 20 October 2019).

Antoniades, Andreas, Alister Miskimmon and Ben O'Loughlin (2010), 'Great Power Politics and Strategic Narratives', *Working paper No. 7*, Centre for Political Economy at the University of Sussex.

Bay, Michael (2014), Film: *Transformers: Age of Extinction*. USA/China: Paramount Pictures.

Baysinger, Tim (2019), '"South Park" Ratings Down for Season 23 Premiere – But It's Still the Top Cable Comedy in Young Adults (Exclusive)', *The Wrap*, <https://www.thewrap.com/south-park-season-23-premiere-ratings-crank-yankers/> (last accessed 30 September 2019).

Belluz, Julia (2020), 'China Hid the Severity of its Coronavirus Outbreak and Muzzled Whistleblowers – Because it Can', *Vox*, 10 February, <https://www.vox.com/2020/2/10/21124831/coronavirus-outbreak-china-li-wenliang-world-health-organization> (last accessed 3 March 2020).

Bernstein, Matthew H., and Gaylyn Studlar (eds) (1997), *Visions of the East. Orientalism in Film*. New Brunswick, NJ: Rutgers University Press.

Cho, Joshua (2020), 'Why It's Wrong (and Racist) to Blame Covid-19 on Chinese "Wet Markets"', *FAIR*, 7 May, <https://fair.org/home/why-its-wrong-and-racist-to-blame-covid-19-on-chinese-wet-markets> (last accessed 4 August 2020).

Collin, Robbie (2014), 'Transformers: Age of Extinction, review: "spectacular junk"', *The Telegraph*, 3 July, <https://www.telegraph.co.uk/culture/film/filmreviews/10931655/Transformers-Age-of-Extinction-review-spectacular-junk.html> (last accessed 20 July 2019).

CSIS (2009), *Smart Power in U.S.–China Relations: A Report of the CSIS Commission on China*. Washington, DC: Center for Strategic and International Studies.

Cuarón, Alfonso (2013), Film: *Gravity*, UK/USA: Warner Bros.

Daly, Robert (2016), 'Hollywood's Dangerous Obsession with China', *Los Angeles Times*, 7 October, <http://www.latimes.com/opinion/op-ed/la-oe-daly-hollywood-20161007-snap-story.html> (last accessed 16 June 2018).

DeKnight, Steven S. (2018), Film: *Pacific Rim: Uprising*. UK/China/Japan/USA: Legendary Entertainment.

Dittmer, Jason, and Klaus Dodds (2013), 'The Geopolitical Audience: Watching Quantum of Solace (2008) in London', *Popular Communication*, 11, 76–91.

Dittmer, Jason, and Nicholas Gray (2010), 'Popular Geopolitics 2.0: Towards Methodologies of the Everyday', *Geography Compass*, 4:11, 1664–77.

Dollar, David, Ryan Hass and Jeffrey A. Bader (2019), 'Assessing U.S.–China Relations 2 Years into the Trump Presidency', *Brookings*, 15 January, <https://www.brookings.edu/blog/order-from-chaos/2019/01/15/assessing-u-s-china-relations-2-years-into-the-trump-presidency/> (last accessed 25 October 2019).

Emmerich, Roland (2016), Film: *Independence Day: Resurgence*. USA: 20th Century Fox.

Escobar, Natalie (2020), 'When Xenophobia Spreads Like a Virus', *npr*, 4 March, <https://www.npr.org/2020/03/02/811363404/when-xenophobia-spreads-like-a-virus?t=1596619532797> (last accessed 04 July 2020).

Ford, Christopher A. (2019), 'Technology and Power in China's Geopolitical Ambitions', Testimony to U.S.–China Economic and Security Review Commission Washington, DC, *U.S. Department of State*, <https://www.state.gov/technology-and-power-in-chinas-geopolitical-ambitions/> (last accessed 23 October 2019).

Ge, Celine (2017), 'Soft Power: China's Hollywood Dreams Not Just About Making Money, Says Media Tycoon Li Ruigang', *South China Morning Post*, 19 January <https://www.scmp.com/business/companies/article/2063471/chinas-hollywood-dreams-not-just-about-making-money-says-tycoon> (last accessed 26 July 2018).

Haas, Benjamin (2018), 'China Bans Winnie the Pooh film After Comparisons to President Xi', *The Guardian*, 7 August, <https://www.theguardian.com/world/2018/aug/07/china-bans-winnie-the-pooh-film-to-stop-comparisons-to-president-xi> (last accessed 7 August 2018).

Hartig, Falk (2015), 'Communicating China to the World: Confucius Institutes and China's Strategic Narratives', *Politics*, 35:3–4, 245–58.

Hendricks, Scotty (2018), 'The Silent Chinese Propaganda in Hollywood Films', *Big Think*, 10 December, <https://bigthink.com/politics-current-affairs/china-hollywood-influence> (last accessed 11 May 2019).

Hewitt, Duncan (2011), *International Media Coverage of China: Chinese Perceptions and the Challenges for Foreign Journalists*, Reuters Institute Fellowship paper, University of Oxford, <https://reutersinstitute.politics.ox.ac.uk/sites/default/files/2018-11/International_media_coverage_of_China.pdf> (last accessed 28 July 2019).

Higgins, Tucker, and Yelena Dzhanova (2020), 'Pompeo Says More Trade Talks with Chinese Possible Even as he Accuses Them of Coronavirus Coverup', *CNBC*, 7 May, <https://www.cnbc.com/2020/05/07/pompeo-accuses-china-of-coronavirus-coverup-but-says-trade-talks-possible.html> (last accessed 8 October 2020).

Homewood, Chris (2018), '"Directed by Hollywood, Edited by China"? Chinese Soft Power, Geo-imaginaries, and Neo-orientalism(s) in Recent U.S. Blockbusters', in R. A. Saunders and V. Strukov (eds), *Popular Geopolitics: Plotting an Evolving Interdiscipline*. New York: Routledge, pp. 174–96.

Horton, Helena (2016), 'Chinese Teen Couple Sold Their 18-day-old Baby Daughter Online for £2,500 to Buy an iPhone', *The Telegraph*, 8 March,

\<https://www.telegraph.co.uk/news/newstopics/howaboutthat/12187726/Chinese-teen-couple-sold-their-baby-daughter-online-to-buy-an-iPhone.html\> (last accessed 23 October 2019).

Huang, Yu, and Christine Chi Mei Leung (2006), 'Western-Led Press Coverage of Mainland China and Vietnam during the SARS Crisis: Reassessing the Concept of "Media Representation of the *Other*"', *Asian Journal of Communication*, 15:3, 302–18.

Johnson, Rian (2012), Film: *Looper*. USA/China: TriStar Pictures.

Kaplan, Sarah, Gerry Shih and Rick Noack (2019), 'China Lands Spacecraft on the Far Side of the Moon, a Historic First', *The Washington Post*, 3 January, \<https://www.washingtonpost.com/science/2019/01/03/china-lands-spacecraft-far-side-moon-historic-first/\> (last accessed 13 October 2019).

Kennedy, John F. (1962), *Moon Speech*, 12 September, \<https://er.jsc.nasa.gov/seh/ricetalk.htm\> (last accessed 16 November 2020).

Leong, Karen J. (2005), *The China Mystique: Pearl S. Buck, Anna May Wong, Mayling Soong, and the Transformation of American Orientalism*. Berkeley and Los Angeles: University of California Press.

Molter, Vanessa, and Graham Webster (2020), 'Virality Project (China): Coronavirus Conspiracy Claims, *Stanford Cyber Policy Center*, 31 March, \<https://cyber.fsi.stanford.edu/news/china-covid19-origin-narrative\> (last accessed 31 March 2020).

Morley, Nicole (2016), 'Man Narrowly Escapes Death After Another Horrific Escalator Accident in China', *Metro*, 30 May, \<https://metro.co.uk/2016/05/30/man-narrowly-escapes-death-after-another-horrific-escalator-accident-in-china-5913990/\> (last accessed 18 August 2019).

Naremore, James (1998), *More than Night: Film Noir in its Contexts*. Berkeley and Los Angeles: University of California Press.

Nye, Joseph S., Jr (2004), *Soft Power: The Means to Success in World Politics*, New York: Public Affairs.

Nye, Joseph S., Jr (2008), 'Public Diplomacy and Soft Power', *The Annals of the American Academy of Political and Social Science*, 616:1, 94–109.

Pamuk, Humeyra, and David Brunnstrom (2020), 'Pompeo Blames China for Hundreds of Thousands of Virus Deaths, Denies Inconsistency', *Reuters*, 6 May, \<https://uk.reuters.com/article/uk-health-coronavirus-china-pompeo/pompeo-blames-china-for-hundreds-of-thousands-of-virus-deaths-denies-inconsistency-idUKKBN22I253\> (last accessed 6 May 2020).

Park, Jane Chi Hyun (2010), *Yellow Future: Oriental Style in Hollywood Cinema*. Minneapolis: University of Minnesota Press.

Parker, Ryan, and Karen Chu (2019), 'Notorious "South Park" China Episode Screened on the Streets of Hong Kong', *The Hollywood Reporter*, 9 October, \<https://www.hollywoodreporter.com/news/south-park-notorious-china-episode-screened-streets-hong-kong-1246561\> (last accessed 10 October 2019).

Pulver, Andrew (2013), 'China Demands "Positive Images" in Return for Access to Markets', *The Guardian*, 6 November, \<https://www.theguardian.com/

film/2013/nov/06/china-hollywood-positive-images-movies> (last accessed 19 May 2019).

Purse, Lisa (2011), *Contemporary Action Cinema*. Edinburgh: Edinburgh University Press.

Roselle, Laura, Alister Miskimmon and Ben O'Loughlin (2014), 'Strategic Narrative: A New Means to Understand Soft Power', *Media War & Conflict*, 7:1, 70–84.

Said, Edward W. (1978), *Orientalism*. New York: Vintage Books.

Saunders, Robert A. (2015), 'Imperial Imaginaries: Employing Science Fiction to Talk About Geopolitics', in Federica Caso and Caitlin Hamilton (eds), *Popular Culture and World Politics: Theories, Methods, Pedagogies*. Bristol: E-International Relations, pp. 149–59.

Savitsky, Shane (2019), 'Hollywood's Cave to China on Censorship', *Axios*, 10 October, <https://www.axios.com/hollywood-movies-china-censorship-bba26aa9-b122-4b2c-80e1-054394414698.html> (last accessed 26 October 2019).

Scott, Ridley (2015), Film: *The Martian*. UK/USA/Hungary/Jordan: 20th Century Fox.

Shackleton, Liz (2019), 'China's Box Office Increases by 9% to $8.9bn in 2018', *Screen Daily*, 2 January, <https://www.screendaily.com/news/chinas-box-office-increases-by-9-to-89bn-in-2018/5135508.article> (last accessed 23 July 2019).

Singer, Bryan (2014), Film: *X-Men: Days of Future Past*. USA: 20th Century Fox.

Sparks, Colin (2010), 'Coverage of China in the UK National Press', *Chinese Journal of Communication*, 3:3, 347–65.

Steinberg, James B. (2008), 'Real Leaders Do Soft Power: Learning Lessons of Iraq', *Washington Quarterly*, 31:2, 155–64.

Tsui, Clarence (2014), '"Transformers: Age of Extinction": Film Review', *The Hollywood Reporter*, 22 June, <https://www.hollywoodreporter.com/review/transformers-age-extinction-film-review-713864> (last accessed 27 November 2019).

Turteltaub, Jon (2018), Film: *The Meg*. USA/China: Apelles Entertainment.

Vazquez, Marietta (2020), 'Calling COVID-19 the "Wuhan Virus" or "China Virus" is Inaccurate and Xenophobic', *Yale School of Medicine*, 12 March, <https://medicine.yale.edu/news-article/23074/> (last accessed 4 August 2020).

Vukovich, Daniel (2012), *China and Orientalism: Western Knowledge Production and the PRC*. London and New York: Routledge.

Weldes, Jutta (2003), 'Popular Culture, Science Fiction, and World Politics', in Jutta Weldes (ed.), *To Seek Out New Worlds: Exploring Links between Science Fiction and World Politics*. Basingstoke: Palgrave Macmillan, pp. 1–22.

Yang, Yanling (2016), 'Film Policy, the Chinese government and Soft Power', *New Cinemas*, 14:1, 71–91.

Zhang, Jenny G. (2020), 'Pinning Coronavirus on How Chinese People Eat Plays Into Racist Assumptions', *Eater*, 31 January, <https://www.eater.com/2020/1/31/21117076/coronavirus-incites-racism-against-chinese-people-and-their-diets-wuhan-market> (last accessed 4 August 2020).

CHAPTER 6

The Second World War, Soviet Sports and Furious Space Walks: Soft Power and Nation Branding in the Putin 2.0 Era

Stephen M. Norris

> Russia is a state that created a great culture. Throughout Russia's history, it was culture that focused on and passed on to new generations the spiritual experience of the nation, ensured unity among the multinational people of Russia and largely determined Russia's influence in the world. ('Proekt' 2014)

So begins the May 2014 'Foundations of the State Cultural Policy', authored under the auspices of the Russian Ministry of Culture, headed by Vladimir Medinskii. The document goes on to state that the 'national catastrophes' Russia experienced during the twentieth century mean that this state cultural policy is needed more than ever, as its 'most important social mission' contains a 'tool for transferring to new generations a set of edifying, moral and ethical values that constitute the basis of national identity'. 'Culture', it declared, 'should help to bring about the government's desired policy of a strong, united Russia' (ibid.).

Among the values the policy hoped to instil is 'love for the Motherland', advanced through a strategic plan of implementation. It called for promoting Russia's cultural heritage, developing and protecting the Russian language, supporting domestic literature, creating a 'more favourable informational environment for the emergence of personality (*lichnost'*)', increasing children's participation in a host of activities (including the Russian Historical Society and the Russian Military Historical Society) and much more. In a section devoted to promotion of the arts, the document stated 'the state pays a great deal of attention to the development of domestic cinema and considerable funds are spent for this purpose' (ibid.).

The 2014 document serves as a perfect entryway to the themes covered in this chapter, where I argue that Russian blockbuster historical cinema has played a key role in domestic soft power and nation branding exercises since 2012 (a role it has performed for the entire Putin era, but one that became more pronounced after 2012). The key political contexts that shaped this document were the protests of 2011–12 against Russian corruption and the subsequent return of Vladimir Putin to the Presidency. In response to the protests, the Putin state became even more repressive, with media outlets launching attacks against any perceived opponents and police launching more crackdowns, policies that in turn characterised the second Putin Presidency (and which Maria Lipman has dubbed Putin 2.0).

The timing of the document also reflects important political concerns, coming just three months after the Sochi Winter Olympics and the Russian annexation of Crimea. 'Foundations of the State Cultural Policy' sought to lay the groundwork for using soft power methods, particularly cinematic narratives, in order to shore up domestic support for the Putin system. While the President himself mattered in these efforts, as this chapter will make clear, other players mattered too, including Medinskii and the Minister of Defence, Sergei Shoigu. The more specific policies that these two men and their ministries authored established guidelines for domestic filmmakers that sought to instil patriotism through cinema. Even more specifically, as will be analysed below, these guidelines favoured funding for movies about the Second World War, the successes of Soviet sport, and the space race. Although international recognition was mentioned at the outset as an aim of the programme, it was mainly concerned with domestic soft power: patriotic movies, in short, could shore up support for Putinism.

A Short History of Russian Patriotic Cinema and Nation Branding, 1991–2012

The May 2014 document captured concerns from that time, yet it also in many ways updated a cultural project under way since the late 1990s, one that aimed to turn Russian culture away from a perceived focus on negativity and towards more positive narratives, heroes and ideas that would restore a patriotic spirit. Russian popular cinema after 1998, and particularly during the first Putin presidency (2000–8), sought to model itself on Hollywood techniques and productions but with 'Russian' content in order to bolster domestic movies, and with it, to foster a renewed sense of Russianness among audiences. The movies that followed frequently mined the past to do so, offering up heroes from the ancient, early modern, tsarist and Soviet eras as models for the present. Russian films after 1998 and particularly during Putin 1.0, in other words, engaged in a form of soft power, aimed mostly at domestic audiences but with an eye toward promoting success abroad.

In the well-known words of Joseph Nye, soft power is the ability to get what you want through attraction rather than coercion or payments. It arises from the attractiveness of a country's culture, political ideals and policies

(Nye 2004: x). Soft power resources, as Nye writes, are the assets that produce such attraction (ibid.: 6). Films, and more specifically Hollywood films, run through Nye's analysis (ibid.: 8, 12, 17, 33, 47); so too does criticism of how the USSR allegedly 'lost' its soft power after its hard power actions in 1956 and 1968, when Soviet-led armed forces crushed revolts in Hungary and Czechoslovakia (ibid.: 9, 11, 73, 101). Nye's argument that the US in part 'won' the cultural Cold War because it managed hard and soft power best, while 'Soviet culture did not generate many soft-power resources' (ibid.: 74), is one echoed in a more thorough analysis by Tony Shaw and Denise Youngblood of Cold War era films. In their estimation, Shaw and Youngblood conclude that American cultural officials and Hollywood films proved better at promoting an American way of life than their Soviet counterparts. The 'Soviet mode' in this cultural war, they conclude, 'was therefore defensive rather than offensive', reacting to what the US government and American cinema said about the USSR (Shaw and Youngblood 2010: 217). The Cold War thus had a crucial cultural, soft power component to it that would fundamentally shape Russian cinematic ideas after 1991.

The post-Soviet Russian cultural dilemma consisted in part of shedding the perception of its Soviet era hard over soft power persona. To do so also required a move away from the so-called *chernukha* culture that dominated late Soviet and early post-Soviet society, a term that can best be translated as 'blackening', and one applied to the seeming dominance of films and books that focused on violence and poverty while conveying messages of hopelessness and despair (see Graham 2013). Post-Soviet cultural figures began to call for a change, culminating in a famous 1998 speech by the newly elected President of the Filmmakers' Union, Academy Award-winning director Nikita Mikhalkov, that claimed Russia needed new heroes for new audiences and an end to all the darkness.

As a result, Russian directors and producers began to make more 'audience-friendly' films, modelled on Hollywood but with 'Russian' content (see Norris 2012). The efforts began to bear fruit in the early 2000s, as Vladimir Putin began his first term as President. The rise in oil prices and recovery of the Russian economy allowed the government to invest more in cinema. Under the auspices of then Minister of Culture Mikhail Shvydkoi, an open-ended 'Culture of Russia, 2001–2005' initiative saw 20 billion rubles invested in cultural productions that would help create more positive, even patriotic, products. Beyond the general desire to promote culture that was not *chernukha*, Shvydkoi's Ministry did not prioritise specific themes. The result, at least in terms of movies, produced narratives that ranged from critiques of the Soviet state during the Second World War to animated movies glorifying the

Kivan Rus' Prince Vladimir to comedies of the good life in contemporary Russia.

What these early 2000s efforts amounted to was a form of domestic nation branding, an attempt to foster a better image of Russia in the present by reminding viewers of heroic pasts, with the aim of creating a better future. Following the works of Keith Dinnie (2016), Melissa Aronczyk (2013), and Robert Saunders (2017), this project might best be understood as the attempt to brand a nation, even for domestic audiences, as a crucial part of soft power and public diplomacy. Cinema can act as a means to promote a more coherent and cohesive national identity, to animate its citizens in the service of national priorities. A 'national brand', as Dinnie has argued, is 'the unique, multidimensional blend of elements that provide the nation with culturally grounded differentiation and relevance for all of its targeted audience' (Dinnie 2016: 5). Aronczyk has written that nation branding is often a solution to perceived contemporary problems affecting the space of the nation-state, particularly national visibility and legitimacy amid the multiple global flows of late modernity (Aronczyk 2013: 3). Nation branding efforts are ultimately about 'territorial attachments and the ways these are made and remade through ideational and material means' (ibid.: 9), or how 'enduring cultural symbols of national identification are brought into play in ways that are not reducible to the particular self-serving objectives of a given political party or leader' (ibid.: 9–10).

The remaking of Russian cinema after 1991 can be seen as an effort in domestic nation branding and, with it, an exercise in domestic soft power, where Russian filmmakers, cultural officials and government officials have all played parts in promoting a sense of patriotism among the population. Indeed, 'patriotism' has been the watchword of the Putin era since 2000, so much so that it has almost lost all meaning and become a catch-all for everything positive about Russia: Putin himself declared it to be our 'national idea' in February 2016 ('Putin Declares' 2016). Cinema has played no small role in promoting this brand, one captured quite well in the 2014 'Foundations of the State Cultural Policy' mentioned above.

As this short history of a main current in contemporary Russian cinema has suggested, the promotion of patriotism, or what might else be called the exercise of Russian domestic soft power, has coincided with the consolidation of power in the Kremlin by Vladimir Putin and his associates. Putinism, particularly Putin 2.0 (after 2012), as Maria Lipman has argued (2016), centres on stability, unity, social consensus, sovereignty and patriotism. It has also, as Mikhail Zygar has pointed out (2016), evolved over the years, becoming more authoritarian and creating in the process more of an echo chamber in the Kremlin. It is not monolithic across time, in other words, nor does it involve only actions by Putin himself. The 'Foundations of the State Cultural Policy' of May 2014 speaks to the evolution of Putinism and the ways that cultural policy also shifted, becoming more government-centric and more authoritarian, and yet also creating different forms of opposition. This shift is best understood as one overseen by Vladimir Medinskii, who became Russia's Minister of Culture in May 2012, shortly after Putin returned to the Presidency following Dmitrii Medvedev's term and in the midst of ongoing protests against Russian political corruption. Medinskii oversaw a cultural project that tapped into the general trends initiated under his predecessor, Shvydkoi, but one that became much more in tune with Kremlin policy. Russian cinema since 2012, and by extension, the project of domestic soft power meant to promote patriotism, became more interventionist, more aligned with the other crackdowns of Putin 2.0. It thus became a form of *belukha*, or a 'whitening' of Russian culture.

Medinskii's Ministry: Rewriting History, Revising the Patriotic Brand

In September 2013, Medinskii sat down for an interview with the radio station Echo Moscow. The talk came after the protests against government policies had died down, after opposition leader Aleksei Navalny had been sentenced to five years' imprisonment and after the Russian government had staged pro-government rallies. Medinskii did not talk about these events, but they certainly formed an important subtext to his appearance and to the policies he was beginning to enact. Instead, interviewer Elena Iampol'skaia wanted Medinskii to talk about the recent decision he had made not to fund Aleksandr Mindadze's film about the Second World War, *My Good Hans*.

The film was set in the last months of the Nazi–Soviet Pact and focused on a handful of German engineers who had come to the USSR under its terms to work in a factory that aimed to create better lenses. The dialogue was mostly in German, and the titular character helped to finish the project, later to return to the very same place in the USSR as a Wehrmacht officer, making use of his lenses to wage total war. In its interpretation of history and rejection of Soviet era mythic narratives about the Great Patriotic War, *My Good Hans* followed in the footsteps of recent Russian films such as Aleksei German, Jr's, *Last Train* (2003), Aleksei Karelin's *A Time to Gather Stones* (2005). Artem Antonov's *Twilight* (2006) and Mikhail Segal's *Franz + Polina* (2006). All had received funding from the Ministry of Culture and all had featured German characters that humanised the enemy.

By the time Mindadze finished his film, however, the cultural climate had changed, in part because of the political protests, yet also because of an increasing backlash against the initial wave of historical films released in the 2000s that were deemed not 'patriotic enough'. Medinskii was a vocal critic of this view, serving on the committee established under then President Dmitrii Medvedev to investigate so-called 'falsifications' of history: the committee, which disbanded in 2012, particularly focused on anyone who would seemingly deny the Soviet contribution to victory. Just after the committee disbanded, Putin tapped Medinskii as his new Minister of Culture. From that position, he worked with pro-government organisations such as the Russian Military Historical Society (RVIO) to continue the aims of the 2009 commissions. The RVIO was founded in December 2012 by an order from the President in order to combat attempts to distort the history of Russian military actions and to promote patriotism. Headed by the Defence Minister, Sergei Shoigu, the Society has overseen the erection of a host of new monuments, worked with museums, and engaged in a wealth of educational projects, all designed to promote patriotism.[1] The Society also sends members to act as consultants on feature films. In this climate, Medinskii decided not to offer state funding to Mindadze's film because the Society declared it 'falsified history'.

In his Echo Moscow interview, the Minister of Culture underscored that another historians' committee vetting Mindadze's film had also rejected it, joining the RVIO. Medinskii further elucidated that it is 'essential' to consult historians on proposed historical films 'if it touches on painful historical themes' (Iampol'skaia 2013). Medinskii was forced to admit that 'truth' about the past was often difficult to pinpoint, stating that when dealing with ancient times, it 'is ridiculous to seek historical truth' because 'no one knows anything, everything is based on legends' (ibid.). The Minister had particularly harsh words for contemporary critics, whom he characterised as wanting to prove that 'we are just crap'. To illustrate this claim, Medinskii referenced the 2005 TV series *Penal Battalion* (*Shtrafbat*), a popular and critically acclaimed account of the use of Gulag prisoners as cannon fodder in the Second World War (and one that had received state funding). Medinskii declared that *Shtrafbat* was one of the 'most vivid' series in post-Soviet TV history, but also that 'it's generally not true', adding that 'the only truth in this film is that we fought against Germany'. To take its claims as 'truth' meant that, after watching it, people would just want to go to Moscow's Sheremetyevo airport and leave 'because it's not worth living in a country that treated people who won the war that way'. 'Yes, we have a terrible, bloody, difficult history,' Medinskii concluded, but 'if the film *Shtrafbat* was true, Russia would not have existed for a thousand years. Therefore I am convinced that the state should not finance such pictures' (ibid.).

The radio interview captured a number of important trends in the culture of the Putin 2.0 era, also the era of Medinskii. It also helps to explain the May 2014 document outlining the role of culture in promoting state patriotism. In his comments, Medinskii deliberately conflates historical truth with strict accuracy, a policy he employed in regard to Mindadze's film. *Penal Battalion* contained episodes that were, strictly speaking, not 'true' (among them, the commanding officer of the battalion was himself a Gulag prisoner, which would not have been allowed), but the series revealed a deeper 'truth', exposing the fact that the Soviet state did employ prisoners in battalions that suffered heavy casualties (facts the state had remained silent about for decades). In a similar vein, Mindadze's film delved into an era that the Soviet state had deliberately ignored, offering a truth not just confined to whether or not certain German engineers worked in the USSR at a certain time, only for one to return as invader. Medinskii's policy and the way he explained it on air thus deliberately tried to muddy the waters of what historical truth means.

Medinskii's views on what is false and what is true should be the lens through which we view the 2014 policy he authored. His ideas characterised the state's allocation to historical cinema under the Ministry, a policy that particularly focused on the Second World War. The same year he denied funding to Mindadze's film, Medinskii's Ministry also declined to fund and support Khusein Erkenov's 2013 film about the 1944 deportation of Chechens during the Second World War, *Ordered to Forget* (*Prikazano zabyt'*). Medinskii claimed that historians could find no archival documentation that supported the film's narrative about events in the village of Khaibakh, where agents from the NKVD, the Stalinist era secret police, rounded up and then set fire to Chechens in a barn.[2] Medinskii and his Ministry rendered this judgement, despite the fact that Soviet era forensic investigations determined that the Khaibakh massacre had taken place. Claiming no archival documents existed provided convenient cover to apply the 'falsification' label and therefore discredit what the Ministry believed to be an 'unpatriotic' film.

The decision about Erkenov's film soon proved ironic. In July 2015, Sergei Mironenko, the head of the State Archive of the Russian Federation (GARF), published documents that exposed the legend of the 28 Panfilov guardsmen as partially untrue. The story of the 28 became widely known after a 1941 newspaper article extolled the sacrifice the soldiers made while defending

Figure 6.1 A Soviet team forms. Members of the famous Panfilov's 28 come together and prepare to defend Moscow in *Panfilov's 28* (2016).

Moscow against the German invaders (Fig. 6.1). The documents Mironenko made public demonstrate that the Soviet journalist who first reported the tale invented part of the story, covering up more uncomfortable facts, most notably that some of the guardsmen wanted to surrender and that not all had died. In response to this exposé, Medinskii retorted that Mironenko was 'not a writer, not a journalist and not a fighter against historical falsifications', and declared 'if he wants to change profession, we will understand this' (quoted in Balmforth 2016). In March 2016, Medinskii's ominous warning took on new meaning when it was announced that Mironenko had been demoted from head of GARF.

One of the reasons for Medinskii's ire, as several reports noted, was that he had already announced that the Ministry of Culture officially backed a 'military–patriotic film' entitled *Panfilov's 28*.[3] Released on 24 November 2016, the film technically falsified history in the way Medinskii had defined it (see Norris 2017). Because of the intense coverage of Mironenko's exposé, however, Andrei Shal'opa, the co-director and scriptwriter, had to acknowledge the ways that the story of Panfilov's 28 blurred the lines between history and myth.

Medinskii, responding after the film had debuted and after Putin had watched it with Kazakh President Nursultan Nazarbayev, stated that 'even if this story was invented from start to finish, if there had been no Panfilov, if there had been nothing, this is a sacred legend that shouldn't be interfered with. People that do that are filthy scum' (quoted in Bone 2016). Writing in late 2013 for the newspaper *Gazeta*, Igor Karev and Aleksei Krizhevskii declared that the most important cultural trend of that year was 'the Minister of Culture went to the cinema (Minkul'tury idet v kino)', creating a 'vertical of power' that echoed Putin's own

(Karev and Krizhevskii 2013). The Mindadze case, mentioned in their article, demonstrated that it is now necessary to depict historical events 'only in the way that the state remembers them', not in the ways they actually took place.

Russian Heroism, Russian 'Firsts': A Short Course in Russian Patriotic Cinema, 2012–18

The Ministry of Culture under Medinskii issued orders that prioritised how government funding should be used. In its *prikaz* (order) for 2016 (no. 1040), Medinskii aimed to motivate filmmakers and film viewers to create and embrace models for behaviour in contemporary Russia. More specifically, Medinskii's Ministry prioritised films that focused on Russia's military history, specifically Russian military heroes and acts of heroism, the theme of 'first in the world', explained to mean instances where Russia had pioneered something in world culture, and films about the Revolution and Civil War as long as they emphasised its tragic history.[4] The priorities echoed those expressed in earlier proclamations. The films that resulted further fostered a 'history' on screen that resembled 'mythistory' more than serious interpretation of the past.

One key to evaluating the sort of patriotic branding that characterised the Medinskii era is not to look deeply into the actual histories of events depicted in blockbuster historical films, but to examine how they distort facts and offer palatable narratives for the present. Andrei Kravchuk's *Viking* (2016), Dzhanik Faiziev's and Ivan Shukhorvetskii's *Furious* (2017) and Rustam Mosafir's *Scythian* (2018) all presented history as *Game of Thrones*, transforming Prince Vladimir (who brought Christianity to Kievan Rus'), Evpatii Kolovrat (who led a resistance against Batu Khan) and a Tmutarakan Prince named Oleg (as well as a motley cast of fellow steppe warriors) into manly defenders of Russianness, however ill defined this concept may be. What mattered in all three films is not any adherence to factual truths (they all veered wildly from historical accounts), but that all the heroic men in the movies fought for something resembling Russia. Women fought too: Anton Sivers's *Vasilisa* (2014) recycles the story of a peasant woman who defended her motherland in 1812, Dmitrii Meskhiev's *Battalion* (2015; Fig. 6.2) narrates the story of the so-called 'Women's Battalion of Death', who defended their Russian motherland in 1917, Sergei Mokritskii's *Battle for Sevastopol* (2015) recounts the heroism of Soviet sniper Liudmila Pavlichenko (and conveniently has her defend Crimea) and Renat Davlet'iarov's *The Dawns Here are Quiet* (2015) is an update on a Soviet era classic about women gunners training for battle in the Second

Figure 6.2 A Russian team forms on the Eastern Front. Members of the Women's Battalion of Death head into battle in Dmitrii Meskhiev's *Battalion* (2015).

World War. Frederick Corney has aptly described the latter as 'an updated but nostalgic treatment of an original nostalgic treatment of a wartime episode' (Corney 2016). The point of all four is more or less the point of the previous three: Russians, now including women, fight to defend their motherland. Any other deeper meaning is not worth exploring. All these films declare some sort of 'victory', whether one occurred in history or not (in the case of the Women's Battalion, it did not), the triumph being mostly an expression of patriotism. As the film critic Elena Kravtsyn concluded when writing about *Viking* – thoughts that could be applied to all the films mentioned in this paragraph – it is a 'fairy tale', one that has 'an indirect relationship to historical reality but captures the style of historical stories of the current Minister of Culture' (Kravtsyn 2016).

This 'victory through patriotism' trope applies to two of the most commercially successful films of the Medinskii era, both about Soviet sports. The first, Nikolai Lebedev's *Legend No. 17*, debuted in April 2013 and earned USD 29.5 million at the box office, placing it in the top ten highest-grossing films of all time in Russia at that point.[5] The film is a biopic of the great Soviet hockey player, Valerii Kharlamov (played by Danila Kozlovskii, who also played Prince Vladimir in *Viking*), following his journey as he first garners attention, breaks into the CSKA Moscow team, and then plays in the 1972 Summit Series between the USSR and Canada. In between, audiences learn about Kharlamov's family, his on-again, off-again love life, his love–hate relationship with the great Soviet coach Anatolii Tarasov, and his run-ins with cartoonishly bad Soviet officials. The film successfully lifts most of the plot themes from Gavin O'Connor's 2004 *Miracle*, which was about the 1980 American Olympic hockey team, and transfers them to the 1970s Soviet Union. A difficult coach becomes the centre of attention, working his team too hard to the point of making them initially hate him, only for his methods to pay off and cultivate a love among the team. The coach deals with reluctant bureaucrats who want to manage defeat, not try to win, but eventually the coach institutes his desired new style of play, which borrows from the successes of the opponent (in *Miracle*, it was American hockey adopting Soviet methods; in *Legend No. 17* it is Soviet hockey adopting Canadian styles). Before the style can work, team differences have to be overcome (Boston versus Minnesota in *Miracle*, Spartak versus Dynamo in *Legend No. 17*). Masculine comradery and love for a game trumps love between men and women in both films. To triumph requires hard work and the acceptance of new methods within a team ethos, but also a miracle. At the end of *Legend No. 17*, the miracle is the 7–3 victory over the Canadian team in the first game of the 1972 series. The miracle of *Miracle* is the 4–3 victory over a Soviet team that featured Kharlamov, with the subsequent 4–2 victory over Finland that guaranteed the Gold Medal barely mentioned (the Finns are not as fearsome a foe as the Soviets).

Russian President Vladimir Putin, accompanied by a number of Soviet hockey greats, watched a special screening of *Legend No. 17* in Sochi during the run-up to the 2014 Winter Olympics. Putin praised Kharlamov's character, stating he became a great player 'not only for our national team, but for world hockey' ('Vladimir Putin' 2013). In doing so, Putin claimed, 'Kharlamov became one of those people who demonstrated the success and greatness of our country' (ibid.).

Like the other historical blockbusters of the Medinskii era, the absences and diversions from historical fact matter a great deal. The film ends with a miraculous victory on ice, but does not mention the result of the series itself, one won by the Canadians and secured in the final match in Moscow. Here the 'victory' comes in the 'fact' that the 'amateur' Soviet team could win at all against the hardened professionals from Canada (Fig. 6.3). To help convey the miraculous victory, the film transforms Canadian players Phil Esposito and Bobby Clarke into ridiculously bad enemies: one critic described them as 'hairy apes chewing gum and using their hockey sticks mostly to beat and maim the Soviet players' (Dobrynin 2013). Lebedev's film played fast and loose with other facts: the onscreen Kharlamov had a serious car crash in 1972, in order to suggest he overcame more adversity before the series and also to suggest the Soviet state victimised patriotic sportsmen as much as helped them, while the real Kharlamov suffered a crash in 1976. Kharlamov's rearranged car crash comes after a match between the Soviet team and Spartak Moscow, Leonid Brezhnev's favourite club team, one that the Soviet team is asked to throw in order to please

Figure 6.3 A Soviet team celebrates victory. The 1972 USSR hockey team defeats the Canadians because of their iron will, not through a miracle, in Nikolai Lebedev's *Legend No. 17* (2013).

the Soviet leader. The match never happened in real life. Clarke's play in the actual series was praised by the Soviet coach. while on film he was brutish. Clarke's infamous slash, one out of character with the player, came against Kharlamov in game six, an act that broke Kharlamov's ankle and forced him out of the rest of the series. The act is left out of the film, for showing it would require admitting that the Canadians won the series.

Russian critics more or less liked the film, with 29 of 34 giving it positive reviews (as collated on the site *Kinopoisk*). In a minority opinion, Ekaterina Barabash called *Legend No. 17* 'an attack of patriotism', noting not just the film's messages, but its reviews, which 'read like a mantra, with repeated chauvinistic nonsense about the inherent patriotism in it' (Barabash 2013). Andrei Kolesnikov called it 'myth no. 17' and noted how much the filmmakers juggled facts to bestow on it a 'propagandistic meaning' (Kolesnikov 2013). Elena Stishova, writing in the influential journal *The Art of Cinema*, acknowledged this critical backlash, but wrote that she more or less liked the film, highlighting how 'adrenaline' was key to understanding it, both as conveyed on screen but also among popular reaction, where she saw spectators applaud and cry out (Stishova 2013). Sergei Sychev, in another positive review, claimed that the film was 'conceived of as part of a great national idea', not about hockey, but 'how to live on Russian soil' (Sychev 2013). In all instances, critics interpreted the film through the patriotism it attempted to espouse, thus reinforcing the aims of the filmmakers and inadvertently highlighting the nation-branding significance of the movie.

The same producers behind *Legend No. 17* – Leonid Vereshchagin, Nikita Mikhalkov and Anton Zlatopol'skii – also produced the blockbuster *Going Vertical*, which set box office records after its 28 December 2017 debut. The story, co-written by Nikolai Kulikov, who also co-wrote *Legend No. 17*, covers the 1972 Olympic basketball championship, won by the USSR over the USA in controversial fashion after the Soviet team was twice awarded extra time at the end of the Gold Medal game. The defeat was the first for the Americans in Olympic basketball play. While the story is recounted from a Russian perspective, inaccuracies abound. Once again, the basic plot roughly follows that of *Legend No. 17*, which followed that of *Miracle*. This time the controversial coach wants to play more like the Americans. He has to convince recalcitrant Soviet bureaucrats and a mishmash of Soviet nationalities (Russians, Ukrainians, Georgians, Uzbeks and Lithuanians) to believe in this concept and embrace a renewed team. Once again, love for the team and, with it, the Soviet motherland, is more important than love for wives and girlfriends.

Much like *Legend No. 17*, *Going Vertical* takes real-life characters and plays fast and loose with the facts of their lives. The cinematic version of Modestas Paulauskas, a Soviet Lithuanian star for the 1972 team and his club Zalgiris Kaunas, nearly defects in Munich during the games but changes his mind at the last minute in order to play for his team. The real Paulauskas, as numerous reports testified after the film debuted, did no such thing, coaching Soviet youth teams after he retired. Aleksandr Belov, who would make the game-winning basket, has a heart defect detected during the team's American tour before the games in the film version, a health issue that the real-life Belov did not know about until after the games (and one that would kill him at the age of twenty-six in 1978). In the film Belov also has a girlfriend, who plays for the Soviet women's basketball team in Munich; unfortunately, women's basketball debuted only in 1976 in Montreal. And so on: many more tidbits are altered to fit within the template of a miracle victory that promotes timeless patriotism. Perhaps the two most glaring inaccuracies come in the depiction of the American team, who are all presented as ruthless thugs (much like the Canadian hockey players), and in the style of basketball depicted, which consists of the sort of high-flying dunks more associated with the 1980s than Olympic basketball in the 1970s. Still, 18 of 21 reviews were deemed positive on *Kinopoisk*.[6]

Vedomosti critic Larisa Iusipova, who liked the film, summed it up by saying that twenty years after the decision in domestic cinema to go Hollywood,

Going Vertical was 'a great Hollywood film in the best sense about a great national victory' (Iusipova 2017). Anton Dolin of *Vesti*, in another positive review, wrote that the film used Hollywood templates but broke with them to create 'a conversation about what real patriotism is' (Dolin 2017). The film's inaccuracies took a back seat to the successful patriotism promoted on screen, a theme that also characterised the coverage in both *Sport Express*, a popular daily sports newspaper, and *Argumenty i Fakty*, the most widely read paper in Russia. In the latter, journalists highlighted seven serious errors: the real coach was Kondrashin, not 'Garanzhin'; the real Aleksandr Belov was not mortally ill; the real Paulauskas was not anti-Soviet; the real Soviet delegation did not plan to abandon the final after Israeli athletes were murdered by Palestinian terrorists at Munich (as shown on screen in order to highlight how bad Soviet bureaucrats were), 1972 era basketball was not full of dunks, and the women's basketball team was not in Munich. Still, both papers simply noted these flaws without commenting meaningfully on whether or not they had any deeper meanings. In one interview, director Anton Megerdichev, responding to similarly mild criticisms about these factual errors, simply claimed 'we cannot make a blockbuster documentary' (quoted in Tsulaia 2018).

In one of the few critical reviews, Anna Moskvina placed the film's errors up front and asked questions about why the filmmakers made Paulauskas anti-Soviet when he had given numerous interviews where he expressed nostalgia for his Soviet life, why Belov had to be sick, and why a contrived love story had to be woven into the plot when this all but ensured further errors. Above all, Moskvina questioned, 'why are films about the past being shot in a seemingly endless stream? Are there no present-day sporting heroes?' (Moskvina 2018). Moskvina only touches on an answer, stating that the film fits within a recent cinematic pattern of focusing on the past as a source of nostalgia, 'when the trees were bigger and the candy was sweeter' (ibid.). Left unmentioned is the programme that Medinskii oversaw, explicitly asking for historical heroes and 'firsts', as well as the way both *Legend* and *Vertical* appeared as Russia hosted the Winter Olympics. The build-up to Sochi came with worldwide coverage of the Russian doping scandal: the films and their celebration of past sporting glories served as ideal distractions. Marat Basharov, who played a Soviet bureaucrat in *Going Vertical*, unwittingly provided a better answer to the questions Moskvina posed when he recoiled at the notion that the movie 'blackened the image of the enemy', by stating 'they are already all black' (a not-so-thinly veiled racist remark regarding the American team). Basharov concluded that the film would remind Americans that they are not a great power (quoted in Iakovleva 2017). Given that the film was not released in the US, nor was it planned to be, Basharov's statement aimed at the same audience that the film's patriotic story did: a domestic one.

These, then, are the main messages *Legend No. 17* and *Going Vertical* aimed to provide. The Soviet system produced some champions, but mostly because people felt patriotic about their motherland. This patriotism was not necessarily state-driven during the Soviet era, because if it was, it might suggest that things were entirely better than they are under Putin. Then, as now, however, heroic deeds and patriotic triumphs came against 'the West', even if facts might state otherwise. Then and now, pride in the motherland, love for it, and a willingness to sacrifice for it, matter more than truth.

Megerdichev's film vividly visualises the revived imaginary community that Medinskii's Ministry hoped for: in the end sequence, which recreates the famous replay offered to the USSR basketball team after a series of controversial and questionable refereeing decisions, the director employs a slo-mo montage technique. We watch as the ball arcs across the court towards its inevitable end in the hands of Belov, who makes the buzzer-beating layup on screen, as he did in 1972. As we watch the ball's path, we also see the reactions of the crowd spliced in with reactions from Soviet citizens cheering them on at home as they watch on television. The drama of the Gold Medal game, in other words, brings people together across various republics and across the vast country. In case anyone missed this visual messaging, the end scene in the celebratory Soviet locker room sees the team turn down their monetary bonuses in order to give them to their coach, who needs the money to help his sick son. Belov declares: 'To be honest, we played for the motherland' (Fig. 6.4).

Figure 6.4 Envisioning team success: the recreation of the last three seconds of the game in Anton Megerdichev's *Going Vertical* (2017). The Soviet team is about to triumph; the American team literally lies on the floor, defeated.

Legend No. 17 contained a similar sequence. The Soviet team's last goal, one orchestrated by Kharlamov, is spliced with scenes from home, where family members, friends and fans watch on screen. The triumph over a sporting foe awakens a patriotic spirit, even among Soviet jailers, who release their drunken arrestees so they too can celebrate victory. Again, the message is driven home via visions and words: the Soviet announcer states that his Canadian counterpart wonders whether the victory is a miracle or magic, to which he retorts, 'no, it is not a miracle, just an iron will to win.'

In a sense, every film evaluated in this chapter contained a roughly similar scene: 'Russians' of all stripes unite as a unit, despite regional, ethnic and cultural differences, in order to engage in a patriotic deed, whether it be fighting on the frontlines in the Great War, defending Moscow in 1941, working in the space programme or playing a sport. Across time and space, Russian patriotic films made in the Medinskii era cast and recast timeless behaviours that, in turn, hoped to inspire present-day viewers to do the same. And the films contained scenes where others watched this mythic patriotic behaviour, whether on television or through newspapers or via oral epics.

Medinskii's Ministry also meddled with films that did not alter facts. Dmitrii Kiselev's *Spacewalk* (*Vremia pervykh*, or 'the time of the first' in Russian) certainly fulfilled the Ministry's film priorities, for it narrated the story of Aleksei Leonov, who became the first person to conduct a spacewalk on 18 March 1965. The film recounts Leonov's journey to becoming a cosmonaut, his (and his fellow cosmonauts') relationship to Sergei Korolev, the rocket engineer, and their conflicts with Soviet authorities, including military leaders who wanted the 'first' regardless of any human costs in order to stick it to the Americans and the authentic patriotic sentiments that guided Leonov, Korolev and others. The critic Aleksandr Trofimov wrote that he liked the movie in spite of the fact that everything pointed otherwise, including the heavy advertising campaign, that it was billed as 'patriotic' and little else, and that it seemed to be made under a state order. Where it went wrong, he concluded, was when it stressed too obviously the 'be proud of the motherland'/heroic/patriotic themes (Trofimov 2017). Sasha Shchipin more or less concurred, noting that the film was predictable after 'war, hockey, Orthodoxy, ballet' films (the last comment referenced Aleksei Uchitel's controversial film *Matilda*), and worked in part because it was not too patriotic (Shchipin 2017).

The film generated a controversy none the less, not because of its appeals to patriotism, but because it was slated to appear on 13 April 2017, the day after Cosmonaut Day in Russia. Unfortunately, this was the same day that *Fast and Furious 8: The Fate of the Furious* (dir. F. Gary Gray) was due to debut. When faced with the likelihood that the patriotic Russian film might be trounced at the domestic box office by the continued exploits of Vin Diesel and Dwayne Johnson, Medinskii decided to postpone *Furious*. Theatre owners protested against the decision, citing a potential loss in profits, so Medinskii allowed *Spacewalk* to appear on 6 April, a week early. *Spacewalk* made just under USD 10 million and topped the box office for one week. *Furious 8* knocked it off its temporary perch on the way to earning USD 29.2 million. Not learning the lesson, Medinskii ordered the release of *Paddington 2* (dir. Paul King) to be pushed back two weeks after its scheduled release in January 2018 so that *Scythians* could do better. Again, theatre owners balked, again Medinskii relented a bit, but forced them to release the Russian blockbuster two days before the British bear. *Scythians* 'won' the two days, making back only half of its USD 2 million budget, while *Paddington 2* eventually took in six times more.

Conclusions: Protectionist Patriotism

While films such as *Legend*, *Viking*, *Spacewalk* and *Going Vertical* all did well commercially and critically, Medinskii's policies of promoting patriotism through cinema eventually came to dominate coverage of other films. Kim Druzhinin, who co-directed *Panfilov's 28*, followed up its mythic history of the Second World War with another film that Medinskii promoted, *Tanks*. Originally titled *Tanks for Stalin* and promoted with the tagline 'the first invincible', the film, conceived of by Medinskii himself, purports to tell the history of the famous T-34 tank and its creator, Mikhail Koshkin. The real story of the tank's creation is relatively boring: in early 1940, Koshkin, who operated a factory in Kharkov, drove two prototypes to Moscow to prove its worthiness. The journey was long, and deemed nearly impossible to make, but succeeded without incident. The tank would go on to help the Red Army win the Second World War.

This prosaic tale was not enough for cinema audiences, however, and Druzhinin's team applied even more refashioning to it than they had with *Panfilov's 28*. Koshkin had to fight saboteurs, White guardists who apparently remained a fighting force in 1940, Nazis who had somehow embedded themselves into the USSR and would-be traitors (not to mention technical problems involving roads and weather) before arriving miraculously in Moscow to show off the goods for Stalin. Anton Aleksandrov, writing in the paper *Zavtra*, stated that even though it claimed to be based on real events, the 'only things from reality were the T-34 tank and its designer, Koshkin. Everything else is clearly the fruit of the abundant narcotic experiments of the producers and screenwriters' (Aleksandrov 2018). He continued:

> And yet, while watching it, the feeling of déjà vu never left me. And then at some point, the clouds parted and I realised, God yes, this is *Mad Max Fury Road*! At that point, I turned off the TV. I didn't wait for the aliens to arrive and defeat the experimental T-34s from Baron Wrangel's battalion. (ibid.)

Writing for *Meduza*, Anton Dolin interpreted *Tanks* as an answer to Armando Iannucci's black comedy *The Death of Stalin* (2018), which Medinskii's Ministry banned because it 'lampooned the history of our country' and 'blackened the memory of our citizens who conquered fascism' (according to a news release). Dolin, in his review of *Tanks*, saw Medinskii's hands all over the film as a means to counter *The Death of Stalin*, writing that while the cinematic story of the T-34 tanks tells us nothing about history, 'It is impossible to imagine a more frank self-portrait of the people ruling Russia today (or at least Russian culture)' (Dolin 2018). Medinskii, Dolin argues, chose Druzhinin because he supports the 'construction of "correct" myths as defined by the minister himself'. As the critic saw it, *Panfilov's 28* offered the first proof of this view, while *Tanks* 'confirms the hypothesis' (ibid.).

Medinskii's policies clarify the aims of Russian nation branding, at least in the use of domestic cinema to promote an image of 'Russianness'. The Minister of Culture and his Ministry sought to manage cultural production, to shape the narratives about the past that are offered on screen as 'patriotic', and to shape the discussions about cinema and the past to reflect what the Kremlin wanted: namely, promoting a timeless patriotism and timeless heroism that can inspire the present. Medinskii's mission aimed to denounce anything deemed negative, anything that 'blackened' the country, and to replace it with visions of the past that 'whiten' history. Medinskii instituted what some call a 'protectionist policy'. When the Minister moved *Paddington 2* and other recent Hollywood blockbusters in order to 'help' Russian films such as *Going Vertical*, he sounded a patriotic note, saying he was 'protecting the interests of domestic cinema'. Theatre owners strongly objected, prompting important film industry figures such as Fedor Bondarchuk, Andrei Konchalovsky, Karen Shakhnazarov and others to write a letter in support of the state's policy.[7] In this sense, the Ministry's missions gained important cheerleaders, who in turn amplified the message of patriotism for patriotism's sake. And in one important sense this is all that mattered: Medinskii's Ministry asked for patriotic products, funded patriotic films, promoted patriotism when the films appeared, and amped up calls for more patriotism. In doing so, the Putinist state and its cultural arm sought to define, police and protect what it meant to be a 'patriotic Russian' after 2012 and to connect these actions with support for the system.[8]

Notes

1. See their web page, available at <https://rvio.histrf.ru/activities/news-en/item-4711> (last accessed 16 November 2020).
2. I have explored these topics in two other publications: 'My Good Hans', in Rimgaila Salys (ed.), *The Russian Cinema Reader*, vol. III (Boston: Academic Studies Press, 2019): 344–61; and 'War, Cinema, and the Politics of Memory in Putin 2.0 Culture', in Anton Weiss-Wendt and Nanci Adler (eds), *The Future of the Soviet Past* (Bloomington: Indiana University Press, forthcoming, 2021).
3. The sponsorship was announced in an official TASS report, available at <http://tass.ru/kultura/2015358> (last accessed 16 November 2020).
4. The *prikaz* can be found online: <https://www.mkrf.ru/upload/mkrf/mkdocs2016/приказ%20№%201040%20от %2012.05.2016%20о%20приоритетных%20темах.pdf> (last accessed 16 November 2020).
5. See the statistics on the film site *Kinopoisk*, available at <https://www.kinopoisk.ru/film/601564/> (last accessed 16 November 2020).
6. The statistics are on the *Kinopoisk* site, available at <https://www.kinopoisk.ru/film/840817/> (last accessed 16 November 2020).
7. Reported on <www.kinopoisk.ru/news/3111457/> (last accessed 16 November 2020).
8. This chapter requires a short postscript: in between drafts, a January 2020 government shake-up reshuffled the Cabinet. Putin did not reappoint Medinskii as Culture Minister; instead, his former subordinate, Olga Liubimova, received the post. Under Medinskii, Liubimova had served as head of the Ministry's cinema wing, so the new appointee did not change much in how the Ministry used soft power techniques. Medinskii also did not go away: Putin tapped him as an aide responsible for developing the Kremlin's policies on history.

Works Cited

Aleksandrov, A. (2018), 'Marazm krepchal i tanki nashi bystry', *Zavtra*, 6 June, <http://zavtra.ru/blogs/marazm_krepchal_i_tanki_nashi_bistri> (last accessed 16 November 2020).
Aronczyk, M. (2013), *Branding the Nation: The Global Business of National Identity*. Oxford: Oxford University Press.
Balmforth, T. (2016), 'Russian Archive Chief Out after Debunking Soviet WWII Legend', *Radio Free Europe/Radio Liberty*, 17 March, <http://www.rferl.org/content/mironenko-state-archive-chief-removed-from-post-panfilov-legend/27619460.html> (last accessed 16 November 2020).

Barabash, E. (2013), 'Pristup patriotizma', *Profil'*, 4 May, <https://profile.ru/article/pristup-patriotizma-film-legenda-%E2%84%96-17-vyshel-v-prokat-75704> (last accessed 7 July 2020).
Bone, H. (2016), 'Putin Backs WW2 Myth in New Russian Film', *BBC*, 11 October, <https://www.bbc.com/news/world-europe-37595972> (last accessed 16 November 2020).
Corney, F. (2016), 'Review of *The Dawns Here are Quiet*', *KinoKultura*, 51, <http://www.kinokultura.com/2016/51r-zori.shtml> (last accessed 16 November 2020).
Dinnie, K. (2016), *Nation Branding: Concepts, Issues, Practice*. New York: Routledge.
Dobrynin, S. (2013), 'Review of *Legend No. 17*', *KinoKultura*, 42, <http://www.kinokultura.com/2013/42r-legenda17.shtml> (last accessed 16 November 2020).
Dolin, A. (2017), 'Patriotizm na iazyke sporta', *Radio vesti*, 27 December, <https://radiovesti.ru/brand/61178/episode/1607793/> (last accessed 16 November 2020).
Dolin, A. (2018), 'Tanki Kima Druzhinina: nash otvet fil'mu "Smert Stalina"', *Meduza*, 23 April, <https://meduza.io/feature/2018/04/23/tanki-kima-druzhinina-nash-otvet-filmu-smert-stalina> (last accessed 16 November 2020).
Graham, S. (2013), 'Tales of Grim: Seth Graham on the Dark Side of Russian Cinema', *The Calvert Journal*, 18 January, <https://www.calvertjournal.com/articles/show/57/chernukha-little-vera-cargo-200> (last accessed 16 November 2020).
Iakovleva, E. (2017), 'Marat Basharov: "Dvizhenie vverkh" napomnit SShA, chto oni ne velikaia derzhava', *Argumenty i fakty*, 27 December, <https://aif.ru/culture/movie/marat_basharov_dvizhenie_vverh_napomnit_ssha_chto_oni_ne_velikaya_derzhava> (last accessed 16 November 2020).
Iampol'skaia, E. (2013), 'Vladimir Medinskii: Bez ideologii chelovek stanovitsia zhivotnym', *Ekho Moskvy*, 8 September, <https://echo.msk.ru/blog/statya/1152670-echo/> (last accessed 16 November 2020).
Iusipova, L. (2017), 'Fil'm o basketbole poluchilsia v polnyi rost', *Vedomosti*, 27 December, <https://www.vedomosti.ru/lifestyle/articles/2017/12/27/746668-film-o-basketbole> (last accessed 16 November 2020).
Karev, I., and A. Krizhevskii (2013), 'Perm'iu men'she', *Gazeta.ru*, 27 December, <https://www.gazeta.ru/culture/2013/12/26/a_5821217.shtml> (last accessed 16 November 2020).
Kolesnikov, A. (2013), 'Mif No. 17', *Gazeta.ru*, 30 April, <https://www.gazeta.ru/comments/column/kolesnikov/5286537.shtml> (last accessed 16 November 2020).
Kravtsyn, E. (2016), 'Chto skryvaet kniaz'', *Kommersant'*, 29 December, <https://www.kommersant.ru/doc/3184780> (last accessed 16 November 2020).
Lipman, M. (2016), 'How Putin Silences Dissent', *Foreign Affairs*, May/June, pp. 38–46.
Moskvina, A. (2018), 'Dvizhenie vniz', *Vecherniaia Moskva*, 7 January, <https://vm.ru/news/449555.html> (last accessed 16 November 2020).

Norris, S. (2012), *Blockbuster History in the New Russia: Movies, Memory, Patriotism*. Bloomington: Indiana University Press.
Norris, S. (2017), 'Review of *Panfilov's 28*', *KinoKultura*, 56, <http://www.kinokultura.com/2017/56r-28panfilovtsy.shtml> (last accessed 16 November 2020).
Nye, J. S., Jr (2004), *Soft Power: The Means to Success in World Politics*. New York: Public Affairs.
'Proekt "Osnov gosudarstvennoi kul'turnoi politiki"' (2014), *Rossiskaia Gazeta*, 16 March, <https://rg.ru/2014/05/15/osnovi-dok.html> (last accessed 16 November 2020).
'Putin Declares Patriotism Russia's Only National Idea' (2016), *The Moscow Times*, 4 February, <https://www.themoscowtimes.com/2016/02/04/putin-declares-patriotism-russias-only-national-idea-a51705> (last accessed 16 November 2020).
Saunders, R. (2017), *Popular Geopolitics and Nation Branding in the Post-Soviet Realm*. New York: Routledge.
Shaw, T., and D. Youngblood (2010), *Cinematic Cold War: The American and Soviet Struggle for Hearts and Minds*. Lawrence: University Press of Kansas.
Shchipin, S. (2017), 'Vremia pervykh: k zvezdam v kandalakh', *Snob*, 7 April, <https://snob.ru/selected/entry/122952> (last accessed 16 November 2020).
Stishova, E. (2013), 'Adrenalin Legenda 17', *Iskusstvo kino*, 1 May, <http://old.kinoart.ru/archive/2013/05/adrenalin-legenda-17-rezhisser-nikolaj-lebedev> (last accessed 24 November 2020).
Sychev, S. (2013), 'Kak zasluzhit liubov' rodinu legenda 17', *Iskusstvo kino*, 1 May, <https://kinoart.ru/ru/archive/2013/05/kak-zasluzhit-lyubov-rodiny-legenda-17-rezhisser-nikolaj-lebedev> (last accessed 16 November 2020).
Trofimov, A. (2017), 'Retsenziia na "Vremia Pervykh"', *Kanobu*, 7 April, <https://kanobu.ru/articles/retsenziya-na-vremya-pervyih--370264/> (last accessed 16 November 2020).
Tsulaia, D. (2018), 'Prokat rassudit', *Kinopoisk*, 16 January, <https://www.kinopoisk.ru/article/3108147/> (last accessed 16 November 2020).
'Vladimir Putin prisutstvoval na pokaze fil'ma "Legenda No. 17"' (2013), *Kremlin.ru*, 17 April, <http://kremlin.ru/events/president/news/17919> (last accessed 16 November 2020).
Zygar, M. (2016), *All the Kremlin's Men: Inside the Court of Vladimir Putin*. New York: Public Affairs.

CHAPTER 7

Popular Geo-politics, Strategic Narratives and Soft Power in *Viking* (2016) and *Guardians* (2017)

Robert A. Saunders

Introduction

Since its introduction in the late 1980s, Joseph Nye's concept of soft power has become increasingly fashionable in its application to myriad elements of International Relations (IR). Extrapolating from Antonio Gramsci's (2001 [1929–35]) theory of cultural hegemony, Nye's concept of soft power stems from the notion that states can set international agendas by influencing the discursive framework of IR. Such manipulation depends on a given polity's capacity to entice other states into 'desirable' behaviours, in terms of either bilateral relations or global engagement. According to Nye, 'Soft power is more than persuasion or the ability to move people by argument. It is the ability to entice and attract. And attraction often leads to acquiescence or imitation' (Nye 2002: 9). Thus, the soft power of a country rests primarily on three resources: culture, political values and foreign policy. Hence, soft power derives from intangible elements such as a state's (or nation's) cultural reservoir, its ideological orientation, and its capacity to achieve outcomes via international trade and intergovernmental institutions (see Chitty et al. 2016). However, the concept is frequently misunderstood, and, in certain cases, knowingly misapplied by political elites in an effort to achieve foreign policy outcomes conducive to the national interest. In international politics, the practices of policymakers are frequently girded by their own national self-images (*Selbstbilder*) and the images they associate with other nations or cultures (*Fremdbilder*) (see Rusciano 2003). Nye stresses that national image is an important channel to exercise a country's soft power by claiming that if a country's culture and ideology are attractive, others are more willing to follow. Such concerns are especially heightened in the current global information age, wherein the spread of the popular culture and new information and communication technologies, combined with the 'deepening of complex economic interdependence', has made governments 'more attentive to their national images' (Saunders 2008: 114).

Perhaps no country has a more complex relationship with what has been labelled soft power than the Russian Federation. During the 1990s, the Yeltsin administration attempted to retrofit certain Western foreign policy mechanisms to the Federation's activities on the international stage, most notably the ill-conceived adaptation of the Monroe Doctrine into the 'Monroeskii Doctrine', with aim of making Moscow's exercise of power in its so-called 'near abroad' more palatable to Berlin, London and Washington. A decade later, the political technologists of Vladimir Putin's first Presidency jettisoned this doctrine, instead embracing a peculiarly inventive notion of Russian 'soft power' as a binding agent for the various states that constitute post-Soviet Eurasia, thus refocusing attention on cultural power rather than 'boots on the ground'. Russia is thus in somewhat of a 'Catch-22': its national image is compromised by its post-imperial legacy of threatening and coercing its neighbours (most notably with the invasion of Georgia and Ukraine in the first two decades of the twenty-first century), yet Moscow constantly seeks to use its civilisational attractiveness to achieve what it cannot accomplish with hard power. Naturally, this leads us to a discussion of what has come to be called 'smart power' (CSIS 2007), or the combined application of 'hard' and 'soft' power, a theme I will return to shortly.

As one of the most important components of a country's soft power, culture attractiveness not only influences various aspects of people's lives and plays a vital part in social development within a country, but also has 'direct impacts on relations between countries and helps a country to achieve important foreign policy goals' (Ding 2008: 62). Within this process, the factor of 'image' plays a crucial role. For Russia, this has proved problematic since, as the geo-politician Dmitri Trenin has noted in *Foreign Affairs* magazine, 'By and large . . . Russian leaders do not care much about acceptance (abroad); even the Soviet Union worried more about its image' (2006: 93). Under Putin's presidencies and prime ministership, Russia has attempted to use a variety of what Peter van Ham (2001) calls 'postmodern' foreign policy initiatives, including nation branding, sports diplomacy and soft power to buttress its international reputation; however, in all cases, whether we speak of the state-controlled international television network RT's efforts to strengthen the Kremlin's voice in international affairs (Yablokov 2015), or the impact of the Sochi Olympics on Russia's standing in the international community (Müller 2014) or the government-sponsored culture promotion agency Russkiy Mir's advocacy of the Russian language around the world (Gorham 2014), the results have been – at best – mixed (see Rutland and Kazantsev 2016). With this in mind, I shall now turn to the medium of film, focusing on how the Russian Federation – a constituent member of the geo-economic bloc known as the BRICS – and its increasingly internationally orientated cinema serve as a fruitful, if sometimes problematic mechanism for promoting Russia's power and interests beyond its borders.

The Russian Federation, Cinema and Geo-politics

From a theoretical perspective, my analysis relies on methods employed in the burgeoning field of popular geo-politics, and particularly on how popular culture artefacts like videogames, television series and film inform everyday understandings of geo-politics. As a space for world building and meaning making, entertainment media increasingly inform and influence myriad aspects of foreign policy, from consensus building to trade negotiations to diplomacy (cf. Nexon and Neumann 2006; Shepherd 2013; Dyson 2015; Moïsi 2016). As Stacy Takacs states: 'Popular culture is not just a weapon. It is also a field of engagement upon which opposing groups fight to make their particular views seem less particular and more like common sense' (2015: 90). Such sentiments echo Russian film scholar Stephen Norris's assertion that the modern-day movie multiplex is a 'battleground', a place where post-Soviet politics and the very meaning of patriotism is forged (2012: 1). Consequently, this essay focuses on film as one such 'field of engagement', wherein Russia's particular worldview gains purchase as the influence of its cinematic output moves over its borders. In terms of methodology, my chapter retools Roselle, Miskimmon and O'Loughlin's (2014) discussion of 'strategic narratives' in IR.[1] Here, I take the foundational components of 'real-world' foreign policy – that is, firstly, characters/actors; secondly, setting/environment/space; thirdly, conflict/action; and fourthly, resolution – and apply these to popular geo-political interventions: namely, *Viking* (dir. Andrei Kravchuk, 2016) and *Guardians* (dir. Sarik Andreasyan, 2017). In adapting this model, it is important to pay close attention to the country in question, especially the state's political history, human and physical geography and its ideology (where applicable); hence a few words on Russia as place, space and idea are in order.

Despite massive territorial losses resulting from the demise of the tsarist empire (1917–22) and the dissolution of the USSR (1990–1), the Russian Federation remains the largest country in the world by a substantial margin. Consequently, Russian space is one which includes nearly a dozen time zones and every biome except tropical rainforests, thus providing a massive canvas upon which stories can be told.² Due to the historical linkages associated with the USSR and the tsarist empire before it, other lands are often connected with the territorial imaginary that is 'Russia', from the Kazakh steppe to Ukraine to the South Caucasus. Despite the vastness of this geographic setting, the Eurasian realm – which is dominated by the Russian Federation – is rather spare in terms of urban spaces, thus privileging a small number of cities, with Moscow enjoying the unquestioned status of metropole (though St Petersburg, Kyiv and Nur-Sultan certainly function as pretenders to the throne) (see Kolossov et al. 2013). Ethnography mirrors geography with regard to this imaginary. While the geo-political construct of 'Eurasia' is dominated by the eastern Slavs (Russians, Ukrainians and Belarusians), more than 150 nationalities claim post-Soviet space as their territorial homeland. Thus, the ethnicities of the region represent a diverse tapestry of Indo-European, Turkic, Finnic, Ugric, Caucasian and Mongolic peoples, espousing a variety of faiths including Christianity (particularly the Eastern Orthodox tradition), Islam, Lamaist Buddhism, Judaism, shamanism and various polytheisms (see Blinnikov 2011). Bound together by language (Russian) and history (a post-Soviet past), the region provides a natural space for cultural exchange. Consequently, contemporary Russian film presents a fecund field of analysis in terms of setting, environment and space, especially when the scope of analysis uses film culture as a framework for exploring what is put in and what is left out (see Dennison and Lim 2006).

As an emerging node in global motion picture production, Russia is steadily becoming an important player in the popular culture–world politics continuum (Saunders and Strukov 2017; see also Grayson et al. 2009), with film functioning as a key plank in the country's repetitive/recursive national dialogism (Hutchings 2017). Initiated with the international success of Russo-Kazakh director Timur Bekmambetov's *Night Watch* (2004) and reaching a new high-water mark with Andrey Zvyagintsev's award-winning *Leviathan* in 2014, Russian filmmakers are making their mark on the world stage. And, as Norris (2012) argues, the new Russian 'blockbuster' is very much modelled on the American form, but filled with Russian content that is deeply rooted in the country's history. Moreover, as the case of *Leviathan* demonstrates, the content of big-budget Russian films is being carefully scrutinised in the West for geo-political content, explicit or otherwise. This is especially true of those films designed to attract audiences beyond Russia's borders (Strukov 2016). Consequently, the production and release of *Viking* and *Guardians* deserve interrogation, especially in the wake of the annexation of Crimea, Russian adventurism in the Donbass and the inauguration of the Eurasian Economic Union (EAEU) binding together the Russian Federation, Kazakhstan, Belarus, Armenia and Kyrgyzstan.[3] This is particularly relevant, given the fact that high-profile Russian political figures, including Konstantin Kosachev, head of Rossotrudnichestvo,[4] have publicly decried 'Hollywood' for impugning the Russian people via derogatory stereotyping which promotes a deleterious 'anti-brand' for the country (quoted in Mäkinen 2016). Recognising what Takacs labels as a 'relational struggle' to define social (as well as geo-political) realities (2015: 105), Russian cultural producers are now taking advantage of the lack of any genuine dominance in pop-culture world making to present their own arguments for viewing the past, engaging with the present and preparing for the future. Given the contemporaneous rise of the Russian blockbuster and Putin's solidification of his mark on the Russian Federation, the links between nationalist cinema and rising nationalism are 'far from coincidental, but not always connected' (Norris 2012: 2). Yet, as Saunders and Strukov (2017) have pointed out, Russian popular culture, while diverse by any measure, strongly reflects a 'feedback loop' that cannot be discussed independently of Western film, comics, television and other popular media, as my discussion of *Viking*'s similarity to the cinematic television series *Game of Thrones* (HBO, 2011–19) and *Guardians*' resemblance to the *Avengers*-centric Marvel Cinematic Universe (MCU) franchise will argue.

Synopses of the Films (with an Eye Towards Soft Power)

Viking – *a medieval metaphor for Putin's foreign policy*

Loosely based on the *Primary Chronicle* (Повѣсть времѧньныхъ лѣтъ), director Andrei Kravchuk's[5] USD 20 million *Viking* is a historical action film about the medieval prince, Vladimir the Great (Danila Kozlovsky), who expanded Kievan Rus' and converted from Slavic polytheism to Orthodox Christianity. Yoked to the current 'Viking wave' in film and television production (see Haugan 2016), the early part of the motion picture focuses on the power dynamic between the three sons of Sviatoslav I. When the eldest brother, Yaropolk (Aleksandr Ustyugov), is held responsible for the death of Oleg, the youngest brother, Vladimir must – according to Varangian custom – avenge his dead sibling, even though it means killing Yaropolk. Under the tutelage of the semi-legendary warrior Sveneld/Sveinaldr (Maksim Sukhanov), Vladimir amasses a mercenary army of Norsemen, gathered during his sojourn in Scandinavia, and takes Kyiv. After his brother's death, he does battle with Yaropolk's retainer, Variazhko (Igor Petrenko), who has allied with the semi-nomadic Pechenegs, a Turkic people originally from inner Eurasia. During this period, Vladimir is torn between two women, his pagan wife, Rognega/Ragnhild of Polotsk (Aleksandra Bortich), and his eldest brother's widow, Irina (Svetlana Khodchenkova), a former Byzantine nun who tutors the prince in Christianity. Ultimately, he shuns his wife, who rightly tries to kill him for raping her in front of her parents (before murdering his would-be in-laws), and embraces the Orthodox faith upon conquering Kherson (with the implied promise that this will lead to his wedding with the Roman Emperor's daughter, Anna Porphyrogenita). The film ends with a chastened Vladimir repenting his violent rise to power, and overseeing the mass baptism of Rus' in the Dnieper river below the Starokyivsky Hill.

In Vladimir's state-building efforts, which unified the domains of the eastern Slavs against invaders from both east and west, and his embrace of monotheism, which resulted in the hierarchical diffusion of Christianity to the pagans of Eastern Europe, the Rurikid prince represents a handy ideologeme for the current era of Russian geo-politics, regardless of the rampant historical revisionism of the film. Despite his reluctant leadership at the beginning of the film, Prince Vladimir finds his (geo-)political footing and leads his people to greatness, thus establishing a space for the audience's potential conflation with a real-world politician with the same given name (a particularly meaningful scene shows Vladimir trying in vain to stop the human sacrifice of a young boy, who is being protected by the Kyivan Varangians' sole Christian warrior). Indeed, the future saint begins his career in a chaotic world devoid of God but slavishly devoted to 'false idols', ultimately finding peace when he is baptised and forgiven for his many sins (in his first confession, he provides a list of personally motivated murders, but fails to mention the myriad lives he took on the field of battle).

Viking clearly mimics the look of the current Viking wave on Western screens, including the sub-genre's visual–textual valorisation of the masculinist ethos of the *Männerbund* (Fig. 7.1) [6] Indeed, critics and viewers repeatedly compared it to HBO's fantasy drama *Game of Thrones* (2011–19), as well as the History Channel's quasi-fictional series *Vikings* (2013–20). However, *Viking* makes a dramatic departure from these artefacts in its depiction of religion, in that it hews to a traditional binary of good/evil, with paganism serving as a scourge of the human spirit, while Christianity is presented as a bastion of selflessness and goodwill to mankind. This is very different from the positive depictions of European native faith in *Vikings* and its fantastical analogue, the faith of the Old Gods in *Game of Thrones* (see Saunders 2014). Through its imagery, which contrasts miserable, dirty and

Figure 7.1 Opening credits of *Viking* – 'Pagan Europe, 977'.
Source: *Viking*, dir. Andrei Kravchuk (2016).

starving polytheists with the newly baptised Christians who are smiling, radiant and healthy-looking,[7] *Viking* makes it clear that Orthodoxy is an internal binding agent for the Slavs and a mechanism for connecting the rough-and-tumble Varangian-ruled lands to a genuine civilisation (Byzantium). That being stated, *Viking* cleverly taps into the New Right's *au courant* obsession with medievalism and particularly pre-Christian value systems, which are increasingly extolled by populist identitarian movements across the European continent and farther afield (S. N. 2017; Whitaker 2020; Saunders 2020); this is particularly evident in the marketing of the film, as its IMDb description refers only to events in the first quarter of the film, thus highlighting 'Vikingness' and carefully avoiding any reference to the pro-Christian message of the work, which occupies the majority of the screen time. Moreover, the crass orientalism of *Viking*'s depiction of the Pechenegs (speaking a reimagined Turkic-like language) reinforces hoary notions of a mythical unified Europe under siege by a 'racially' alien invader from the East (Table 7.1).

In terms of its geo-political framing, *Viking* can be seen as sculpting a world where intrigue, cunning and raw power determine the fate of nations, from the fractious Rurikids to the mercenary Northmen to the ruthless Pecheneg hordes to the avaricious Greeks. In doing so, the film echoes the Kremlin's public position on contemporary international relations, which argues that all states act in their own interest, often cloaking their motives in the flowery language of 'democracy' (Foer 2016). Yet, as the film lays bare, it is tangible outcomes that actually matter, and a little blood and dirt never hurt any ruler who was on the rise.

Table 7.1 Potential sources of soft power in *Viking*.

	Element	Analogue	Narrative Essence/Symbolic Contribution to Soft Power
Personality	Vladimir the Great	Vladimir V. Putin	A strong, steadfast leader is necessary for Russia as the indispensable power-centre of Eurasia
Space	Novgorod + Kyiv + Drevlian Lands + Taurida	Russian Federation + Crimea and eastern Ukraine	A single state for the eastern Slavs is 'natural'; Ukraine belongs in union with Russia; Russian adventurism is valid
Faith	Paganism → Christianity	Sovietism → (resurgent) Russian Orthodoxy	Monotheism strengthens the state; the Soviet modus was soulless; validation of pan-Orthodox ties (Russia, Ukraine, Serbia, etc.)
Identity	Varangian vs Turkic	Russians as a 'northern European' people (not a Eurasian mélange)	Russian 'purity' via performative Nordicism; the Viking-era *Männerbund* finds parallels in contemporary 'Russian masculinity'; Russia *qua* 'Europe' via medievalism

Guardians – *a superhero manifestation of the Eurasian Union*

The product of Moscow-based Armenian director Sarik Andreasyan, *Guardians* is a USD 5 million science fiction/fantasy film which brings together a formerly disbanded troop of genetically enhanced Soviet super-soldiers to save Moscow from annihilation. Under the leadership of Major Elena Larina (Valeriya Shkirando), the Armenian telekinetic Ler (Sebastian Sisak-Grigoryan), the teleporting Kazakh sword-master Khan (Sanjar Madi) and the Siberian were-bear Ursus (Anton Pampushnyy) join forces (Fig. 7.2). Subsequently, the team recruits Xenia (Alina Lanina), a martial artist with the power to turn herself invisible. Together, the Guardians provide a post-Soviet continuation of the 'Patriot' project, intended to protect the USSR from supernatural threats. However, the immediate danger to Russia comes from within the Patriot project, in the form of the rogue government scientist August Kuratov, who, transformed by a chemical accident, can control any machine through the manipulation of its electrical signals. Jealous of a fellow scientist and resenting the Soviet government's takeover of his work, the supervillain Kuratov lays waste to parts of Moscow. Using a clone army, he relocates the Ostankino Tower to the Moscow International

Figure 7.2 Major Larina comes to recruit Ler at the Khor Virap monastery in Armenia.
Source: *Guardians/Zashchitniki*, dir. Sarik Andreasyan (2017).

Business Centre (MIBC) in an effort to employ a high-orbit weapon known as the 'Hammer Space Station'. Built by the US as part of President Ronald Reagan's 'Star Wars' missile defence scheme, the space station is key to Kuratov's plans to utilise the entire extra-terrestrial satellite network to extend his control of machinery to a global level (a conceit that is similarly employed in DC Films' *Wonder Woman 1984* (2020)). After initially being defeated by Kuratov, the team learns to work together, and, augmented by the state-issued supersuits, defeats the mad scientist by blowing up the Federation Towers and all the other buildings in the vicinity.

The nomenclature of the first three members of the team (Ler, Khan and Ursus) borders on literal, with the rock-wielding Armenian taking his name from his people's word for 'mountain', the Asiatic warrior labelled a 'ruler' in any Turkic language, and the ursine Siberian sporting the Latin name for 'bear'. The name of the only superpowered female on the team paradoxically marks her out as a 'visitor' or 'foreigner', despite the fact that she is a Muscovite, unlike the others who hail from three bits of the outer edges of the old USSR. In terms of semiotics, the audience is not left pondering the otherness of the non-Russian members of the team, as Ler's chest is emblazoned with a seven-pointed Armenia wheel of eternity, and the black-clad Khan (complete with face covering) cuts his way through his enemies with crescent-moon scimitars, reminding the viewer of his Islamic origins.[8] The two Russian members of the team are clean-cut, blond(e) and blue-eyed, in sharp contrast to the tawny, heavily bearded Ler and the dark-eyed, black-haired Khan. Geographically, each team member's locale connects to their identity, from Ler's location in the Khor Virap monastery near Ararat, to Khan positioned

Table 7.2 Guardian team member characteristics.

	Geographical Origin	Powers	Personality Traits	Narrative Essence/ Symbolic Contribution to Soft Power
Ler (Lernik)	Armenia/ mountains	Telekinesis; rock-armour exoskeleton; superstrength	Selfless, meditative, protective	Religiosity via ancient Christian Orthodoxy connection
Khan (Temirkhan)	Kazakhstan/ steppe	Superspeed bordering on teleportation; strength; enhanced perception; sword mastery	Inscrutable, standoffish, serious	Eurasianism via Islamic–Turkic–Asian identity
Ursus (Arsenii)	Siberia/ boreal forests	Lycanthropy (half-bear and full-bear); dense skin; strength; speed	Bold, brash, loyal	Organicism via the manifestation of the symbol of Russia (a European brown bear)
Xenia	Moscow/ metropolis	Invisibility; resistance to elements; enhanced manœuvrability; martial arts	Naïve, subtle, emotional	Glamour/ cosmopolitanism via association with wealth and pomp of Moscow
Major Elena Larina	Russian Federation	None (or, alternatively, soft power)	Commanding, focused, unwavering	Managed democracy via strong leadership persona

on the desiccated steppes adjacent to the Aral Sea, to Ursus's Siberian redoubt on the Putorana Plateau, to Xenia's performance in a Moscow Cirque du Soleil-style performance (Table 7.2).

The film reprises a plethora of elements from the MCU superhero film franchises (to date, grossing USD 122.5 billion globally) and larger Marvel universe,[9] including, firstly, the vengeful 'mad scientist', bald techno-villain and electro-whip technology from the *Iron Man* films (2008–13); secondly, the geographical diversity, *genii loci* and genetic mutation tropes of the *X-Men* franchise (2000–); thirdly, the banal nationalism and government superteam aspects of *The Avengers* series (2012–); fourthly, the *Guardians of the Galaxy Vol. 1* (2014) climax, in which the team serves as conduit for a mysterious pulse of power that destroys the otherwise invincible enemy, as well as the farcical image of a snarling human–animal hybrid wielding a massive machine gun; and fifthly, the use of a post-credits scene to prime the viewer's anticipation of the sequel.[10] In terms of its individual characters, *Guardians* likewise borrows heavily from Marvel Comics (both film and print). with Ler resembling the rock-man The Thing/Ben Grimm and Xenia paralleling Susan Storm-Richards, also known as the Invisible Girl/Woman, both members of Marvel's inaugural superhero team, *The Fantastic Four* (1961–).[11] While the

Kazakh hero Khan embodies a variety of Marvel's orientalist tropes associated with the 'mysterious East', the combination of teleportation, mastery of the sword and his 'outsider' status is reminiscent of the X-Men character Nightcrawler. The were-bear Ursus is even more derivative, being nearly identical to Mikhail Ursus, also known as Ursa Major, a Soviet superbear who first appeared in Marvel Comics' *Incredible Hulk* #258 (April 1981). Collectively, the team is a retrofitted manifestation of Marvel's Supreme Soviets (1989), quickly rechristened as the Soviet Super-Soldiers (1989–91), and most recently as Winter Guard (1998).[12] In addition to the aforementioned Ursa Major, this state-sanctioned band of metahumans has included the thunder-god Perun, as well as a host of Sovietesque-named characters such as Crimson Dynamo, Red Guardian, Vanguard and Sputnik (the team was originally led by Professor Phobos, who convinced the Politburo to stop euthanising mutants and instead use them in defence of the state).

Reception and (Geo-)Politicisation of *Viking* and *Guardians*

Viking

Produced by the director general of Channel 1 (*Perviy kanal*), which labelled it in a news report as the 'most anticipated Russian film of the year' (Braynin 2016), and receiving the informal government stamp of approval, *Viking* – while the creation of a filmmaker – invariably functions as a tool of (geo-)politics. This is particularly true, given the emotionally charged environment in which it was released. Most notably, this politicisation stems from the sitting president's accolades for the motion picture, as well as his geo-historical contextualisation of its subject, Prince Vladimir. On 4 November 2016, less than two months before the film's release, Putin inaugurated a massive statue of his namesake some 100 metres from the Kremlin's walls, remarking to assembled government officials: 'Prince Vladimir has remained in history forever as the unifier and defender of Russian lands, a visionary politician who laid the foundations of a strong, unified, centralized state' (quoted in Kernelyd 2017). Seen as a 'metaphor' (MacFarquhar 2016) for Putin's own fundamental role in unifying the new Russian state, the statue prompted praise among religious conservatives (who venerate Vladimir as a saint, whose requirement of conversion for his subjects established the faith in the Slavic realm) and nationalists (who view him as a font of Russian greatness). While unconnected to the film's release, the unveiling of the statue in the centre of the capital, as part of what the *Moscow Times* (Muchnik 2016) has labelled a 'state-sponsored Prince Vladimir lovefest',[13] the erecting of a giant Vladimir I served as a poignant marketing promotion for *Viking*. More directly connecting state power to popular culture, the Russian president, accompanied by the Minister of Culture, Vladimir Rostislavovich Medinskii, attended a private screening of *Viking*. The President's Office subsequently tweeted about his meeting with the film's cast and crew, noting the film's basis in a 'Tale of Bygone Years' (Putin 2016). Yet, the president quipped that his viewing partner, a trained historian, would likely find 'issues that from the point of view of experts can be challenged' (Lenta.ru 2016). Putin went on to clarify that *Viking* is 'a work of art, not a documentary', which he 'would like to see again' (quoted in Kernelyd 2017).

In its narrative rhetoric and visual storytelling, *Viking* presents a 'stark contrast between Rus' and Europe', yet affirms the intertwining factors of these 'civilisations', not least of which is a shared history of pagan conversion to Christianity and foundational identity linked to the rise of medieval kingdoms (Katty-Bri 2017). As *Perviy kanal*'s film reviewer Kirill Braynin (2016) characterised the project, it has a singular goal:

> (T)o tell the story of Prince Vladimir so that the viewer not only was stimulated from the first to the last frame, but also thought about what the country was like a thousand-odd years ago, and how the choices made by the prince determined (Russia's) path for many centuries to come.

Obviously, the most important of these decisions was to embrace Christianity and mass-baptise his people. According to historian Vladimir Petrukhin, 'There were people, as (Nestor the) Chronicler writes, who remembered baptism. This remains a living memory (in Russia) as it seems to me that the ceremony was (widely) observed' (quoted in Yaroslavtseva 2016).[14] The historical event is widely venerated as a holiday known as Day of Baptism of Rus' (*Den Khreshchenia Rusi*) (Fig. 7.3). Supported by an international organisation backed by the Russian Orthodox Church (ROC), this mass ceremony promotes the 'gathering of the Russian lands', a geo-political end that the ROC explicitly supports (Lutsevych 2016: 24). While religion is the indispensable thread running through *Viking*, geo-politics also pervades the narrative; as Petrukhin notes, 'The geopolitical situation in the world is quite accurately shown in the film' (qtd in Yaroslavtseva 2016), with Rus's contacts with Byzantium, Scandinavian earldoms and the nomadic Pechenegs all being shown. The centrality of Crimea, both as a subject of the tale of Vladimir and as a filming location, cannot be overstated, despite the declarations of the filmmaker that his epic was in development years before the Russian Federation's annexation of the Ukrainian

Figure 7.3 The Mass Baptism of Kyivan Rus' in the Dnieper river.
Source: *Viking*, dir. Andrei Kravchuk (2016).

republic in 2014. Not insignificantly, the film's initial depiction of an abandoned Kyiv (save for a few emaciated pagan priests living amongst a circle of wooden idylls representing their gods) can be read as geopolitical intervention, suggesting that, without the dynastic linkage to the ultimate Russian state, the city is an empty signifier.

For Ukrainians, who claim Volodymyr as their own, *Viking* is 'an ideal tool to rewrite Russian history' (Nychyk 2017) in the midst of a contentious period for the Federation, which has troops in the Donbass and is – at the time of writing – under international sanctions for its adventurism in Ukraine. Moreover, film critic Alina Nychyk (2017) makes the subtle argument that Kravchuk operationalises the 'Varangian versus Khazar' frame (see Lipovetsky and Etkind 2010; Oushakine 2015) to present audiences with the (fictive) impression that Russia is a genuinely 'European' state with medieval origins, rather than the scion of a later process built on imperial conflation of many ethnicities. Moreover, the privileging of Viking heritage, with its northern European ethnos and masculinist *Männerbund* ethos, some twenty-five years after the end of the USSR, places Russia in clear opposition to the corporatist ideals of the Asiatic Turkic nomads, thus reaffirming a certain trend evident in some forms of post-Soviet fiction (Oushakine 2015). In his review of the film, Per Anders Johansen (2017), Norway's largest printed newspaper *Aftenposten*'s Moscow correspondent, highlighted the bloodlust, rape and filth of the Rurikids, arguing that, despite the ROC's condemnation of the depiction of its inaugural saint and some nationalists' invective about the role of Northmen in establishing Kievan Rus, the film is a testament that many 'Russians want to be Scandinavians', however fraught or spurious such an identity formation might be.

Guardians

In advance of *Guardians*' release in cinemas, various iterations of the trailer made the rounds on the internet, including in the US and UK, where Russian and English-language versions were made widely available. The prospect of an *Avengers*-style film which inverted Marvel's ongoing obsession with the Cold War origins of its own superhero narratives – especially prevalent in *Iron Man 2* (Jon Favreau, 2010), *Captain America: The Winter Soldier* (Anthony Russo and Joe Russo, 2014) and *Ant-Man* (Peyton Reed, 2015) (see Saunders 2017) – made headlines in the West, particularly given the 'inherently political nature' of comic book superheroes (O'Neil 2016). One commentator from *The Guardian* even went as far as to frame Ursus as a cinematic rendering of Putin himself (Hyde 2016). *Guardians* was released on 23 February 2017, which, not insignificantly, was also a public holiday known as Defender of the Fatherland Day. Topping the market on its opening weekend, the film quickly plummeted in ticket sales, later being declared a box office 'bomb'. Critical reviews within Russia were particularly harsh; however, despite the poor reception and fleeting box-office performance, the franchise has been greenlighted for a second motion picture. *Guardians 2* will be funded in part by its Chinese distributor, Turbo, which necessarily guarantees the film's inclusion in the extremely limited list of some thirty-four international films per annum that show on Chinese screens (Kozlov 2016). The deal is reported to include the use of Chinese characters and will be partly filmed in China (Ryan 2017), thus reflecting the latter's increasing influence in shaping positive depictions of 'Chineseness' in world cinema through lucrative access to its screens (see Homewood 2018).

Guardians' lacklustre showing in the Russian market, however, does not necessarily portend its failure as a tool of soft power. Indeed, in the current social media environment, the buzz around a box-office flop can serve as para-text with more political, social and cultural influence than the film itself (see, for instance, Bryan and Clark 2019). As a commentator from SOFREP News, an online publication featuring reports from US special operations veterans, noted:

> [*Guardians*] was clearly marketed as a Russian Avengers, meaning just like the American version, it's a movie intended for a wide audience to enjoy but aimed specifically at children. Marvel does this to impart the importance of buying the new Captain America Happy Meal at McDonalds. Russia, on the other hand, wants to make sure you know the government is the good guy. Not only does Major Elena Larina provide each of the heroes with her solemn word that she'll help them save their great motherland, but she demonstrates time and time again that the Russian government has altruistic intentions that are hindered by external forces beyond their control. (Hollings 2017)

The respected Russian-funded, English-language publication *The Calvert Journal* echoed the sentiments of the SOFREP in a somewhat less conspiratorial manner, suggesting that, by mimicking the superhero genre, *Guardians* has – at the very least – succeeded in pushing Soviet meta-humans out of the shadows and into the spotlight, trading their villainous past for a more heroic future. As James Luxford (2017) notes: '[*Guardians*'] approach is simultaneously subversive and traditional – moving away from the era of the darker, more self-aware superhero film, and going back to what the icons of comic book lore once stood for' – that is, patriotism and maintaining the status quo of whatever country they call home (see Dittmer 2013). Importantly, the derivative qualities of *Guardians* are front-and-centre, with both the Russian and Western press making it clear that there is nothing genuinely original about the format or these 'Hollywood-like' characters; moreover, the director was at pains to stress that his film uses 'familiar' subjects to tell his stories, specifically referencing filming locations in Moscow, rather than some distant and intangible future (REN 2016).

Analysis of the (Pop-culture) Power of Strategic Narratives

Strategic narratives are omnipresent in the conduct of IR, guiding efforts at persuasion and the efficacy of influence in a world knitted together by an increasingly deterritorialised media ecosystem (Roselle et al. 2014). Within this chaotic battlefield of ideas and ideology, filmic narratives function as trenchant tools of power, producing everyday understandings of how IR really works, creating 'consensus around shared meaning' (ibid.: 72) and 'ordering the chaos' of everyday geo-political events (ibid.: 74). Recognising the utility of Roselle et al.'s adaptation of Burke's (1969) discussion of narratives, I have refocused this analytical framework on its origins, thus concentrating on 'symbolic action' in popular culture as a *reflexion* of geo-political aspirations in the so-called 'real world'.[15] Through a reflexive restructuration, I contend that we can better understand the role of film in contributing to the 'smart power' of international actors. Thus, in the popular linking together of filmic depictions of historical/fantastical events with ongoing IR concerns in Russia's near abroad, Kravchuk and Andreasyan – wittingly or not – contribute to Russia's status in the contemporary geo-political realm, with their films serving as popular geo-political interventions in the Ukraine crisis (2014 to the present) and the establishment of the EAEU in 2015.[16] Consequently, I employ *Viking* and *Guardians* as case studies of soft power-based geo-political interventions via this adapted typology.

Characters/actors

The first of these components is characters or actors; in IR, examples include states, non-state actors, non-governmental organisations and multinational corporations. As Roselle et al. (2014) argue, *behaviour* is the paramount factor for analysis. In contemporary IR circles, Russia is often seen as an inheritor of its Soviet legacy (both positive and negative), and shaped by its neo-authoritarian political system, which is often labelled as a form of 'managed democracy' (Colton and McFaul 2003). Due to the perception that Putin is a latter-day tsar (Myers 2016), the Russian state's behaviour on the international stage is generally seen through the prism of his personality; however, other actors include Russia's military–security apparatus, state-owned corporations, media outlets, oligarchs and its sizeable hacker/hactivist community. In terms of soft power, RT, Rossotrudnichestvo, Russkiy Mir, and the nation's widespread and influential diaspora have been recognised as invaluable contributors, particularly in terms of mobilising the power of the Russian language and shaping news reporting of events within and beyond the country (cf. Kudors 2010; Ćwiek-Karpowicz 2012; Dolinsky 2013; Kureev 2015; Dolinsky 2015; Rutland and Kazantsev 2016).

Turning from Russia's real-world characters and actors to their popular culture counterparts in *Viking* and *Guardians*, we find interesting parallels in Vladimir the Great, also known as Saint Vladimir and Vladimir the Baptist. As a former pagan who revelled in violence, rape and political backstabbing, he is redeemed in Kravchuk's film upon taking the cross and baptising the people of Rus. In shedding his heathenism, we can see a dramatic parallel with the life of his namesake, Vladimir Putin, who began his political life as a KGB agent stationed in East Germany (therein metaphorically mapping on to Vladimir's sojourn in Scandinavia) before returning to the motherland to unite the Slavs under the banner of Orthodoxy (tracking with Putin's growing affiliation with the ROC and its leadership). While always destined to lead, the two Vladimirs must pass through a period of impurity before being bestowed with the mantle of 'saviour'. Behaviour in the past certainly may be judged harshly, but the final outcome is what really matters.

In *Guardians*, the actors are (former) agents of the Soviet state, now led by a major in the Russian armed forces. Each team member evinces symbolic elements of Eurasia, from Ler's performance of Orthodox Christianity to Ursus's embodiment of the boreal realm to Khan's 'Eastern' (*vostochnyy*) qualities to Xenia's urban(e) glamour and cosmopolitanism. In their collective action, they are able to defeat the (post-)Soviet monster, a latent American technological threat and the

Figure 7.4 *Guardians*' 'faceless enemies' as a stand-in for the 'opposition forces'.
Source: *Guardians/Zashchitniki*, dir. Sarik Andreasyan (2017).

faceless enemy (poignantly labelled as 'opposition forces' by the Russian news media) on the streets of Moscow (Fig. 7.4). As a reformed unit, the Guardians (who still operate under the banner of the 'Patriot' programme, itself a highly charged word in contemporary Russian political discourse) demonstrate that, when they work as individuals, they fail (being swiftly defeated by Kuratov), but when they train together and accept Russian-state augmentations (specifically technology transfer), they are a formidable force, eventually discovering an unknown *collective* power, a mysterious force blast that wipes out any threat: the parallels to the EAEU are so obvious as to provoke laughter.

Setting/environment/space

The second component is the 'stage' upon which action takes place, as well as the (geo-)political environment in which actors must operate (Roselle et al. 2014: 75). Contemporary Russia is defined by its large size, petrowealth and mixed Euro-Asian geo-political location. Such situatedness is key to Moscow's contentious relationship with its many neighbours *and* its seeming inability to function as a 'normal country' in the international system (see, for instance, Trenin 2002; Blinnikov 2011; Laruelle 2012). Historically speaking, Russia is arguably the most 'geo-political' of states, being the holdfast of the world-island's 'Heartland' (Mackinder 1904) and perennially defined by the connection between the state's messianism and the landmass, from tsarist anti-republicanism to the Soviets' Marxism–Leninism to Putin's *katechon*-based Eurasianism (see Engström 2014).

In *Viking*'s focus on place, it is plausible to view the pre-Christian lands of the Slavs as analogous to the USSR, whereas the expanding Rurikid princedom represents the Russian Federation with its Tauridian adjunct of Kherson, therein functioning as a metaphor for the 2014 annexation of Crimea. Another thread of setting analysis allows the Russian Federation to become analogous to the lands of Sviatoslav I, with all its incumbent ties to Nordic Europe thus buttressing the problematic construct of Russia as an eastern adjunct of Scandinavia, a realm forged in fiery Viking funerals, shaped by the worship of Norse gods and defined by a *Männerbund* ethos. Thirdly, *Viking*'s orientalist geo-imaginary, which hinges on the delimitation of the 'Pecheneg border', presents a visual essay of whiteness/Europeanness against the threat of ethnic (if not necessarily religious) otherness/Asianness.

Guardians, by contrast, roots its spatial dynamics in a world that requires little in the way of allegory, providing the viewer with extremely specific places and spaces that produce meaning when connected to the history of the USSR. Ranging from secret military facilities in Moscow, to a monastery in the shadow of Mount Ararat, to the dry seabed of the Aral basin, to the north Eurasian taiga to the glimmering halls of Moscow's ultrarich, the early scenes of the film sketch a postmodern, highly variegated Eurasia defined by its contradictions as much as its commonalities. The only time the setting shifts out of Eurasia, it is to go into (near) outer space, a zone that Strukov and Goscilo (2017) argue is something of a private reserve for the (post-)Soviet imagination, as well as new zone for geo-political adventurism, something only underscored by the Trump administration's launch of the United States Space Force in late 2019. Lastly, the gratuitous destruction of the MIBC represents, on one hand, a feedback-loop manifestation of the 'Hollywood' trope of destroying parts of the Russian capital for no apparent reason (Saunders 2017) and, on the other, a regionally and generationally informed reification of the desire to unwrite the capitalist transformation of the once-proud Soviet capital into a gleaming mirage of globalised cupidity.

Conflict/action

The third component revolves around actions, reactions and interactions, with temporality (that is, real and imagined pasts, presents and futures) informing and framing how these engagements are interpreted by the audience. As referenced above, the Russian Federation tried and failed to achieve what post-Soviet Russian politicians posited as 'normalcy' after independence. Following an abortive attempt at Atlanticist integration under Yeltsin's early administration, Putin continued trends pioneered under Foreign Minister Yevgeny Primakov (1998–9), challenging the norms of a unipolar world led by the US. As a consequence, the Russian Federation emerged as a resurgent geo-political power in global affairs, particularly through its resumption of long-range bomber missions, Arctic expansion and politico-economic integration with post-Soviet states (via the Commonwealth of Independent States, Eurasian Customs Union and so on). Most dramatically, Russia under Putin transitioned from using its troops as 'peacekeepers' in the near abroad (Transnistria, Tajikistan and so on) to being an invading force in Georgia (securing the independence of Abkhazia and South Ossetia) and Ukraine (annexing Crimea and supporting anti-Kyiv forces in the Donbass). Acting against terrorism (which proved a rather malleable concept vis-à-vis separatists in the North Caucasus), Russia also emerged as a paradigm of the security state in the new millennium (Soldatov and Borogan 2011).

Such trends bubble up in both *Viking* and *Guardians*. In the former, the challenge to rightful governance and fraternal alliance is shattered by Yaropolk's purported 'murder' of his brother, resulting in the saintly Vladimir's bloody-yet-righteous reunification of the east Slavic lands, a metaphor for Putin's actions in Crimea and eastern Ukraine (as well as his articulated goals for Novorossiya). By placing these actions under the protective sign of the Cross and international solidarity (accusing Kyivan loyalists of fascism, anti-Semitism and terrorism by turns), Putin – like his namesake Vladimir I – is the manifestation of the strong leader in a time of chaos, holding back the forces of evil. Alternatively, the Guardians must emerge from the shadows to address the legacy of the Cold War (something they themselves literally embody). By choosing to work together, the five members of the team – just like the five states of the EAEU – can overcome even the most dangerous foe, meanwhile dispatching lingering, if hitherto unknown, threats like Reagan's 'space weapon'. In both films, the 'heroes' are reactive, responding to existential threats thrust upon them by the outside world, therein reprising established themes related to the Axis invasion in 1941 (see Souch 2017). In the case of Vladimir, he is bound by the Varangian code to avenge his brother, but in doing so is eventually drawn into a larger campaign to expand the state and Christianise it in the process (thus lending support to Putin's own expansionist efforts, which are often draped in religious language). With Ler, Khan, Ursus, Xenia and their leader Larina, all are called to duty due to the actions of the mad scientist and his faceless minions (later, we learn that Larina's superior is in league with Kuratov, thus suggesting that fifth columns exist not only 'on the street' but in the very heart of the Russian security apparatus). Only through collective action can the threat be countered, and, when challenged, the team (qua the EUAU) finds new powers never thought possible (or, as one reading of the text would suggest, lost since the dissolution of the USSR).

(Suggested) resolution

The final component centres on human beings' agency (individually or collectively) to change reality, whether in a conservative or progressive way. This may come as a return to the status quo (as is common in superhero tales) or the invocation of a new world order (more frequent in historical or religiously charged narratives). In IR, a discipline defined by its reverence for internationally recognised (read Western) 'norms' (Ferguson and Mansbach 1988), the resolution is usually achieved when violators of the established system are removed from the scene or successfully contained (interestingly mirroring comic-book narrative structures, and perhaps explaining the enthusiasm in popular geopolitics for studying that particular medium). In 'fixing' things, through either a return to the past or the making of a new way, such stories – like other forms of folklore that preceded them – explain the world and how it works, therein establishing the limits of what 'bounds the possible' in terms of international engagement (Roselle et al. 2014: 71). Each state engaged in such a process is guided by an established 'biographical narrative', which explains a given polity's 'spatio-temporal situatedness and structures its orientation in the world' (Berenskoetter 2014: 264). The Russian Federation, as inheritor of the tsarist (Third Rome) and Soviet (world revolution) legacies, possesses a quiddity unrivalled in foreign affairs. Consequently, this allows for the possibility of acting quite differently from other states (recent examples include the Syrian intervention, claims to the undersea Arctic basin and the annexation of Crimea) (see Satter 2013).

In its historical revisionism of the founding of the Russian state (an admittedly problematic construct, but one nevertheless reinforced in the film), *Viking* addresses everyday Varangian politics as a 'disruption' rather than a norm, situating Vladimir as the 'chosen one' who will unify the eastern Slavs, stop Turkic expansion and bring his flock to the Lord Jesus. The resolution is achieved first with Vladimir's cathartic confession of his sins, and finally with the mass baptism of Kyivan Rus'. As a Viking (Varangian), Vladimir is shown as tentative, even doubtful in his actions, but when he finally embraces the risen Christ, he is resolute to the point of offering himself up to Sveneld's blade as a sacrificial lamb for his new 'big-G' god. In its cinematic didacticism, *Viking* inculcates its audience in the values of Christianity, promising a new/Third Rome, ruled by a benevolent prince (despite his earlier tendencies towards ultra-violence). Such an ending presents a resolution that finds an analogue in the 'real world' via a proposed resolution: namely, that Russia is special, Kyiv (symbolising Ukraine) is integral to the state's identity and strong leaders must be forgiven their youthful errors and chequered pasts.

Guardians achieves its resolution in fantastical fashion, with the team coming together to save Moscow by destroying an iconic part of it (a Marvel Cinematic Universe trope if there ever was one).[17] Like the American exceptionalism that powers the Avengers, X-Men, Justice League and lesser-known superhero teams, the Guardians pool their powers (each of which draws strength from a specific *genius loci*) to erase the threat that Kuratov embodies (driven by his (anti-Soviet) egotism, backed up by his (anti-Kremlin) toadies and made globally lethal by his appropriation of (US) space weaponry). Unlike Kravchuk's film, Andreasyan's *Guardians* promises a sequel with its post-credits teaser (further mimicking the Marvel Studios *modus operandi*), thus demonstrating that there is a seemingly unending font of heroes and villains swelling up in post-Soviet Eurasia. In doing so, *Guardians* can be read as an advertisement for enlargement of the EAEU, targeting fence-sitters like Tajikistan and Moldova, and warning more reticent partners such as Azerbaijan and Uzbekistan of the dangers of going their own way (obviously, Western 'stooges' like Georgia and Ukraine need not apply).

Conclusion: Strategic Narratives and Feedback Loops

With the deepening of complex global interdependence, particularly via the protean communication/information/media ecology enabled by the internet and the deterritorialisation of delivery platforms (such as Netflix, YouTube and so on), popular culture – when linked to a nation's strategic narrative – is a key plank of soft power projection. This comes through in one review of *Guardians*, which labels the message of the film as such: 'They are all representatives of the Soviet republics, which tell the viewer: we are different, but we fight on one side of the barricades' (REN 2016). In this cogent, even parsimonious framing, it becomes obvious that certain forms of Russian cinematic production are specifically intended to massage reality through a repositioning of Russia/post-Soviet Eurasia as a force for good in the ongoing struggle against the 'opposition' (however defined). Pseudo-historical and fantastical Russian films, in addition to impacting the country's 'structure of the Self', can assist in (re)configuring the Russian Federation's 'being-in-the-world' (Berenskoetter 2014: 271). Partly shaped by an iterative feedback loop that binds 'Hollywood' to Russian popular cultural production, *Viking* and *Guardians* represent exemplars of 'new patterns and dimensions of exchange that "explain" variations triggered by the vagaries of globalisation' (Saunders and Strukov 2017: 306), from tapping the Viking wave to frame Russia's interests in Ukraine to co-optation of Marvel's Soviet Super-Soldiers (and its cinematic aesthetic) to market the EAEU. While it would not be appropriate to describe these films as examples of propaganda (unless one were to apply the same descriptor to *Game of Thrones* or *The Avengers* franchise), such artefacts lay bare the interconnectedness of popular culture, international affairs and geo-politics, with the media being one of the most effective tools of any state's soft power (see Press-Barnathan 2013). By contouring their cinematic and storytelling qualities to established norms that have proven popular on a global scale, these two films reflect the increasing influence of feedback loops of cultural production. In this chapter, I have endeavoured to demonstrate how application of the four components of strategic narrative (characters, setting, action and resolution), when refracted back through the prism of international affairs, help explain the formation, projection and reception of soft power in a globalised media ecosystem.

Notes

1. Their work is, in fact, an adaptation of Burke's (1969) analytical framework of the components of rhetoric applied to foreign policy.
2. As discussed later, outer space is also very much part of Russia's territorial imagination. My thanks to Vlad Strukov for his encouragement to expand my field of gaze to the heavens.
3. According to its official website (<http://www.eaeunion.org/>), the EAEU is 'an international organization for regional economic integration (which) provides for free movement of goods, services, capital and labour, pursues coordinated, harmonized and single policy in the sectors determined by the Treaty (on the Eurasian Economic Union) and international agreements within the Union'.
4. The English-language title of the organisation is the Federal Agency for the Commonwealth of Independent States, Compatriots Living Abroad and International Humanitarian Cooperation.
5. Internationally known for his acclaimed drama *The Italian* (2005), about a young orphan's search for his birth mother, Kravchuk also directed the historical biopic *Admiral* (2008), telling the story of Aleksandr Kolchak, a vice-admiral in the imperial navy and prominent leader of the Whites in the Russian Civil War (1917–22).
6. Proponents of the *Männerbund* argue that the organic, competitive and hierarchal bonds between a group of men provide the foundation organisational unit for European (and thus Western) civilisation, shaping everything from sexual morality and property rights to military action and state building (see a fuller description at Yuray 2015).
7. As I have explored elsewhere (Saunders 2014), the first season of History's *Vikings* sculpts Norse paganism as a noble, beautiful and meaningful faith

system against the Saxons' rapacious and ignorant Catholicism. In subsequent seasons, the main certain characters gravitate towards Christianity, but only as a tactical measure to expand their personal power; the series generally continues to paint monotheism as corrupt and corrupting.
8. Although the shape of Khan's swords is also reminiscent of the sickle, thus evincing Soviet era iconography.
9. This figure includes only films distributed by Marvel Studios. Due to licensing agreements, the 20th Century Fox-distributed *X-Men*, *Deadpool* and *Fantastic Four* series are not included, yet these narratives take place in the same conceptual 'universe' with some overlap; likewise, Sony's *Spider-Man* franchise falls outside of the Marvel Studios franchise, though the character has been integrated into the MCU in recent films. Since Disney's acquisition of Marvel Studios in 2009, the corporate giant has steadily brought more of the outstanding Marvel characters under its control.
10. Notably, *Guardians* differs from these films due to the absence of non-stop bickering among these various teams, which function as dysfunctional families that ultimately come together to counter some existential threat. Alternatively, this can be read as an update of WWII-era Soviet tropes, which featured a collectivist gathering of strangers, who come to serve as an ersatz family in the context of a major conflict (see Souch 2017).
11. The inaugural Marvel team of the Fantastic Four is deeply grounded in the Cold War space race, with the members gaining their powers from a blast of cosmic rays on an extra-terrestrial mission. Creator Stan Lee famously remarked on the Fantastic Four's origin story: 'The rate the Communists are progressing in space, maybe we better make this a flight to the STARS, instead of just to Mars, because by the time this mag goes on sale, the Russians may have already MADE a flight to Mars!' (quoted in Alexander 2012: 27).
12. Interestingly, the team's name reverted to the Supreme Soviets in Marvel Comics' Black Widow (Natasha Romanoff) miniseries *Widowmaker* (2010–11), in which the former KGB operative takes on her old teammates with the help of fellow Avenger, Hawkeye.
13. The effigial geo-politics of the monument are worth noting, given that Vladimir is symbolically pointing towards Kyiv, inverting the directionality of the tsarist era Vladimir statue erected in Kyiv, which pointed towards Moscow. The earlier statue was meant to reinforce the centrality of Kyiv to the Russian state, whereas the more recent one is perceived by many as a manifestation of Russia's territorial designs on an independent Ukraine. My thanks to Stephen Norris for this observation.
14. In examining the historiography of the event, it is relevant to consider the work of White (1980), particularly his connections between narrativity and the perception of reality.
15. Here I use the variant spelling of 'reflection' to flag up the flexibility inherent in the 'throwing back by a body or surface of light, heat, or sound' of some force.

16. The links between *Viking* and the state are fairly straightforward, given the film's backing by *Perviy kanal*, whereas *Guardians* was produced outside any explicit state structures. However, as Alford (2010) has demonstrated with Hollywood blockbusters, there need not be any direct relationship between the cultural producer and the state for nationalist narratives to shape the content of film production, themes and reception.
17. *Captain America: Civil War* (Anthony Russo and Joe Russo, 2016) hinges on the ramifications of the Avengers' destructive tactics, which trigger a United Nations' measure bringing them under the supervision of an intergovernmental body to ensure that these metahumans do not wreak any more havoc.

Works Cited

Alexander, Mark (2012), *Lee & Kirby: The Wonder Years*. Raleigh: TwoMorrows.
Alford, Matthew (2010), *Reel Power: Hollywood Cinema and American Supremacy*. New York: Pluto Press.
Berenskoetter, Felix (2014), 'Parameters of a National Biography', *European Journal of International Relations*, 20:1, 262–88.
Blinnikov, Mikhail S. (2011), *A Geography of Russia and Its Neighbors*. New York: Guilford Press.
Braynin, Kirill (2016), "Владимир Путин посмотрел фильм «Викинг» и встретился со съемочной группой (Vladimir Putin Watched the Film *Viking* and Met the Film Crew)', *Perviy kanal*, <http://www.1tv.ru/news/2016-12-30/317162-vladimir_putin_posmotrel_film_viking_i_vstretilsya_so_s_emochnoy_gruppoy> (last accessed 3 June 2017).
Bryan, Peter Cullen, and Brittany R. Clark (2019), '#NotMyGhostbusters: Adaptation, Response, and Fan Entitlement in 2016's *Ghostbusters*', *Journal of American Culture*, 42:2, 147–58.
Burke, Kenneth (1969), *A Rhetoric of Motives*. Berkeley: University of California Press.
Chitty, Naren, Li Ji, Gary D. Rawnsley and Craig Hayden (eds) (2016), *The Routledge Handbook of Soft Power*. London and New York: Routledge.
Colton, Timothy J., and Michael McFaul (2003), *Popular Choice and Managed Democracy: The Russian Elections of 1999 and 2000*. Washington, DC: Brookings Institution Press.
CSIS (2007), *CSIS Commission on Smart Power: A Smarter, More Secure America*. Washington, DC: Center for Strategic and International Studies.
Ćwiek-Karpowicz, Jarosław (2012), 'Limits to Russian Soft Power in the Post-Soviet Area' by the German Council on Foreign Relations/DGAPanlyse, Berlin (8 July).
Dennison, Stephanie, and Song Hwee Lim (eds) (2006), *Remapping World Cinema: Identity, Culture, and Politics in Film*. New York: Columbia University Press.
Ding, Sheng (2008), *The Dragon's Hidden Wings: How China Rises with its Soft Power*. Lanham, MD: Lexington Books.

Dittmer, Jason (2013), *Captain America and the Nationalist Superhero: Metaphors, Narratives, and Geopolitics*. Philadelphia: Temple University Press.

Dolinsky, Alexey (2013) 'How Moscow Understands Soft Power', *Russia Direct*, <https://www.russia-direct.org/analysis/how-moscow-understands-soft-power> (last accessed 5 June 2017).

Dolinsky, Alexey (2015), 'Hard Thinking about Russian Soft Power: What to Do Next', *Russia Direct*, <https://www.russia-direct.org/analysis/hard-thinking-about-russian-soft-power-what-do-next> (last accessed 5 June 2017).

Dyson, Stephen Benedict (2015), *Otherworldly Politics: The International Relations of Star Trek, Game of Thrones, and Battlestar Galactica*. Baltimore: Johns Hopkins University Press.

Engström, Maria (2014), 'Contemporary Russian Messianism and New Russian Foreign Policy', *Contemporary Security Policy*, 35:3, 356–79.

Ferguson, Yale H., and Richard W. Mansbach (1988), *The Elusive Quest: Theory and Global Politics*. Columbia: University of South Carolina Press.

Foer, Franklin (2016), 'Putin's Puppet', *Slate*, <http://www.slate.com/articles/news_and_politics/cover_story/2016/07/vladimir_putin_has_a_plan_for_destroying_the_west_and_it_looks_a_lot_like.html> (last accessed 20 June 2017).

Gorham, Michael (2014), *After Newspeak: Language Culture and Politics in Russia from Gorbachev to Putin*. Ithaca, NY: Cornell University Press.

Gramsci, Antonio (2001) [1929–35], *The Prison Notebooks*, trans. Joseph A. Buttigieg and Antonio Callari. New York: Columbia University Press.

Grayson, Kyle, Matt Davies and Simon Philpott (2009), 'Pop Goes IR? Researching the Popular Culture-World Politics Continuum', *Politics*, 29:3, 155–63.

Haugan, Iden (2016), 'Viking Movie Will Be Entirely in Old Norwegian', *Science Nordic*, <http://sciencenordic.com/viking-movie-will-be-entirely-old-norwegian> (last accessed 8 June 2017).

Hollings, Alex (2017), 'Propaganda the Cinema: "Guardians" Depicts Russia's *Avengers* Taking on an America Stand-in', *SOFREP News*, <https://sofrep.com/80826/propaganda-the-cinema-guardians-depicts-russias-avengers-taking-on-an-america-stand-in/> (last accessed 30 May 2017).

Homewood, Chris (2018), '"Directed by Hollywood, Edited by China"? Chinese Soft Power, Geo-Imaginaries and Neo-Orientalism(s) in Recent U.S. Blockbusters', in Robert A. Saunders and Vlad Strukov (eds), *Popular Geopolitics: Plotting an Evolving Interdiscipline*, London and New York: Routledge, pp. 174–96.

Hutchings, Stephen (2017), 'Projecting Putin's Russia on the International Screen: Cinema, Cultural Diplomacy and Recursive Nationhood', conference paper presented at Cinema, Soft Power and Geo-political Change, University of Leeds (20 June).

Hyde, Marina (2016), 'Russia's New Movie Superhero: A Bear Called Arsus that Looks like Putin', *The Guardian*, <https://www.theguardian.com/lifeandstyle/lostinshowbiz/2016/sep/02/russias-new-movie-superhero-a-bear-called-arsus-that-looks-like-putin> (last accessed 11 June 2017).

Johansen, Per Anders (2017), 'Викинги, изнасилование и человеческие жертвоприношения — самый крупный российский киноуспех (Vikings. Rape and Human Sacrifice – The Largest Russian Film Success)', *INOSMI*, <http://inosmi.ru/social/20170120/238541024.html> (last accessed 3 June 2017).

Katty-Bri (2017), 'Рецензия к фильму "Викинг" – Ваши ожидания – Ваши проблемы (Review of *Viking* – Your Expectations Are Your Problems)', *Kinonews*, <https://www.kinonews.ru/userreview_1463/> (last accessed 3 June 2017).

Kernelyd, Par (2017), 'Russie – Le film "Viking" navigue entre scandale et succès', *Idavoll – Art, culture et histoire Vikings*, <http://idavoll.e-monsite.com/blog/evenements/russie-le-film-viking-navigue-entre-scandale-et-succes.html> (last accessed 24 May 2017).

Kolossov, Vladimir, Olga Vendina and John O'Loughlin (2013), 'Moscow as an Emergent World City: International Links, Business Developments, and the Entrepreneurial City', *Eurasian Geography and Economics*, 43, 170–96.

Kozlov, Vladimir (2016), 'Russian Cold War Superhero Film to Get China Release Under Import Quota', *The Hollywood Reporter*, <http://www.hollywoodreporter.com/news/russian-superhero-film-china-release-868671> (last accessed 30 May 2017).

Kudors, Anders (2010), '"Russian World" – Russia's Soft Power Approach to Compatriots Policy', *Russian Analytical Digest*, 81:10, 2–4.

Kureev, Artem (2015), 'Russian Diaspora: A Tool of Soft Power?', *Russia Direct*, <https://www.russia-direct.org/opinion/russian-diaspora-tool-soft-power> (last accessed 5 June 2017).

Laruelle, Marlène (2012), *Russian Eurasianism: An Ideology of Empire*. Baltimore: Johns Hopkins University Press.

Lenta.ru. (2016), 'Путин оценил фильм «Викинг» (Putin Appreciated the Film *Viking*)', *Lenta.ru News*, <https://lenta.ru/news/2016/12/30/viking/> (last accessed 3 June 2017).

Lipovetsky, Mark, and Alexander Etkind (2010), 'The Salamander's Return: The Soviet Catastrophe and the Post-Soviet Novel', *Russian Studies in Literature*, 46:4, 6–48.

Lutsevych, Orysia (2016), *Agents of the Russian World: Proxy Groups in the Contested Neighborhood*. London: Chatham House.

Luxford, James (2017), '*Guardians*: Is the World Ready for the First Superhero Blockbuster from Russia?' *The Calvert Journal*, <http://www.calvertjournal.com/opinion/show/7796/russias-first-superheroes> (last accessed 30 May 2017).

MacFarquhar, Neil (2016), 'A New Vladimir Overlooking Moscow', *New York Times*, <https://www.nytimes.com/2016/11/05/world/europe/vladimir-statue-moscow-kremlin.html?_r=0> (last accessed 24 May 2017).

Mackinder, Halford J. (1904), 'The Geographical Pivot of History', *The Geographical Journal*, 23:4, 421–37.

Mäkinen, Sirke (2016), 'Russia as an Alternative Model: Geopolitical Representations of Russia's Diplomacy – The Case of Rossotrudnichestvo', in Mikhail Suslov and Mark Bassin (eds), *Eurasia 2.0: Russian Geopolitics in the Age of New Media*. Lanham, MD: Lexington Books, pp. 101–21.

Moïsi, Dominique (2016), *La Géopolitique des séries ou le triomphe de la peur*. Paris: Stock.

Muchnik, Andrei (2016), 'Russian Historical Revisionism Goes to the Movies', *Moscow Times*, <https://themoscowtimes.com/articles/russian-historical-revisionism-goes-to-the-movies-56828> (last accessed 6 June 2017).

Müller, Martin (2014), 'After Sochi 2014: Costs and Impacts of Russia's Olympic Games', *Eurasian Geography and Economics*, 55:6, 628–55.

Myers, Steven Lee (2016), *The New Tsar: The Rise and Reign of Vladimir Putin*. New York: Knopf Doubleday.

Nexon, Daniel H., and Iver B. Neumann (eds) (2006), *Harry Potter and International Relations*. Lanham, MD: Rowman & Littlefield.

Norris, Stephen M. (2012), *Blockbuster History in the New Russia: Movies, Memory, and Patriotism*. Bloomington: Indiana University Press.

Nychyk, Alina (2017), '"Viking" is Yet Another Way to Annoy Ukraine', *Emerging Europe*, <http://emerging-europe.com/regions/ukraine/viking-is-yet-another-way-to-annoy-ukraine/> (last accessed 3 June 2017).

Nye, Joseph S., Jr (2002), *The Paradox of American Power: Why the World's Only Superpower Can't Go It Alone*. New York: Oxford University Press.

O'Neil, Tegan (2016), 'How the Cold War Saved Marvel and Birthed a Generation of Superheroes', *A.V. Club*, <http://www.avclub.com/article/how-cold-war-saved-marvel-and-birthed-generation-s-233993> (last accessed 30 May 2017).

Oushakine, Serguei A. (2015), '(Post)Ideological Novel', in Evgeny Dobrenko and Mark Lipovetsky (eds), *Russian Literature Since 1991*. Cambridge: Cambridge University Press, pp. 45–65.

Press-Barnathan, Galia (2013), 'Does Popular Culture Matter to International Relations Scholars? Possible Links and Methodological Challenges', in Nissim Otmazgin and Eyal Ben-Ari (eds), *Popular Culture and the State in East and Southeast Asia*. London and New York: Routledge, pp. 29–45.

Putin, Vladimir (2016), 'Meeting with Film Crew of Viking', *President of the Russian Federation*, <http://en.kremlin.ru/events/president/news/53679> (last accessed 2 June 2017).

REN (2016), '"Guardians": The First Film about Russian Superheroes Will Be Released on Big Screens February 23', *REN Novosti*, <http://ren.tv/novosti/2017-02-21/zashchitniki-pervyy-film-o-rossiyskih-super-geroyah-vyydet-na-bolshie-ekrany-23> (last accessed 11 June 2017).

Roselle, Laura, Alister Miskimmon and Ben O'Loughlin (2014), 'Strategic Narrative: A New Means to Understand Soft Power', *Media War & Conflict*, 7:1, 70–84.

Rusciano, Frank L. (2003), 'The Construction of National Identity – A 23-Nation Study', *Political Research Quarterly*, 56:3, 361–6.

Rutland, Peter, and Andrei Kazantsev (2016), 'The Limits of Russia's "Soft Power"', *Journal of Political Power*, 9:3, 395–413.
Ryan, Fergus (2017), 'China, Russia Team up to Take on "The Avengers" with Communist Superheroes', *China Film Insider*, <http://chinafilminsider.com/china-russia-team-take-avengers-communist-superheroes/> (last accessed 30 May 2017).
S. N. (2017), 'Medieval Memes: The Far Right's New Fascination with the Middle Ages', *Economist*, <http://www.economist.com/blogs/democracy-inamerica/2017/01/medieval-memes?spc=scode&spv=xm&ah=9d7f7ab945510a56fa6d37c30b6f1709> (last accessed 4 January 2017).
Satter, David (2013), 'The Curse of Russian "Exceptionalism"', *Foreign Policy Research Institute*, <http://www.fpri.org/article/2013/10/the-curse-of-russian-exceptionalism/> (last accessed 8 June 2017).
Saunders, Robert A. (2008), *The Many Faces of Sacha Baron Cohen: Politics, Parody, and the Battle over Borat*. Lanham, MD: Lexington Books.
Saunders, Robert A. (2014), 'Primetime Paganism: Popular Cultural Representations of Europhilic Polytheism in Game of Thrones and Vikings', *Correspondences: Online Journal for the Study of Western Esotericism*, 2:2, 121–57.
Saunders, Robert A. (2017), *Popular Geopolitics and Nation Branding in the Post-Soviet Realm*. London and New York: Routledge.
Saunders, Robert A. (2020), '*Völkisch* Vibes: Neofolk, Place, Politics, and Pan-European Nationalism', in Tim Nieguth (ed.), *Nationalism and Popular Culture*. London and New York: Routledge, pp. 36–58.
Saunders, Robert A., and Vlad Strukov (2017), 'The Popular Geopolitics Feedback Loop: Thinking Beyond the "Russia Versus the West" Paradigm', *Europe-Asia Studies*, 69:2, 303–24.
Shepherd, Laura J. (2013), *Gender, Violence and Popular Culture: Telling Stories*. London and New York: Routledge.
Soldatov, Andrei, and Irina Borogan (2011), *The New Nobility: The Restoration of Russia's Security State and the Enduring Legacy of the KGB*. Washington, DC: Public Affairs.
Souch, Irina (2017), *Popular Tropes of Identity in Contemporary Russian Television and Film*. London: Bloomsbury.
Strukov, Vlad (2016), 'Russian "Manipulative Smart Power": Zviagintsev's Oscar Nomination, (Non-)Government Agency, and Contradictions of the Globalised World', *New Cinemas: Journal of Contemporary Film*, 14:1, 31–49.
Strukov, Vlad, and Helena Goscilo (2017), 'Introduction: The Aerial Ways of Aspiration and Iinspiration, or the Russian Chronot(r)ope of Transcendence', in Vlad Strukov and Helena Goscilo (eds), *Russian Aviation, Space Flight and Visual Culture*. London and New York: Routledge.
Takacs, Stacy (2015), *Interrogating Popular Culture: Key Questions*. London and New York: Routledge.
Trenin, Dmitri (2002), *The End of Eurasia: Russia on the Border between Geopolitics and Globalization*. Washington, DC: Carnegie Endowment for Global Peace.

Trenin, Dmitri (2006), 'Russia Leaves the West', *Foreign Affairs*, 85:4, 87–96.
van Ham, Peter (2001), 'The Rise of the Brand State: The Postmodern Politics of Image and Reputation', *Foreign Affairs*, 80:5, 2–7.
Whitaker, Cord J. (2020), 'The Problem of Alt-Right Medievalist White Supremacy, and Its Black Medievalist Answer', in Louie Dean Valencia-García, *Far-Right Revisionism and the End of History: Alt/Histories*. London and New York: Routledge.
White, Hayden (1980), 'The Value of Narrativity in the Representation of Reality', *Critical Inquiry*, 7:1, 5–27.
Yablokov, Ilya (2015), 'Conspiracy Theories as a Russian Public Diplomacy Tool: The Case of Russia Today (RT)', *Politics*, 35:3/4, 301–15.
Yaroslavtseva, Yulia (2016), 'Драма «Викинг» (2016): история и вымысел (Drama *Viking* 2016): History and Fiction)', *BelInFilm*, <http://belinfilm.by/1096/viking-istoriya-i-vymysel/> (last accessed 3 June 2017).
Yuray, Mark (2015), 'Mannerbund 101', *The Future Primaeval*, <https://thefutureprimaeval.tumblr.com/post/135086851938/mannerbund-101#:~:text=The%20Mannerbund%20is%20the%20source,from%20the%20male%20competitive%20instinct> (last accessed 17 November 2020).

CHAPTER 8

The South African Soft Power Narrative, Cinema and Participatory Video
Paul Cooke

Introduction

In January 2019, South Africa's President Cyril Ramaphosa stunned the international press at the launch of his party's (the African National Congress, ANC) election manifesto with his impassioned plea to end the growing scourge of gender-based violence that has gripped the country in recent years and dominated the media in 2018:

> We have made huge strides in improving the position of women in society [. . .]. However, gender-based violence is a national crisis that we are determined to end, so that all South African women and girls may live in peace, safety and dignity. (quoted in Harding 2019)

This was a radical and unexpected declaration. As BBC Africa correspondent Andrew Harding notes, the main aim of the speech was 'to mark a clear break with a decade of drift and misrule under his predecessor, Jacob Zuma' (ibid.). Over the course of its nine years in power, the Zuma administration was increasingly gripped by corruption scandals, and ultimately brought down by claims that it had facilitated 'state capture' by the Guptas, a well-connected, wealthy family accused of exhibiting undue influence on the government, to the point that the family could ostensibly even have people appointed to ministerial posts (Cotterill 2018). The corruption and cronyism over which Zuma presided led, in turn, to the downgrading of the country's credit rating to 'junk status'; huge levels of youth unemployment; the failure of the education system and the collapse of school infrastructure (causing, for example, children to drown in school 'pit latrines'; de Greef 2018); large-scale protests by university students, initially focused on decolonising the curriculum (the widely reported #RhodesMustFall campaign) and subsequently on the cost of university education and the social exclusion this fosters (the #FeesMustFall campaign); a rise in xenophobic attacks against migrant workers and, of course, a rise in violent attacks against women and girls. Between April 2017 and March 2018 an average of 110 rapes were reported to the police every day, a number that is probably only a fraction of the actual number of rapes taking place (Africa Check 2018).

This is all a far cry from the early post-apartheid days of the mid-1990s, when the country managed to transform itself swiftly from apartheid pariah into a democratic, outward-looking state with one of the world's most progressive constitutions, defined by strong institutions that embraced the nation's diversity: a constitutional support structure designed to deliver the 'Rainbow Nation', the term coined by Archbishop Desmond Tutu to describe what post-apartheid South Africa should be. It was the first country ever to give up its nuclear arsenal unilaterally, positioning itself on the global stage to represent not only its own interests but also those of Africa as a whole (Tella 2017: 396–7), a position that was shaped by the foundational post-apartheid leadership of Nelson Mandela, an unimpeachable moral authority of global significance. This, in turn, led to a period of economic stability and prosperity, culminating in the country's invitation to join the BRICS grouping in 2011 (Ogunnubi and Okeke-Uzodike 2015: 23–4).

In this chapter I wish to explore the gap between the way South Africa is *experienced* internally by some parts of the nation and the continued power of the story of the nation's transition to democracy under Mandela internationally, a story which, as I shall discuss in more detail below, remains a remarkably resilient factor in the nation's 'soft power' offering. As I shall outline here (and as I have discussed in more detail elsewhere: Cooke 2016), culture generally, and film in particular, are viewed by political elites as an important means of leveraging this narrative internationally. The story of Mandela is, for example, particularly visible in the way the nation is presented on the world's cinema screens. In this chapter, however, I wish to focus my discussion on the less frequently explored internal dimension of national soft power narratives, and how they can be used to construct an 'imagined [national] community' (Anderson 1991: 6). Here I am again interested in film culture, but in particular how community-level filmmaking has been used to contest national soft power narratives – not least in the case of South Africa, the presentation of the state as an inclusive 'Rainbow Nation'. I examine how community-level, participatory video projects have supported certain marginalised communities to advocate for a more inclusive understanding of the 'national narrative', focusing in particular on one such project currently running in townships across Ekurhuleni. In the process, we see how film has been used by these communities to challenge their exclusion, or mistreatment, in order to advocate for change in their lives and so ultimately to reconnect with, and thus to revivify, the nation's soft power narrative.

South Africa's Soft Power Offering

Ramaphosa's speech was an attempt to change the dominant national narrative about South Africa, as it is reported in the international media, and to reconnect with the values of the earlier post-apartheid era. In so doing, the President would seem to acknowledge the importance of South Africa's soft power offering. While India has Bollywood and Brazil has samba and football, South Africa's soft power is rooted in the values that drive its national story. As Elizabeth Sidiropoulos puts it:

> On the continent, setting aside external actors, South Africa is probably the country with the best claim to the exercise of soft power, as defined by Nye [. . .]. Nigeria may have Nollywood (cultural reach through its film industry), and its economy may have overtaken South Africa's as the largest in Africa, after the April 2014 rebasing of its gross domestic product calculations; however, Nigeria still has some way to go in rivalling the South African story. (Sidiropoulos 2014: 197)

The attractiveness of a country's 'story', or as Laura Roselle, Alister Miskimmon and Ben O'Loughlin term it in their re-evaluation of soft power discourses, a nation's 'strategic narrative', is central to understanding the value of soft power as a tool of international influence. So much of the recent discussion of soft power, Roselle et al. argue, has moved a long way from Nye's original formulation. For Nye, soft power is a descriptive term, used to capture what he identified as a shift in international relations in the 1990s towards the instrumentalisation of 'attraction rather than coercion or payment' (Nye 2004: x), his analysis focusing on the ways in which questions of 'culture' and 'values' were playing an ever greater role in foreign policy (ibid.: 11). Roselle et al. point to how the term has been taken up by political elites, in particular, far more normatively. Here it is frequently conceptualised as something that governments can themselves proactively *manufacture*. In the process, the discussion of soft power is increasingly focused on identifying and exploiting potential soft power 'assets', be it Nollywood in Nigeria, Bollywood in India or China's ability to use its economic might to buy a piece of Hollywood's global influence. However, it is the story behind such 'assets', and the values that the story communicates, that are key to their success or failure. 'Strategic narrative *is* soft power in the 21st century' (Roselle et al. 2014: 71; emphasis in original), or as John Arquilla and David Ronfeldt put it, international standing and influence are fundamentally shaped by 'whose story wins' (Arquilla and Ronfeldt 2001: 328).

And despite its recent history under Zuma, South Africa's story is hard to beat and has proven to be remarkably resilient. Moreover, it is clear that the soft power potential of the country's strategic narrative continues to be highly valued by the government, as the country's current National Development Plan (NDP), which sets out the government's goals for 2030, makes very clear (National Planning Commission 2012: 241). Indeed, as the country's economic power has faltered, the soft power of this narrative, as well as the concomitant set of values it communicates to the world, has become all the more important. Miller Matola, Chief Executive Officer (CEO) of 'Brand South Africa' – the national agency tasked with presenting a coherent image of the nation abroad in order to maximise the nation's soft power – speaks for many state representatives: 'we are proud of our history and diversity. [These are] our greatest strengths' (Brand South Africa 2013), a position further underlined in a survey carried out by this organisation in 2016, which found the country's story of democratic transition, along with its strong institutions, to be central to the continuing strength of the national 'brand' (Brand South Africa 2016).

Of course, and of particular interest to this chapter, the role of soft power and nation branding is often not only about generating international influence. Michael Barr, in his analysis of China, notes that in China the use of 'soft power is not only limited to international image building. Rather its deployment is as critical at home within the country as it is abroad.' 'Nation branding', in the Chinese case, is inextricably interconnected with 'nation building' (Barr 2012: 81). A similar dynamic can be found in South Africa. Chapter 15 of the NDP focuses entirely on 'nation building and social cohesion', setting out a strategy for spreading awareness of the values at the centre of 'Brand South Africa' across society, in order to establish 'a united, prosperous, non-racial, non-sexist and democratic South Africa' (National Planning Commission 2012: 65): the 'Rainbow Nation', as conceptualised by Tutu and propagated by Mandela, which, the NDP hopes, might be 'refracted in each one of us at home, in the community, in the city, and across the land, in an abundance of colour' (ibid.: 12).

Film, Media and Soft Power

To remain for the moment with the NDP, the cultural and creative industries – alongside, for example, the nation's ability to attract major international sporting events (Grix and Lee 2013) or the international standing of some of its universities (the recent campaigns mentioned above notwithstanding) – are considered to be pivotal for the delivery of both the internal and external dimensions of the country's soft power. At home, arts and culture generally, and film and media in particular, are seen as crucial to the project of nation building, of helping to unite society by embedding the types of values outlined in the NDP in the general population, on the one hand, while also supporting economic growth and national prosperity on the other (National Planning Commission 2012: 36). Abroad, the NDP suggests, the nation's culture needs to be utilised as a tool for 'South Africa to promote its presence and leadership on strategic issues as part of its "soft power"' (ibid.: 241). 'The country's rich cultural legacy and the creativity of its people mean that South Africa can offer unique stories, voices and products to the world' (ibid.: 35). And as the Government's *Revised White Paper on Arts, Culture & Heritage* – which emerged from the NDP – makes clear, film has a particular role to play in this regard (Department of Arts and Culture 2013), a position emphasised by Paul Mashatile, the Minister of Arts and Culture at the time:

> Film now occupies the centre stage in on-going efforts to foster social cohesion and nation building as well as the economic empowerment of the people of South Africa [...]. It is, among others, through film that we can open powerful spaces for debate about where we are as a society and where we are headed. Film is also one of the mediums through which we can tell our unique and compelling stories to the world. We have seen on many occasions that the world is hungry to hear the South African story; a story of a people that have overcome adversity and are now working together towards a shared and prosperous future. (Mashatile 2013)

If one looks at many of the films that circulate internationally (particularly those that find international co-financing), it does indeed seem to be the case that the (Western) world continues to be attracted to South Africa's ostensible 'national strategic narrative'. Here we might mention *Invictus* (dir. Clint Eastwood, 2009, South Africa (SA)/USA), the story of how Mandela worked with the captain of the national rugby union team to help bring the country together during the sport's World Cup finals in 1995, or the story of Mandela's time in prison, *Mandela: Long Walk to Freedom* (dir. Justin Chadwick, 2014, UK/SA), as well as the Truth and Reconciliation Committee drama *Red Dust* (Tom Hooper, 2004, UK/SA), *Catch a Fire* (Phillip Noyce, 2006, UK/USA/France/SA), a thriller about the anti-apartheid resistance, *Goodbye Bafana* (Bille August, Germany/France/Belgium/Italy/SA, 2007), the story of Mandela's friendship with one of his jailers, or the biopic *Winnie Mandela* (Darrell Roodt, 2011, SA/Canada). And as plans for a new film based on the memoir of Zelda la

Grange, Mandela's personal assistant, *Good Morning, Mr. Mandela*, show, for the international film industry at least, South Africa's story continues to be considered a bankable commodity (Kay 2020).

For the government, then, its support for the film industry has several competing goals. On the one hand, film is seen as an important tool in the country's soft power arsenal, not in the way that other nations, not least some of the BRICS, seek to use film – namely, as a cultural product with a global reach that can be instrumentalised to increase the nation's attractiveness to tourists and investors from the rest of the world – but as a way of better communicating to other countries the essential value of the South African strategic narrative of democratic transition. This, in turn, is viewed as a means to support the government's internal nation-building endeavours. On the other hand, it is viewed as an important part of the culture and creative industries that can support economic growth, contributing, according to the latest available figures, approximately 3.5 billion rand annually to South Africa's gross domestic product and generating over 25,175 jobs (NFVF 2013: 6).

As Ogunnubi and Okeke-Uzodike note, in the literature on soft power there has, until recently, been little discussion of South Africa (Ogunnubi and Okeke-Uzodike 2015: 154). Within this literature there has, however, been some exploration of the regional influence of the South African broadcast media as a soft power tool. Stacy Hardy, for example, examines the significant role played by MultiChoice Africa across the continent in this regard. MultiChoice Africa is a satellite and internet television company owned by the South African company Naspers. Its digital satellite services help to spread South African cultural products across the continent, and with them South Africa's cultural values, be it via local versions of Western reality shows such as *Big Brother Africa* (2003–) or through popular 'Soapies' such as *Generations* (1994–2014) or *Egoli: Place of Gold* (1992–2010) (Hardy 2015). At the same time, DStv, MultiChoice Africa's digital satellite platform, also carries a whole host of competing messages, be they broadcast via Nollywood on its 'Africa Magic' set of channels, the BBC World Service, Russia Today or China's CGTN (formerly CCTV). It can hardly be considered solely as a vehicle for the communication of the ANC's version of the South African story (for more detailed discussion see Milton and Fourie 2015).

Studies on post-apartheid South African Cinema, specifically, have not explored the relationship of the film industry to soft power discourses. That said, scholars have paid a good deal of attention to the role of film as part of the nation-building project. Lindiwe Dovey, for example, in her study, quotes Lionel Ngakane, 'Father of Black South African

Cinema', who argues that the nation 'needs to recognize that at this stage of our history cinema is perhaps the most powerful instrument to foster a stable, democratic and united South Africa through feature films and documentary films about ourselves', noting the extent to which 'contemporary South African filmmakers are playing an important role in narrating the new South African nation into being', for all their heterogeneity (Dovey 2009: 50–2). Martin Botha and Lucia Saks also draw out the role of film as a tool of nation building, while simultaneously highlighting the difficulty of this endeavour, given the diversity of potential narratives available to the post-apartheid nation. Botha, who was a key figure in the development of the 1996 White Paper on film that led to the creation of the National Film and Video Foundation (NFVF), points to the burgeoning diversity of contemporary South African film production, while also lamenting what he sees as the inability of the institution he helped to create to foster and sustain this diversity (Botha 2010: 203; 250). Saks also points to the difficulties faced by the national film infrastructure in delivering on what she sees as the 'incompatible aims' of the country's film policy. On the one hand, she too notes the government's goal to create a 'national cinema [. . .] which reflects the nation's own culture', while also positing what, in her view, is the impossibility of forming a coherent sense of national cinema at a time when there is such a strong need to protect the polyvocality of the national strategic narrative. On the other, she highlights how this is made more complex still due to the government's aim to build an industry which can 'create jobs at home, generate economic spin-offs in local economies, earn foreign revenue by touting locations and production expertise, generate revenue from co-productions and sales abroad, and encourage tourism' (Saks 2010: 6–7). And this is made yet more difficult if one considers the role the government sees for film as an agent of international influence. Saks points to the desire, particularly under the government of Thabo Mbeki, to use film as part of his drive to foster a pan-continental 'African Renaissance' (ibid.: 7), and as we can see from the statements made by the government quoted above, this remains important.

Internal Soft Power and Finding an Audience for South African Film

Central to the rhetoric around soft power and South African film internationally is the importance of filmmakers telling 'authentic stories' about the nation (however 'authenticity' might be defined). For many people working in the industry, however, this is an impossible goal. For example, the screenwriter and director Ntshaveni Wa Luruli argues that 'The South African industry is basically a service industry' that is more focused on providing cheap labour and expertise for Hollywood runaway productions than it is developing local talent (qtd in McCluskey 2009: 77). This has led, so such critics suggest, to a dearth of high-quality indigenous South African stories. Indeed, for some, the structural issues around how the industry has evolved underline, or are even exasperated by, a more disturbing form of implicit censorship. As actor and director Sechaba Morojele puts it:

> The bigger picture is if you talk politics, race, or racism, people go 'Sh-shh.' White people still have a strong hold over our society [. . .] You [have] never really seen a black South African make a true black political film about the past. (qtd in McCluskey 2009: 40)

This appears curious, given the role the past plays in the national strategic narrative. However, it would seem, to some in the industry at least, that funding bodies want a very specific version of the past – such as we see propagated in films like *The Long Walk to Freedom*, mentioned above. A similar claim is made by filmmaker Angus Gibson. He recounts his attempt to encourage take-up of a screenplay which painted a bleak picture of contemporary society: 'Everybody was very kind of saying, "There's not space for this kind of narrative in South Africa right now." They thought it doesn't represent the kind of rainbow nation that is painted' (qtd in McCluskey 2009: 55).

Such comments might well be dismissed as sour grapes from artists unable to find the resources to realise their projects. As I have discussed elsewhere, there is also a strong trend – also, at times, internationally visible – of films that highlight the problems contemporary society faces, be it the Oscar-winning story of a township gangster, *Tsotsi* (dir. Gavin Hood, 2005, SA), the treatment of migrant workers in *Sink* (dir. Brett Michael Innes, 2015, SA) or the sexual exploitation of young women and girls in *Of Good Report* (dir. Jahmil X. T. Qubeka, 2013, SA). What is less open to debate is the relative lack of public funding in South Africa for local film production compared to other countries. Astrid Treffry-Goatley points out that the budget available to the NFVF (around 120 million rand) is far less than that typically available to flourishing national film industries elsewhere, 'such as that of France' (Treffry-Goatley 2010: 42). France spent 74.8 million euros (1.2 billion rand) of public funding on film in 2015 (CNC 2015: 82). As one-time CEO of NFVF Zama Mkosi is at pains to point out, the demand for funding 'currently exceeds the budget by

116% each quarter' (quoted in Wagner 2016). It is unrealistic to expect a developing country like South Africa to be able to fund the industry to the same level as France, even if, according to the NFVF's 2013 *Film Industry Economic Baseline Study*, 'for every R1 spent in the industry, another R1.89 was generated within the South African economy' (NFVF 2013: 6). Despite this claim, it is widely acknowledged that, with regard to the creation of local content, there is a problem.

At the root of this problem, commentators frequently recognise, is the issue of audience development. The majority of the population does not go to the cinema and so the cinema audience for domestic South African films telling South African stories is limited. A report commissioned by the NFVF in 2015 found that while there was a large appetite for South African content amongst the population as a whole, very few people would consider watching such films in a cinema. If they did watch films, wherever the films were from, they tended to be on (frequently pirated) DVDs or on free-to-air television. Part of this is due to the lack of a tradition of going to cinemas in rural areas or in townships, a legacy of the apartheid era. Visiting cinemas is largely an urban activity and is considered to be out of the price range for the majority of the population (NFVF 2015: 20–39).

It is interesting to note in this regard that a far greater proportion of the white population go to the cinema than other communities, an audience that is, in fact, supporting an overall growth in the cinema sector. South Africa's box office hit a record high in 2015 of 1.2 billion rand, up 36 per cent on the previous year. Only 6 per cent of this came from local films, however, and the only one of these to make it into the top twenty-five was the comedian Leon Schuster's 'Candid Camera' movie *Shucks! Pay Back the Money* (2015) (Odek 2016). That said, the market for local productions remains steady, predominantly for Afrikaans film. There have been moments of optimism. The NFVF box-office report for the first half of 2016, for example, saw ticket sales for local films grow by 55 per cent to 43.9 million rand, compared to the same period in 2015 (28.2 million). This was primarily due to the success of a single film, *Vir Altyd* (dir. Jaco Smit, 2016) an Afrikaans romantic adventure (NFVF 2016: 6–8). That said, generally, Afrikaans films are the most popular local films with cinema audiences, accounting for 47 per cent of releases in 2017 (NFVF 2017b: 18).

Given the asymmetrical growth of the South African cinema market, the dominant position (however limited) of Afrikaans films at home would not seem to be supporting the culture of national inclusivity and cohesion that the government's film policy ostensibly wishes to develop. This is why the

NFVF's audience analysis puts such an emphasis in its recommendations on audience development and film education:

> Film education can assist in growing the audiences of today and tomorrow, ensuring that more people have an improved understanding and appreciation of the value of different kinds of film. The young generation can be encouraged to learn through and about film, providing them with a wide range of activities to encourage watching, understanding and making films. (NFVF 2015: 39)

Here we see the report following the direction of travel of similar studies commissioned by national film institutions around the world, such as the UK Film Policy Review of 2012, which also concluded that the future of British film 'begins with the audience' (Smith 2012). Furthermore, it chimes with local initiatives designed to raise awareness of South African films beyond the cities, such as the 'New Spaces for African Cinema' project, which took place as part of the 2013 Durban International Film Festival (Govindasamy 2013). Similarly, one might mention 'Sunshine Cinema' or 'Kasi Movie Nights', mobile cinema projects that seek to bring cinema to the townships, building an audience for South African stories in order 'to empower local communities and to share the industry with regular South Africans', an initiative that, like the NFVF audience report, sees teaching filmmaking skills as an important means of growing an audience for local product (Mokoena 2014), an idea that is also set to shape the NFVF's approach to audience development. The NFVF is currently creating 'a series of digital content generation hubs for local content provision' (NFVF 2017a: 16). The aim of these regional film 'hubs' is to bring exhibition spaces and production facilities to more rural areas in order to increase access to films and also to encourage the making of films (Khumalo 2016).

How effective the NFVF's regional film strategy will be in the medium term is still to be determined. Although not always very successful, it should be noted, of course, that South Africa does have a wide variety of regional film practices, ranging from the Hollywood-type co-productions mentioned above to a very small-scale Nollywood-like industry that apes the low-budget, quick-turn around production and distribution ethos of Nigeria (for example, 'Sollywood' Productions in Kwa-Zulu Natal or 'Vendawood' in the country's northernmost province) (Smith 2010). One area of the country's film production that has received very little discussion in this context, but that would seem to be particularly helpful to the NFVF as it seeks to develop regional filmmaking hubs, is the wide variety of community-level, participatory video projects that have been set up in recent years, often funded by international non-governmental organisations (NGOs) as part of wider development initiatives.

Participatory Video

Participatory video (PV), along with 'participatory arts' (PA) more generally, have become something of a 'go-to' methodology within the international development sector, considered by Craig Zelizer, for example, to be an 'an essential component of peacebuilding work' in post-conflict societies (2003: 62), or, as Matthew Flinders and Malaika Cunningham suggest, playing a key role in the production of civil society in the developing world, helping to 'nurtur[e] engaged citizenship' (2014: 5). The starting point for the contemporary surge in PV activity is frequently traced to a community filmmaking project set up by the National Film Board of Canada in the 1960s to support the inhabitants of the Newfoundland island of Fogo in their efforts to avoid resettlement by the government (Crocker 2003). Filmmakers worked with the residents to make films about their lives, the aim of which was, firstly, to raise awareness across the island of the shared nature of the inhabitants' plight. Here film became an extension of the way Benedict Anderson describes newspapers functioning in the eighteenth and nineteenth centuries. The circulation of film images of, and by, the inhabitants of Fogo helped them to see themselves as part of a larger 'imagined community' with a collective purpose (1991: 6). Central to what became known as the 'Fogo Process' was collective, critical self-reflection by the islanders of the images produced, which were generally either short pieces of direct cinema capturing everyday life or single-shot, individual interviews that attempted to create what Colin Low, the main external filmmaker involved in the process, called 'vertical films', or films which presented non-hierarchical, inclusive images of life that avoided relativising the voice of participants as, he argued, can happen in multivoice, what he termed 'horizontal', films, where one interviewee is contrasted, or indeed played off, against another (Crocker 2003: 129). Through their production, and more importantly their collective consumption, of the films, participants claimed they gained in 'confidence [and] self-worth', developing a 'better self-image' that valued their local knowledge (ibid.: 130). In turn, the 'Fogo Process' allowed this community, with its new collective sense of identity, to project itself externally in order to advocate for change with the government (ibid.: 123; Corneil 2012; Walker and Arrighi 2012: 410; Bell 2017).

While the Fogo Process was clearly hugely influential on PV practice, the *global* growth of PV can be traced to a set of practices emerging in the 1960s around the world. In the UK, for example, the development of PV came as part of the wider community arts movement that grew out of an activist culture that also emerged in the 1960s (Kelly 1984: 15–36; Dickinson 1999: 17–61), ultimately being co-opted, to a degree at least, by the establishment under New Labour in the 1990s (Bishop 2012: 38). The question of co-option can be found in discussion of PV, as well as PA more broadly, as a development tool. As PV/PA have been adopted by major organisations such as UNESCO and the World Bank, what is seen by these organisations as a 'scaling up' of practice, and so an increase in the impact of these projects, others see, again, as a form of co-option that provides a placebo which, at best, ignores the structural inequalities between the Global North and South, and at worst helps to maintain them. As Matt Rogers puts it,

> Often championed for its democratic, critical and counter-hegemonic potential, participatory video has steadily gained favour in academic, developmental, and educational contexts. However, practitioners implementing participatory approaches often fail to engage with issues of power. [Looking at how power operates in a given project] accents the importance of challenging taken-for-granted assumptions about participatory video by showing how the method can be shaped by, and play into, marginalising discourses. (Rogers 2016)

Furthermore, what is particularly interesting about accounts of the development of PV, and which also reflects a lack of engagement with questions of power, or in this case with the *agency* of the participants, is that PV is rarely seen as part of a wider tradition within, particularly, documentary filmmaking, identified by Bill Nichols as the 'Participatory Mode' (2012: 115–24). This is a trend which foregrounds the active participation of both the filmmaker and her/his subjects in the production of the film, a trend which can, in fact, be traced back as far as the work of Dziga Vertov and Robert J. Flaherty (Cain 2009: 28–35). A particularly important point of reference for my argument in this regard is 'Third Cinema', the movement that emerged out of the extraordinary growth in experimental, underground filmmaking found across Latin America from the late 1950s, for which a particular version of participation was central. In their definition of the term, Fernando Solanas and Octavio Getino famously saw a two-fold role for participation in their form of revolutionary film practice. Firstly, the material shown on screen is drawn directly from the everyday experience of the working classes. It is their oppression which has generated both the footage shown and Solanas and Getino's approach to the edit (1976: 60). On the other, through the active participation of the working classes in their underground screenings of the film, Solanas and Getino sought to provoke their audience to revolution, the projector being paused regularly during screenings to allow political discussion (Chanan 1997). Here we again find echoes of the 'Fogo Process'. However, unlike the Fogo films, Solanas and Getino's *La hora de los hornos* (*The Hour of the Furnaces*, 1968) is seen as a canonical film text that would never be considered, as Walsh points out, as a 'participatory film' (2016: 409), even as Solanas and Getino themselves define their practice as an act of collective participation with the working-class masses ('We thus discovered a new facet of cinema: the participation of people who, until then, were considered spectators': 1976: 62).

In the final section of this chapter I wish to look in more detail at one particular PV project in South Africa that I have been involved with and which looks explicitly at how film can be used to challenge the international representation of the nation, as propagated within the national strategic narrative. In so doing, I also wish to explore some of the particular film 'texts' that have been produced by this project. While such projects invariably make claims for PV as an effective method for 'giving' communities 'voice' (however patronising such a formulation might be) (Bery 2003 108), very little space is given to the exploration of the films produced in such projects: that is, the specific articulation of this 'voice'. Thus, I wish to explore the ways in which this project seeks to communicate the experience of the young people involved through its use of cinematic language. Here I am not looking to make general claims for PV. Instead, I wish to challenge a trend in the analysis of such practice that focuses entirely on questions of methodology and an understanding of PV as a *process*, largely ignoring the *products* made.

PV in South Africa

As Julia Cain notes, the Fogo project had an important influence on the development of PV in South Africa. In the 1970s, delegates from the Canadian project came to the country to meet with anti-apartheid activists in order to explore the potential of PV as a tool of resistance. This led to the creation of the Community Video Resource Association at the University of Cape Town, and subsequently to the Community Video Education Trust (CVET). CVET was initially focused on training and supporting community-based activists in the struggle against apartheid and now houses an archive of footage from that time (Cain 2009: 99–100; see also http://www.cvet.org.za/). There is a large number of PV projects running across South Africa. These range from small-scale interventions looking to raise awareness about 'household food insecurity' and vermin infestation in uMgungundlovu (Makhanya 2016) or the work of Tamara Plush with Cape Town-based Civil Society Organisation (CSO) Sonke Gender Justice that looked to challenge gender-based violence (Plush 2015), to larger-scale initiatives by national and international organisations such as Steps (http://steps.co.za/) or InsightShare (https://insightshare.org/), seeking, for example, to raise awareness of environmental impacts on the country's indigenous communities. In the rest of this chapter I wish to look at the films produced by one PV project that specifically took as its creative stimulus South Africa's soft power strategic narrative.

Changing the Story is an international project using PA to support CSOs to engage young people in social development in post-conflict countries (https://changingthestory.leeds.ac.uk). One of the projects that the South African strand of the project has been running is with the Bishop Simeon Trust, an NGO in Ekurhuleni. This has involved using PV to develop a youth-leadership programme that is supporting young people to raise awareness of a wide variety of issues that they face but that they feel are ignored, or misrepresented, in their communities, be those xenophobia, the question of 'undocumented' children or gender-based violence. The starting point for this project was a series of workshops looking at the gap between the way the nation is presented internationally on world cinema screens and participants' local experience of the nation in their township. As is typical of PV projects, the main function of the films produced was for advocacy. Participants organised a series of events showcasing the films they made as part of the project in order to raise awareness of, and generate discussion about, these issues. Overall, it was clear that participants felt there was a large gap between their experience and the national soft power strategic narrative. However, in the process of making, and most importantly screening, the films, it became clear that PV provided a useful space to create debate that, in turn, had the potential to *reinvigorate* this narrative.

One of the most striking aspects of the films produced by the Changing the Story project is, firstly, that they are frequently not documentaries. They are thus different to many PV projects which, as already suggested, can often be seen to be working within a tradition of participatory documentary. That said, textually, all of the films produced have certain documentary qualities, not least their impulse towards 'denotative' rather than 'connotative' forms of representation. *Tit for Tat* (dir. Tshepo Hope, 2016), for example, a story about the sexual exploitation of a young girl (Amanda) by an older man, culminates in a violent attack on the girl by her boyfriend (Pelican). We see and hear the boy repeatedly stamp on what the film suggests is the girl's head, a reflection, the male actor says, of both the reality of their lives and the way they are frequently presented on screen. As aesthetic points of reference, he refers both to Nollywood, which often has a similarly denotative approach to film communication (Okwuowulu 2015: 106), and to some of the social problem films mentioned above. While the group's insistence on local reference points in their filmmaking reminds us that any cinema which seeks to empower specific communities must be *situated* if it is going to be effective, the group also maintains that its denotative approach to filmmaking is a deliberate strategy. In *Tit for Tat* the group insisted upon showing the violence directly because, they argue, this is the reality of their lives. However, crucially, they also demanded that the film had a happy ending. Amanda eventually marries a doctor who diagnoses her as HIV-positive, having been infected by her boyfriend. Here the film plays on classical forms of theatre. Weddings tend to provide the conclusion for comedies, as opposed to the death and destruction of tragedies. Such an ending would seem to be out of place in this story, which has all the hallmarks of tragedy. None the less, the group insisted that its use here is yet another denotative declaration of the reality of their lives. Their lives are violent and precarious. However, their use of narrative conventions ostensibly out of kilter with the content of their story also suggests a refusal to present their lives as tragic. It is possible for them to continue to survive and have a 'happy ending' (Cooke 2016).

As is suggested in the way these films play with narrative conventions, while there is a deliberate attempt to focus on the power of denotative communication in these films, this can bring with it other *connotations* that speak symbolically to the world in which these young people live. *Heaven Hugged Me* (dir. Tshepo Hope, 2017), for example, is a film made by a group of six- to ten-year-olds that tells the story of a young gangster who wants to rebuild his life after prison. The group again aimed to reflect the kinds of narratives they see on screen about themselves and their communities. However, the fact that the group consisted of young children led them to use a preponderance of low-angle shots, presenting the external world as an overwhelming environment, over which they have little control (Fig. 8.1). It is as if the extra-diegetic reality repeatedly breaks into the diegesis, forcing the spectator into a dialectical relationship with this reality, akin to that suggested by Solanas and Getino, and forcing her/him to reflect upon the film's conditions of production. Similarly, in other films such as *When You Strike a Woman You Strike a Rock* (dir. Boniswe Field, 2017), the film's voiceover is repeatedly drowned out by the sound of the wind, highlighting not only the precarious nature of this community's existence (there was nowhere that they could find shelter to record the soundtrack), but also the symbolism of wind as an irresistible force of nature, just like the powerful women we meet in the film who refuse to acquiesce to the forces of gender-based violence that surround them.

Figure 8.1 The low angle-dominated world of *Heaven Hugged Me* (Tshepo Hope, 2017).

As hinted at above, in their evocation of classical tropes these films can be quite theatrical in their visual composition. Such an approach to cinema tends to foreground the performance of the actors. However, in these films, the use of non-professional actors frequently foregrounds their inability to maintain the suspension of disbelief required for long-take filmmaking. In *Heaven Hugged Me* the voiceover explains that the gangster's sister, Twinky, is seriously ill. But as the camera focuses on her face, Twinky faintly smiles (Fig. 8.2). The young girl playing the role breaks through the illusion of the narrative, reminding us of the incongruity of the situation. These are children playing a role. From a UK perspective, this is a story that one would not expect children to perform, and certainly not to have come up with themselves. This young girl's smile reminds us that she is a participant in a filmmaking project. And yet, it also highlights the potentially distressing nature of her life and the life experience that means she could help to develop this story. The tension between the performance and the story's content often leads to the generation of 'affect'. If, as Deleuze suggests, 'affect' is the product of the space between a movement on screen and its resolution into an emotion in the spectator – what he terms 'the centre of indetermination' (1986: 68) – these films continually generate and extend such 'indetermination'. We are regularly jarred out of the diegesis and into the reality of the filmmakers' lives, which is, of course, the basis *for* this diegesis, maximising the film's affective qualities and forcing the spectator to reflect upon their relationship to the images on screen.

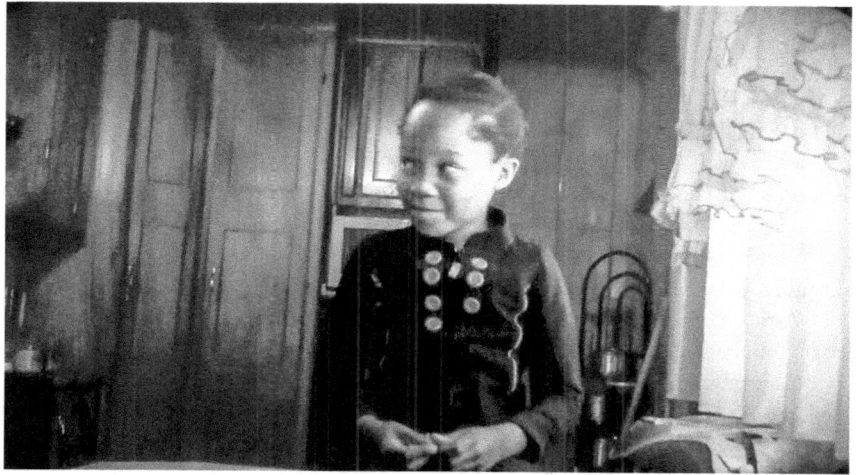

Figure 8.2 Twinky's enigmatic smile in *Heaven Hugged Me* (Tshepo Hope, 2017).

Looking at the products of this PV project as films in their own right, rather than as 'outputs' from a participatory *process*, as they often are, highlights the complex ways in which these films articulate the voice of their makers. On one level, these films would seem to reject categorically the notion of the Rainbow Nation and of South Africa as an inclusive democracy. The films produced by communities across Ekurhuleni speak to social exclusion and the failure of the state to live up to the promises of the post-apartheid transition. At the same time, they also speak to this generation's demand to have their voices heard and for their right to engage in debate. In so doing, in their ostensible rejection of the nation's soft power narrative – indeed, in their implicit declaration of the current failure of any sense of their even being a 'national project' – such films ultimately speak to the continued resilience of the nation, highlighting the robustness of the country's underlying values and, with it, the hope that this generation can help to regenerate this initiative. Moreover, as the Changing the Story project develops, it is hoped that it will be able to help further support the creativity of the young filmmakers with which it has engaged to date, building their skills and, in turn, enhancing their future employability. With this in mind, the project hopes to connect them with the NFVF. This will give them a national platform for their films, while also helping the NFVF to deliver its strategy, supporting the development of a national audience for South African cinema via its regional digital hubs, and its approach to film education rooted in an understanding of filmmaking practice.

Works Cited

Africa Check (2018), 'FACT SHEET: South Africa's Crime Statistics for 2017/18', *Africa Check: Sorting Fact from Fiction*, <https://africacheck.org/factsheets/factsheet-south-africas-crime-statistics-for-2017-18/> (last accessed 30 January 2019).

Anderson, Benedict Richard O'Gorman (1991), *Imagined Communities: Reflections on the Origin and Spread of Nationalism* (revised and extended edn). London: Verso.

Arquilla, John, and David Ronfeldt (2001), *Networks and Netwars: The Future of Terror, Crime, and Militancy*. Santa Monica, CA: RAND Corporation.

Barr, Michael (2012), 'Nation Branding as Nation Building: China's Image Campaign', *East Asia*, 29:1, 81–94.

Bell, D. M. (2017), 'The Politics of Participatory Art', *Political Studies Review*, 15:1, 73–83.

Bery, Renuka (2003), 'Participatory Video that Empowers', in Shirley. A. White (ed.), *Participatory Video: Images that Transform and Empower*. London: Sage, pp. 102–21.

Bishop, Claire (2012), *Artificial Hells: Participatory Art and the Politics of Spectatorship*. London: Verso.

Botha, Martin (2010), *South African Cinema 1896–2010*. Bristol: Intellect.

Brand South Africa (2013), 'South Africa's Global Reputation Remains Stable', 15 November, <http://www.brandsouthafrica.com/news/36-news/releases1/987-south-africa-s-global-reputation-remains-stable> (last accessed 1 January 2019).

Brand South Africa (2016), 'The Impact, Profile, and Reputation of South Africa on the African Continent', 16 March, <http://www.mediaclubsouthafrica.com/images/stories/march_2016/BSA-UJ-Seminar.pdf> (last accessed 1 January 2019)

Cain, Julia (2009), *Understanding Film and Video as Tools for Change: Applying Participatory Video and Video Advocacy in South Africa*. DPhil, Stellenbosch University.

Chanan, Michael (1997), 'The Changing Geography of Third Cinema', *Screen*, 38:4, 372–88.

CNC (2015), *Results 2015: Films, Television Programs, Production, Distribution, Exhibition, Exports, Video, New Media*. Paris: Centre national du cinéma et de l'image animée.

Cooke, Paul (2016), 'Soft Power and South African Film: Negotiating Mutually Incompatible Agendas?', *New Cinemas*, 14:1, 93–109.

Corneil, Marit Kathryn (2012), 'Citizenship and Participatory Video', in E.-J. Milne, Claudia Mitchell and Naydene de Lange (eds), *Handbook of Participatory Video*. Lanham, MD: Altamira, pp. 19–34.

Cotterill, Joseph (2018), 'South Africa's "State Capture" Inquiry Heaps Pressure on ANC', *Financial Times*, 13 December.

Crocker, Stephen (2003), 'The *Fogo Process*: Participatory Communication in a Globalizing World', in Shirley A. White (ed.), *Participatory Video: Images that Transform and Empower*, London: Sage, pp. 122–41.
de Greef, Kimon (2018), 'After Children Die in Pit Toilets, South Africa Vows to Fix School Sanitation', *The New York Times*, 14 August.
Deleuze, Gilles (1986), *Cinema 1*, trans. H. Tomlinson and B. Habberjam. London: Continuum.
Department of Arts and Culture (2013), *Revised White Paper on Arts, Culture & Heritage*, October, <http://www.dac.gov.za/sites/default/files/REVISED-WHITEPAPER04062013.pdf> (last accessed 1 December 2020).
Dickinson, Margaret (ed.), *Rogue Reels: Oppositional Film in Britain, 1945–90*. London: BFI.
Dovey, Lindiwe (2009), *African Film and Literature: Adapting Violence to the Screen*. New York: Columbia University Press.
Flinders, Matthew, and Malaika Cunningham (2014), *Participatory Art and Political Engagement*. Sheffield: The Crick Centre, <http://www.crickcentre.org/wp-content/uploads/2014/03/AHRC_Cultural_Value.pdf> (last accessed 19 February 2019).
Govindasamy, Valencia (2013), 'Taking Cinema to the Township', *IOL*, 30 July, <https://www.pressreader.com/south-africa/daily-news-south-africa/20130730/282312497692539> (last accessed 1 December 2020).
Grix, Jon, and Donna Lee (2013), 'Soft Power, Sports Mega-events and Emerging States: The Lure of the Politics of Attraction', *Global Society*, 27:4, 521–36.
Harding, Andrew (2019), 'South Africa's Cyril Ramaphosa Urges Action Against "Rape Crisis"', *BBC News*, 12 January, <https://www.bbc.co.uk/news/world-africa-46851802> (last accessed 1 February 2019).
Hardy, S. (2015), 'Soft Power South African Style', *Chronic*, 28 July, <https://chimurengachronic.co.za/soft-power-south-african-style/> (last accessed 15 March 2018).
Kay, Jeremy (2020), 'Working Title Films Boards Roger Michell's "Good Morning, Mr. Mandela"', *Screen Daily*, <https://www.screendaily.com/news/working-title-films-boards-roger-michells-good-morning-mr-mandela-exclusive/5152017.article> (last accessed 18 November 2020).
Kelly, Owen (1984), *Community, Art and the State: Storming the Citadels*. London: Comedia.
Khumalo, Terrence (2016), unpublished interview, Rosebank, Johannesburg, 30 June.
McCluskey, Audrey Thomas (ed.) (2009), *The Devil You Dance With: Film Culture in the New South Africa*. Urbana: University of Illinois Press.
Makhanya, Mzwandile (2016), *Using the Participatory Mode of Documentary Filmmaking for Knowledge Exchange and Empowerment: A Case Study of House-hold Food Security in the uMgungundlovu District of South Africa*, MA, University of Kwazulu-Natal.

Mashatile, Paul (2013), 'Address by the Minister Paul on the Occasion of the 4th Film Indaba, Emperors Palace', 14 November, <http://www.gov.za/address-minister-paul-mashatile-occasion-4th-film-indaba-emperors-palace> (last accessed 12 December 2018).

Milton, Viola. C., and Pieter J. Fourie (2015), 'South Africa: A Free Media Still in the Making', in Kaarle Nordenstreng and Daya Thussu (eds), *Mapping BRICS Media*. London: Routledge, pp. 181–201.

Mokoena, Thapelo (2014), 'Redefining Film and Television', *Kasibiz*, <http://kasibiz.co.za/?p=8101>, 6 December (last accessed 18 February 2019).

National Planning Commission (NPC) (2012), *National Development Plan 2030: Our Future – Make It Work*. Pretoria: Sherino Printers.

NFVF (2013), *South African Film Industry Economic Baseline Study Report*, April, <http://nfvf.co.za/home/22/files/Baseline%20study.pdf> (last accessed 1 February 2019).

NFVF (2015), *National Film and Video Foundation Audience Research Report*. Johannesburg: NFVF Policy & Research Unit.

NFVF (2016) *South Africa's Box Office Report (January – June)*, <http://nfvf.co.za/home/22/files/2016%20Files%20Folders%20etc/Box%20Office%20Report_Revised_Version%20%20final%5B2%5D.pdf> (last accessed 1 February 2019).

NFVF (2017a), *Economic Impact of the South African Film Industry: Report 2017*. Johannesburg: Urban-Econ Development Economists.

NFVF (2017b), *South Africa's Box Office Report (January – December)*, <http://www.nfvf.co.za/home/22/files/2018/Research/Box%20Office%20Report%20Jan_Dec%202017.pdf> (last accessed 18 February 2019).

Nichols, Bill (2012), *Introduction to Documentary*. Bloomington: Indiana University Press.

Nye, Joseph S., Jr (2004), *Soft Power: The Means to Success in World Politics*. New York: Public Affairs.

Odek (2016), 'These Films Made the Most Money in South Africa in 2015', *Odek Business Tech*, 9 March, <http://businesstech.co.za/news/business/116080/these-movies-made-the-most-money-in-south-africa-in-2015> (last accessed 1 February 2019).

Ogunnubi, Olusola, and Ufo Okeke-Uzodike (2015), 'South Africa's Foreign Policy and the Strategy of Soft Power', *South African Journal of International Affairs*, 22:1, 23–41, <http://0-dx.doi.org.wam.leeds.ac.uk/10.1080/10220461.2015.1007078> (last accessed 30 January 2019).

Okwuowulu, Charles (2015), 'Semiotic Discourse on Narrative Techniques in Nollywood', *Creative Artist: A Journal of Theatre and Media Studies*, 9:1, 103–20.

Plush, Tamara (2015), 'Participatory Video for Citizen Mobilisation in South Africa', *Media Development*, 3, 12–16.

Rogers, Matt (2014), 'Problematising Participatory Video with Youth in Canada: The Intersection of Therapeutic, Deficit and Individualising Discourses', *Area*, 48:4, 427–34.

Roselle, Laura, Alister Miskimmon and Ben O'Loughlin (2014), 'Strategic Narrative: A New Means to Understand Soft Power', *Media, War & Conflict*, 7:1, 70–84.

Saks, Lucia (2010), *Cinema in a Democratic South Africa: The Race for Representation*. Bloomington: Indiana University Press.

Sidiropoulos, Elizabeth (2014), 'South Africa's Emerging Soft Power', *Current History*, May, 197–202.

Smith, Chris (2012), *A Future for British Film: It Begins with the Audience*, <https://assets.publishing.service.gov.uk/government/uploads/system/uploads/attachment_data/file/78460/DCMS_film_policy_review_report-2012_update.pdf> (last accessed 1 December 2020).

Smith, David (2010), 'Sollywood – South Africa's Fledgling Film Genre', *The Guardian*, 6 May.

Solanas, Fernando, and Octavio Getino (1976), 'Towards a Third Cinema', in Bill Nichols (ed.), *Movies and Methods: An Anthology*. Berkeley: University of California Press, pp. 44–64.

Tella, Oluwaseun (2017), 'South Africa in BRICS: The Regional Power's Soft Balancing', *Politikon*, 44:3, 387–403.

Treffry-Goatley, A. (2010), 'South African Cinema After Apartheid: A Political-Economic Exploration', *Communicatio: South African Journal for Communication Theory and Research*, 36:1, 37–57.

Wagner, Leonie (2016), 'Funding Demand Exceeds the Budget by 116% Each Quarter at NFVF', *FilmContact.com*, 5 May, <http://www.filmcontact.com/news/south-africa/funding-demand-exceeds-budget-116-each-quarter-nfvf> (last accessed 15 May 2016).

Walker, Grady, and Julie Arrighi (2012), 'Participatory Video as a Catalyst for Informal Learning and Expression: A Review of a PV Training in Uganda', *LEARNing Landscapes*, 6:2, 409–23.

Walsh, Shannon (2016), 'Critiquing the Politics of Participatory Video and the Dangerous Romance of Liberalism', *Area*, 48:4, 405–11.

Zelizer, Craig (2003), 'The Role of Artistic Processes in Peace-building in Bosnia-Herzegovina', *Peace and Conflict Studies*, 10:2, 62–75.

CHAPTER 9

New Myths for an Old Nation: Bollywood, Soft Power and Hindu Nationalism

Rachel Dwyer

It is 19 October 2019. The screening of *Baahubali: The Beginning* (dir. S. S. Rajamouli, 2015) at the Royal Albert Hall, London, with a live orchestra, had the cast and crew attend for a preliminary talk (chaired by the present author), making the film not the usual presence of absence but a one-off event, a night of Indian film and music in a spectacular venue in the heart of the former imperial city which is now home to many British people of South Asian origin. Although the tickets were priced at Royal Albert Hall levels rather than those of a film screening – that is, mostly over £50 – it was a full house. The audience was mostly of Indian origin, mainly from the UK, India and the US, with some non-Indians, including several Japanese women dressed in saris. The atmosphere was redolent of a wedding, as strangers shared stories of their travels to witness this major event, while during the screening itself the level of audience interaction with the film recalled the glory days of the single-screen (pre-multiplex) cinemas of India, with whistling and shouting every time the stars gave snappy speeches, cast sharp looks or looked beautiful as they danced. When Baahubali (Strong Arms) flexed his muscles so much that his biceps broke his armlet, the crowd went wild. The presence of the stars brought the spectators together to form an audience, bewitched and dazzled by the stars, the music and a new epic style of Indian cinema. Around 6,000 fans went out into the London night, faces shining with happiness at the story of mythical King Baahubali, victorious in overthrowing the usurper, setting up just rule in Mahishmati, somewhere in India, some time in history. Although India is a modern republic, and the UK its former imperial ruler, the kingdom of Mahishmati was right there in metropolitan, multicultural London.

We can look at this event as an example of India's soft power, using Joseph Nye's concept: namely, that, although it is cultural and hard to measure and assess, it 'rests on the ability to shape the preferences of others' (Nye 2004: 5). Nye states that the soft power of a country depends on three resources: its culture, political values and foreign policies (Nye 1990; Zahran and Ramos 2010: 19; Hayden 2012: 29).

This chapter focuses on the cultural elements of India's soft power, in particular Indian cinema, and mostly the Hindi film industry (although the Hindi-dubbed version of *Baahubali* was screened in London, the original is in Telugu or Tamil; see below), in creating a positive image of India globally and through overseas fan networks. The extent and depth of its role are hard to measure. I examine the wide reach of Bollywood, which brands India globally, before homing in on its recent role in the political agenda of Hindutva, the Hindu nationalist project which seeks to reshape India's culture to one of Hindu primacy – and to represent its ancient and recent history in this vein.

India ought to be easy to market in soft power terms, as it is such a vast and diverse country, which has attracted enormous interest for its history, spirituality, architecture, food, style and design. It can be seen as an Orientalist fantasy of adventure, mystery, ancientness, colour, spice, the world's largest democracy, a worthy but poor country with global leaders such as Jawaharlal Nehru, Mahatma Gandhi and Indira Gandhi, a great centre of world cricket, a vast buzzing urban culture of global significance, and also a homeland for one of the world's largest diasporas.

It is no exaggeration to say that India's view of itself and that from outside changed with Prime Minister Narendra Modi's election in 2014 and his subsequent landslide victory in 2019. His rhetoric of a new India pushes a new cultural agenda that is anti-Nehruvian. Its underlying ideology of Hindu nationalism and anti-secularism is reshaping the idea of Hinduism and equating Hindu with Indian, yet while promoting nativist culture it has also encouraged a more open Indian economy in order to compete globally (*Business Standard* 2020).

This new vision of India seeks to remake it as a sacred homeland for Hindus rather than a secular republic. It aims to cleanse Indian culture of its Muslim history, its colonial mentality and its leftist nationalist leaders, and is fighting its corner in these cultural wars not only through political change but also on social media and on university campuses. Its fervent supporters or *bhakts* ('devotees'), as they are labelled by their detractors, are highly visible on Twitter and other social media, where they are known as the 'Troll Army'. Based in India and overseas, they are supporters of Hindu nationalism, and of a Hindu India, tweeting about a range of issues such as seeking an end to privilege and cronyism, notably that of the Nehru–Gandhi family or 'Lutyens Delhi' (named after the imperial buildings of New Delhi which house the government and its functionaries) in order to make way for rising new social groups. They seek to promote Hindi as the national language over English, the language of the privileged, and to rid India of Urdu with its Muslim associations. They mobilise around symbols such as cow protection, a prohibition on eating beef and cow slaughter, which excludes Muslims and low castes. The Hindu nationalists promote the narrative of Hindus as victims of outsiders who are now claiming their rightful inheritance. This is the backlash against Nehru's socialist vision, which they claim is a postcolonial mindset.

However, the left in India sees this as part of a desire for a strong man, or even a dictator. It sees *Hindutvavadis* (supporters of Hindutva) as oppressors of minorities, in particular of Muslims, who form around 18 per cent of India's population, removers of human rights, or even fascists, with reactionary views on gender, sexuality and religion.

A positive view of India's economic growth was developing abroad post-liberalisation, but sentiment has waned over the last decade following demonetisation in 2016 and the imposition of a General Services Tax (GST), and in the wake of COVID-19. The Indian press has reacted much more strongly in response to changes in the 1950 Constitution, removing Kashmir's special status, and the Citizenship Amendment Bill (CAB, 2019), which its detractors claim gives worse citizenship rights to India's religious minorities. Along with film of student uprisings and police repression being broadcast internationally, a new set of negative images about India has gained prominence, focusing on the government's treatment of minorities, the serial lynching of alleged beef eaters and the country's so-called 'rape culture', made notorious by the 2012 Delhi gang rape and murder of a student on a private bus, alongside images of poverty, of manual scavengers and the like.

This chapter also examines whether Indian soft power can respond to such negative images of India overseas, or whether they are merely ignored, being seen as anti-Indian reporting. In many ways, the new India is an autarky. Questioning the government is regarded as antinational and much international news is seen as anti-Indian. Yet if India wishes to remain a significant force in global economic and political networks, it has to counteract such negative messages and project its importance on the world stage as an emerging power, as a place both to invest and to convey the country's moral and political authority. Soft power, rather than social media trolling or propaganda, would be an ideal way to change the way India is seen abroad, and it is the forms of soft power which the government uses and those which are available to it, whether produced by the government or by non-state actors, that are my concern in this chapter.

The National Democratic Alliance, led by the Bharatiya Janata Party (BJP), which forms the current Indian government, in addition to regular diplomacy, has promoted India overseas through the charismatic and not uncontroversial figure of Prime Minister Modi, who, till COVID-19, travelled globally, meeting leaders, availing himself of photo opportunities that showcased his stylish dress sense, and giving speeches in Hindi that enthralled diasporic and domestic audiences. His savvy use of social media has also allowed Mr Modi to bypass a frequently hostile traditional media in building his image domestically.

The government has also continued to promote soft power institutions such as the Nehru Centres, venues for Indian cultural events established in many other countries, whose directors are appointed by the government. The London Nehru Centre's earlier directors include Gopal Gandhi (the grandson of Mahatma Gandhi) and Girish Karnad, a leading leftist intellectual, writer and actor. The present director is Amish Tripathi, the bestselling author of religio-fantasy fiction, who is more allied to the ideologies of the governing party.

The Nehru and other Indian cultural centres come under the aegis of the Indian Council for Cultural Relations (founded 1950), which also promotes university chairs in Indian studies, student scholarships and so on. Its significance in soft power projection is noted by the Indian government in its Report to the Standing Committee on External Affairs (Report 2016a), entitled 'India's Soft Power Diplomacy Including [the] Role of [the] Indian Council for Cultural Relations (ICCR) and [the] Indian Diaspora'; the committee is chaired by Shashi Tharoor, MP, a Congress Party politician and former international diplomat, who is one of India's leading spokespersons on soft power.

The report gives a detailed view of Indian soft power, its deployment and its potential. Tharoor notes that it is only in the last two decades that India has sought to harness its soft power and it is yet to do so as effectively as it might through cultural diplomacy. Its recommendations include:

> teaching and learning (socialization, language, literature), ideas (identity, Philosophy and way of thinking), value system (democratic and secular), norms (economic systems, traditions, varied art forms and sports) and India's institutional structures (family, Constitution and political systems). (Report 2016a: 6)

and these are carried out through exchanges of people, publications, performance and so on.

The report notes the success of marketing India to foreign tourists, notably the long-running 'Incredible India' campaign, produced by the

Department of Tourism, which has fared very well. It has not notably promoted Hindu sites over Muslim ones, unlike the Hindutva-ruled state of Uttar Pradesh, whose tourism department's booklet omitted the Taj Mahal in 2017 (Bell 2017).

The most successful government soft power initiative of the current government has been 'Yoga Day'. Skirting definitions of what yoga is, how much current ideas of yoga are Indian or foreign, or whether yoga is an aspect of Hinduism that is unacceptable to Christian and Muslim theology, the government has determined that it now symbolises the Indian nation. A discipline of mind and body which connects ancient India to the modern nation, it offers endless opportunities for exploitation as a subtle form of soft power. But has yoga's soft power efficacy been tested with overseas consumers, or is it more about mobilising domestic Indian opinion and strengthening national unity, with soft power merely a spin-off?

Other forms of Indian soft power include ideas of wellness and ayurvedic medicine, which have become popular through spas, and certain aspects of diet and welfare. Indian food, formerly known in Britain as 'curry', has also become very popular overseas, given the growing numbers of vegetarians in Western countries. Indian literature too, especially the Indian English novel, has a wide following outside India, although it is beyond any government control, with many of the most renowned contemporary writers being deeply critical of Hindutva, notably the Booker Prize-winning Arundhati Roy, a fierce critic of the government, in her non-fiction and her fiction. Her latest novel attacked the Indian government's policies in Kashmir even before its special status was abrogated in 2019 (Roy 2017). Indian English popular lowbrow fiction, such as the fantasy novels of Amish Tripathi, sell in their millions in India, yet have not found a Western readership. In the latter, gods and goddesses are characters with inner thoughts who act in familiar narratives told in a novelistic style, making them seem more human while also underlining their divinity.

The report notes two areas which are of key importance to this chapter. One is its recommendation that the government should 'utilize the power of Indian cinema that has been a particularly effective tool over many decades in shaping a positive view of India abroad' (Report 2016a: 4–5); the other is that it should 'leverage the influence of the world's largest Diaspora to advance our interests and improve our global standing' (ibid.: 5). The rest of this chapter looks at Indian cinema overseas in brief, then at the relationship between the Indian government and the film industry, before examining how current cinema may be of particular interest in promoting a positive image of India that differs from that usually seen in the Western media.

The pre-1947 'Empire' films (Jaikumar 2006) had a huge impact on how the West saw India, as did assorted orientalist movies (from Fritz Lang's India films to Spielberg's *Indiana Jones*). In the last four decades, two films which each won eight 'Oscars' further affected the perceptions of India in the West. One is Richard Attenborough's *Gandhi* (1982, a joint Indo-British production; see Dwyer 2011a); the other is *Slumdog Millionaire* (dir. Danny Boyle, 2009; see Gehlawat 2017a). The Merchant–Ivory art films set in India were also widely seen in the West, as are the contemporary films of Mira Nair (an Indo-Canadian director), Deepa Mehta and Britain's own Gurinder Chadha. While all of these films were influenced by Western sensibilities, if not outright foreign productions (*Slumdog Millionaire*), *Gandhi* has remained important *within* India and is broadcast on national television on Gandhi's birthday.

Indian films have rarely penetrated the Western mainstream market beyond the 'festival' circuit, where they have had occasional success overseas, such as *The Lunchbox* (dir. Ritesh Bhatra, 2013), while Western cinephiles are familiar with the work of the great art filmmakers, including Satyajit Ray, whose recognition overseas is confirmed by his many awards, including his honorary award at the 1991 Oscars. However, the audience for art cinema is limited in the West, and even more so in India, and as such it is a limited instrument of soft power. Moreover, within India it was argued that realist cinema depicted India negatively. When the superstar Nargis was given a seat in the Rajya Sabha (Upper House of Parliament) in 1980, she attacked Satyajit Ray in her maiden speech, saying that his films were presenting images of India that the West wanted to see –: namely, those of abject poverty – which were incorrect depictions. When pushed by a journalist about how India ought to be shown on screen, she said she wanted images of modern India to be presented, suggesting these were represented by dams, as indeed occurs in the classic, *Mother India* (Robinson 2003: 327).

It is the popular cinema made in many Indian languages that has massive daily audiences and is preferred to any other form of film, including Hollywood. Indian cinema is known among the diaspora and many countries, but not in Europe and North America. Hindi cinema, made in Mumbai (Bombay), has the widest reach of these cinemas, not least because its language is widely understood in much of northern India and beyond. The cinemas of south India – in particular, Tamil and Telugu – on the other hand, also have massive audiences at home and among the south Indian diasporas, and are often popular when dubbed into Hindi.

Since independence in 1947, the Hindi film itself has tried to forge a national culture, largely avoiding controversy in favour of a consensus on

Indian values and traditions. Most genres created an all-Indian hero, tall, fair and vaguely north Indian, largely avoiding mentions of caste. This was an image of the Indian citizen that was neutral and unreal, and which flattened difference.

Since their origin, Hindi films have been concerned with notions of 'Indianness'. Raj Kapoor's Nehruvian hero sings '*Phir bhi dil hai Hindustani*/My heart remains Indian', the diasporic characters of the 1990s proudly manifest their Indianness, and in today's blockbusters by Rajkumar Hirani the youth struggle with their own desires in the context of the family and the nation. Hindi films also embrace the idea of the 'Overseas Citizen of India' and of India somehow remaining the homeland or *pitribhumi*, and, for many, especially Hindus, the *punyabhumi*, or sacred land (Tharoor 2008; Schaefer and Karan 2012; Devasundaram 2016).

The features of Hindi cinema that make it so loved in India and other parts of the world are perhaps those which have hindered its popularity in northern Europa and America, in particular its use of melodrama, lack of realism, star performances, disruptive and digressive narrative, long scenes and running times, and the style in which song and dance are used (Rajagopalan 2008).

Moreover, mainstream Hindi films are more concerned about striving for emotional accuracy rather than the aesthetics of realism. A Hindi film has to engage the audience not just mentally but physically, so that they are stirred to weep, laugh and be angry by stars embodying emotions or values, their feelings intensified in close-up shots, delivering moving dialogues in a meaningful mise-en-scène where emotions are transferred on to inanimate objects, with spirited background music and, most famously, with songs which condense dialogue to lyrics. One of the feelings that films can arouse in the audience is patriotism, as a heroic star, perhaps in uniform, uses powerful oratory associated with the nation, such as undying enmity to those who dare to insult India. Or we may see the Indian flag, set against stirring music, declaring India's victory over its adversaries.

After economic liberalisation in 1991 and the spread of new media technologies, Hindi film became widely known as 'Bollywood' and was recognised internationally as a style of glamour and kitsch, associated with song and dance. Ashish Rajadhyaksha (2003) and others have argued that Bollywood is a style, a conglomeration of media in which film may be dominant rather than the films themselves. From being seen as something of a national guilty secret, Bollywood has come to mark a new image of modern India, where it continues to hold around 95 per cent of the domestic film market (Thussu 2013: passim), with the new and other media reinforcing rather than detracting from it.

The relationship between government and non-government agencies in the Indian film industry is complex but central to this chapter, if only to enable us to see that the state has mechanisms in place to develop one of the world's few global cinema industries. The Indian government gave little support to cinema in the early years after independence and has yet to set up a national academy for film as it has for the other arts such as literature, theatre, music and so on. India's federal state governments promoted realist cinema, most famously the West Bengal administration's support of Satyajit Ray, but it was not until much later that the government set up institutes to promote what Madhava Prasad (1998) calls 'state-sponsored realism': that is, a kind of cinema separate from mainstream popular cinema, which conforms more to international styles and forms.

Bollywood, while having achieved industry recognition in 1998, receives no direct government support, being a mostly private business. The Ministry of Information and Broadcasting has several organisations which have a significant impact on the industry: namely, the Central Board of Film Certification (CBFC), often referred to as the 'Censor Board'; the Directorate of Film Festivals (DFF); and the National Film Development Corporation (NFDC).

All films screened have to be certified by the CBFC, which creates rules for what is and is not allowed to be seen, using a very loose set of guidelines. The DFF, as well as organising the annual International Film Festival of India (IFFI), selects the Indian Panorama of 'good films', which are awarded tax-free status in India, thereby lowering their ticket prices, and then sent to overseas film festivals, promoted by the Federation of Indian Chambers of Commerce and Industry, including Cannes and Berlin. The DFF also runs the annual National Film Awards (NFA), whose choices define what is 'good' cinema.

The NFDC, created in 1975 from the Film Finance Corporation, produced some of the Indian films that have been most viewed overseas: *Gandhi*, *Salaam Bombay!* (Mira Nair, 1988) and *The Lunchbox*. It no longer funds film but it does host the successful Film Bazaar at IFFI, the aim of which is to bring together directors and producers. Many of its films bagged awards overseas, including several which won 'Un certain regard' at Cannes: *Miss Lovely* (Ashim Ahuluwalia, 2012), *Titli* (Kanu Behl, 2014), *Chauthi Koot* (Gurvinder Singh, 2015) and *Liar's Dice* (Geetu Mohandas, 2013; screened at the Sundance Film Festival in 2014). The NFDC also runs the Film Facilitation Office (FFO), which promotes

India as a destination for film shooting for overseas filmmakers, as well as helping Indian filmmakers.

These governmental organisations have helped promote Indian film overseas, but they have a limited budget and reach. The government uses Bollywood in other ways, such as in its interactions with the US government (Thussu 2013: 148), when meeting overseas delegations from Pakistan, such as President Musharraf's visit to Delhi in 2003, and during the Duke and Duchess of Cambridge's tour in 2016. In 2010, India included a Bollywood-inspired display at the Commonwealth Games opening ceremony instead of traditional folk dances and music.

Bollywood is not a national cinema, but often seems to be one because of its use of the mostly widely understood language of India. However, those involved in the industry and the economics of cinema – filmmakers, producers, distributors and exhibitors – who are non-state actors are important figures in the soft power agendas of their country. Certain actors are closely associated with government, some as elected or nominated politicians, and many others as vocal supporters or detractors, especially on social media.

Given that the state's influence on Bollywood is limited, its filmmakers are not pressured to produce cinema that backs the government's Hindu nationalist agenda. Moreover, many filmmakers strive to be apolitical, albeit with some notable exceptions. They would have to face reduced audiences and limitations if they made films endorsing Hindutva, which would be rejected in many overseas markets. Moreover, such films would not appeal to many in the Mumbai-based film industry, which is made up of mostly family-run businesses, employing a high proportion of Muslim personnel (stars, musicians and directors), with its roots in a syncretic 'Islamicate' culture (Dwyer 2006).

Mainstream filmmakers seek to maximise their audiences, and hence are well aware of how the rhetoric of anti-nationalism is deployed against those who query the government, let alone the nation. The audience too is sensitive to propaganda and being bludgeoned by films carrying too overt a political message, such as Vivek Oberoi's *PM Modi* (dir. Omung Kumar, 2019), and would rather seek entertainment and emotional realism. Just as the politicians must woo the electorate, so must the filmmakers find audiences for their work.

Films mark a shift in the *Zeitgeist*, as they are part of an *imaginaire* of contemporary India (Dwyer 2014b). That is, their understandings of India become common and accepted, and are a powerful way of spreading soft power, especially if these are accepted beyond India itself. It is hard to measure the impact of these understandings on audiences but it seems that they persuade the audience to accept their view, while the texts also pick up on how the audiences themselves see the world. This contemporary cinema produces a positive image of India at home and then travels overseas, presenting an image of India today as part of soft power, but only if the films are able to find audiences.

However, my main focus here is on film genres which have become highly productive in the last decade: namely, hyper-nationalist/war films, biopics and historical dramas. They manifest elements of nationalism, possibly Hindu nationalism, creating a different image of India which is concerned with conflict and its resolution, presenting political history as personal dramas between often cut-out figures, morally firm defenders of the nation against threats from outsiders, for which they sacrifice romance, personal happiness and often their own lives (Dwyer 2019).

These hyper-nationalist films seek to justify war, espionage and state violence, and promote images which have a more overtly political slant, not least as they feature characters active in current politics. *Raazi* (dir. Meghna Gulzar, 2018) is a spy drama based on the true story of an Indian Muslim RAW agent (Research and Analysis Wing, the foreign intelligence agency of India) who marries into a Pakistani military family to spy on them before the 1971 war. It shows the Pakistanis as mostly kind, normal, people but the heroine betrays her husband for her nation, only to realise that her country puts itself before her, thus deflating any patriotic sentiment.

Uri: The Surgical Strike (dir. Aditya Dhar, 2019) features characters who closely resemble Prime Minister Modi and National Security Adviser Ajit Doval, who oversaw the 'surgical strikes' on Pakistan following the assault on Uri in 2016. Its release at the time of the Pulwarma terrorist attack and its aftermath in 2019 no doubt contributed to the huge success of the film. Vicky Kaushal's brilliant performance as a national military hero, Major Vihaan Singh Shergill, elicited from the audience the same response as he does from his men when he asks them how high is their spirit, or *josh*. The use of this word by Manohar Parikkar, who was Minister of Defence at the time, and who was terminally ill during Pulwarma, and by the Minister who succeeded him, Nirmala Sitharaman, suggests they were seeking electoral advantage by exploiting the current government's assertive military stance against Pakistan.

The biopic has become one of the most productive genres in recent Hindi cinema, with two cycles in the first two decades of this century. The first cycle of biopics in the early 2000s were mostly of national leaders (Dwyer 2013a), whereas the second cycle since around 2010 (Dwyer 2014a) were semi-fictionalised biopics of figures whose success was achieved mostly in business, sports or entertainment, the heroes of India's new middle classes (Dwyer 2011b). There is also a new cycle of historical biopics which feature national heroes presented in a more Hindu nationalist manner.

The major stars of Bollywood's heyday in the 1990s have also taken roles in films which have been excessively nationalistic: for example, in the currently popular sports genres. Three of the biggest male heroes of Bollywood, Shahrukh Khan, Aamir Khan and Salman Khan, are Muslims and, although they have been mostly silent on political matters, can be assumed reasonably safely not to be supporters of Hindutva ideology, however careful their relationship with the Prime Minister and other members of the government is. All three have acted in biopics of sports stars, the new icons of Indian nationalism across the political spectrum.

Shahrukh Khan was the biggest romantic hero of Bollywood, hugely popular in the diaspora (Dwyer 2015), when he played the coach of the Indian women's hockey team in *Chak de! India/Go for it, India!* (Shimit Amin, 2007), a film where he had no romantic interest. It was shown at Somerset House, London, on 15 August 2007, the sixtieth anniversary of Indian independence, suggesting a strong soft power opportunity. The London screening was also attended by Indian sports heroes, including Sunil Gavaskar, a well-known figure to any cricket fan.

Aamir Khan, whose films have made him massively successful in China, has focused more on issue-based cinema than romance (Bajpai 2019). His biggest hit to date, *Dangal* (Nitesh Tiwari, 2016), is based on the life of India's champion wrestlers, the Phogat sisters, who are trained by their father, a failed wrestler, who did not have a son. The film queries gender norms and family relationships but its climax is a tear-jerking nationalist moment.

Salman Khan has moved from romantic hero to action/comedy hero. He has a huge fan base among young Muslim men (Dwyer 2017) and played hit roles as an Indian who interacts with Pakistanis, notably as the Indian spy 'Tiger' in *Ek tha Tiger* (dir. Kabir Khan, 2012). In *Bajrangi Bhaijaan* (Kabir Khan, 2015) he plays a Hindutva supporter who is transformed by his love for a young mute girl. When he finds out she is Pakistani, he fulfils an impossible mission by taking her home (ibid.). Salman Khan also acted in a sports biopic, *Sultan* (Ali Abbas Zafar, 2016), as a fictional world wrestling champion, where he trains a wrestler whom he marries. She retires when pregnant and he goes back into the ring.

All of these sports films, all but one a biopic, present a notion of what an Indian sportsman should be, arousing nationalist sentiment which can be enjoyed by all viewers, including the diasporic Indian who can feel proud of India's sporting achievements, which are little known internationally except in cricket.

A possible third cycle of biopics is emerging: namely, the big-budget historical biopic, interwoven with costume drama, in which filmmakers recount seminal moments in India's national history. Recent historical dramas have focused on idealised Hindu women who gave up their lives for their kingdoms or the nation. These include Padmavati, the legendary Rajput queen whose beauty is said to have prompted the Delhi Sultan, Alauddin Khilji, to attack the fort at Chittor, and who led the women of the palace to commit *jauhar* (ritual suicide) rather than be taken captive; and Manikarnika, the Queen of Jhansi, who led an uprising against the British in 1857. Following the success of and controversies surrounding *Bajirao Mastani* (2015), Sanjay Leela Bhansali's reworking of the story of Peshwa Bajirao and his wives Kashibai and Mastani, he then shot *Padmaavat* (2018) (Gehlawat 2017b; Kumar 2018).

The story on which *Padmaavat* is based was composed by Malik Muhammad Jayasi, who wrote *Padmavat* as fiction in 1520, and the film is based on this epic rather than aiming to be historical (Jalil 2018). The film was none the less highly contested and changes were made before it could be released, including the change of title from *Padmaavati* to *Padmavat* to indicate that it is based on Jayasi's epic poem, coupled with a disclaimer that the film did not claim to be historically accurate, as well as saying that it did not support the practice of *jauhar* (*HT Correspondent* 2018; Siddique 2017).

The story could have been told as a tragedy, the tale of a king who lays siege to a city to meet a queen who chooses death rather than see him, but the film tells it as a 'love triangle', though one with resonances of Ram, Sita and Ravan (Ramnath 2018). Though the Muslim Khilji is the 'baddie' and the Rajputs the 'goodies', there are subtle ways in which the film undermines this: 'colour-coded opposites – the amber-hued and gleaming Chittor, where reside Hindu Rajput honour, moral rectitude and courage; and the jet-toned and underlit lair of the Afghan-origin Muslim ruler Alauddin Khilji, which houses deceit and debauchery' (ibid.).

In Hindu nationalism, masculinity is not just physical strength but also strength of character. The ideal Hindu man is disciplined and restrained. This is very different from the derogatory idea of the lustful, aggressive and hyper-masculine Muslim, with his many wives and children. This seems to be what the film is portraying but for many viewers the sympathy lies with the devil.

The world of the Hindu Rajputs, with wordy dialogues about duty and right, looks terribly boring in comparison with Khilji's world of poetry (the great poet Amir Khusrau), music, carousing and fun. Khilji is presented as a wild and amoral animalistic figure but lives up to all the negative images of the lustful Muslim and more. He is never shown as a Muslim or a religious man but rather is a sensual figure, readily displaying his muscled flesh.

Hindu–Muslim relations in the film show a great intimacy, whether romantic or inimical (Siddique 2017), though the film is wary of a romantic Hindu–Muslim sequence, avoiding even a 'dream sequence', a frequent feature of Hindi films. However, the stardom of the couple, Ranveer and Deepika, who had recently appeared together in *Bajirao Mastani*, where she played the Muslim Mastani to his Brahminical Hindu king, brings the focus on them as the central couple in the film, even though they never appear together, overshadowing Shaheed and Deepika, who act as the Rajput king and queen, Ratan Singh and Padmavati, as they have never been a star couple. The star couple were further reinforced when Ranveer and Deepika married a few months after film, to enormous media attention, boosting their star images.

The abiding image of the film is of sumptuous and excessive beauty in the Hindu court (even the moment of the women walking to their death at the end is exquisite) and of wild savagery and debauchery in the Muslim Sultanate court. This allows the film to project soft power as an image of heritage India with a good Hindu king and a degenerate Muslim ruler, as the text, which undermines itself on closer analysis, is overwhelmed by the visuals and music.

Manikarnika: The Queen of Jhansi (dir. Radha Krishna Jagarlamudi and Kangana Ranaut, 2019) returned to the 'First War of Independence' (once known as the Sepoy Mutiny of 1857), in a biopic of the Rani of Jhansi, in which Kangana Ranaut plays a warrior queen who alone defies all odds to resist the British. The film has powerful images of female warriors in red and green, with swords and guns, and men in white forming a celluloid tricolour, again boosting the audience's patriotic sentiments.

Manikarnika contains complex readings which feed into current patriotism, not just about this revered national heroine but also about broader strands of patriotism and nationalism evident in India today. The protagonist is regal but in touch with her people, a loving wife and mother but also a warrior and an educated woman. The film focuses on the splendour of an India oppressed by the wicked and brutal British, who even take a calf away from its mother to kill and eat it. They serve as pantomime villains but speeches in the film about the English in India feed into the patriotic sentiment. It is significant that two of its writers are major figures in the portrayal of nationalistic views of India. The screenplay is by K. V. Vijayendra Prasad, who wrote the *Baahubali* films (Telugu/Tamil and dubbed into Hindi), making nationwide historical/fantasy films which create powerful images of a Hindu Indian past. Some of the dialogues are by Prasoon Joshi, whose exceptional skills in arousing emotions extends beyond the romantic to the nationalistic, his talents deployed in interviewing Prime Minister Modi during his London visit in 2018.

These genres create an image of a powerful struggle that demands attention, where the good Indian/Hindu is focused only on the nation, for which they are willing to sacrifice their lives in a heroic struggle against dastardly enemies, whether Pakistan, the Delhi Sultanate or the British. Perhaps the films merely stir patriotism or perhaps they remind the audience that the Indian nation has always been in peril and the righteous must rise up to defend it. Even in the moment of decolonisation in the West, such struggles and their rhetoric are too localised to speak to wider audiences but they may well appeal to Indian audiences overseas.

Whereas Hindi cinema has found its greatest success in the Indian diaspora, which numbers over 25 million (Dwyer 2013b), The Report (2016a: 55–6) confirms that the Indian government is well aware of the soft power potential of the diaspora and its practices, and has forged ever stronger networks with them, the most recent being the category of Overseas Citizen of India, which extends considerable privileges, though not a passport nor the right to vote.

The Indian diaspora remains avid consumers of Bollywood, and enjoys its view of the country's elite, or at least India's powerful middle class (Athique 2012). Yet even films which have been massively successful in India have evinced little interest beyond the diaspora and so cannot be considered part of India's soft power outreach, except within the diaspora or to neighbouring countries which consume the films. It seems that the current government is focusing on the diaspora, with Prime Minister Modi's tours being aimed mostly at the diaspora and politicians overseas whose constituents have roots among them. For example, Modi's visit to London 2018 was ostensibly for the Commonwealth Heads of Government meeting but he held an onstage public interview – in Hindi.

The growth of Hindu nationalism over the same time period as Bollywood was formed has led some to posit links between its political imaginary with this form of cinema and the emergence of the new Indian middle class. However, these links were often tenuous (Dwyer 2000), although it is undeniable that such new social groups are the major consumers of Bollywood.

Given the state's limited support for cinema, outlined above, it may be surprising that the BJP has not embraced Bollywood for the purposes of soft power projection. Perhaps this is because it expends more energy in an almost obsessive zeal to tame it, especially where depictions of the nation and Muslims are concerned, be they stars, such as Aamir Khan, or sensitive film topics and story lines, as was seen in debates around the release of *PK* (dir. Rajkumar Hirani, 2014; see Dwyer 2017) Perhaps the present government is satisfied with the soft power that arises among the diaspora that enjoys romcoms, promoting Indian family values, and films which glorify martyrdom for the nation: *Raazi*, *Padmaavat* and *Manikarnika*. Films which promote patriotism, notably the sports biopics, are less divisive and stir a gentler national pride.

The two films of *Baahubali* (the second being *Baahubali 2: The Conclusion*, dir. S. S. Rajamouli, 2017) showed that a high-quality Telugu/Tamil film dubbed into Hindi can be successful with many audiences. This fantasy film, which creates an idealised historical kingdom, with elements of the conflict in the great epic, the *Mahabharata*, blends Telugu film traditions with elements of Western cinema in a gripping story with spectacular visuals, music and an all-Indian hero. Baahubali (Prabhas) is the ultimate hero. Intelligent, kind, powerful, beautiful, strong, he is a model of masculinity. He is an obsessed lover and devoted son. To underline the latter, he has three mothers, not just one: his birth mother, Devasena (Anushka Shetty); his adopted mother, Sanga (Rohini); and Sivagami (Ramya Krishna), the woman who saves him as a baby and carries him down river. As Shiva the child, he reinforces his divine links with the deity by carrying a huge lingam, and shows his supernatural strength in the sequence when he climbs the waterfall, before revealing his strength in saving the men putting up the statue of evil Bhallaladeva. Baahubali marks his kingship at this moment, a living icon, while the evil king has to establish his iconicity with a gold statue. Baahubali shows his power not only in the city of Mahishmati but also in dramatic landscapes, waterfalls, jungles, snowy mountains and the dusty battlefield.

Baahubali's screening showcased India's skills in high tech with the special effects of the film, which create an image of spectacular splendour, using the film form with song and dance and heroic fighting stars. The screening attracted viewers beyond the diaspora but the film still has not penetrated the Western market.

Despite its great merits, for Western audiences there are still problems with the film being a long family melodrama, with subtitles, and it not being a Western-style piece set in India. Yet, given the success of the event at the Royal Albert Hall, it seems that the soft power that cinema creates, mostly among the diaspora, but also among small pockets of viewers overseas, could be magnified, were it to be helped by selecting appropriate films to promote: namely, those that would not conflict with Hindutva but present a positive image overseas. For example, in 2016, the year that might have included *Baahubali* (2015), the Indian official entry for the Oscars was *Visaranai* (dir. Vetrimaaran, 2015, in Tamil), which is about interrogation under torture. The NFDC is no longer funded to produce films, even though it has made the kind of cinema that would do well at the Oscars and so reach wider audiences. As the CBFC did not act on the Report (2016b, 'The Benegal Report'), it effectively makes filmmakers self-censor their films to avoid cuts and certifications which would restrict their audiences (Central Board of Film Certification 2018). The IFFI has rejected films that it feels are controversial (such as S. Durga's *Sanak Kumar Sasidharan*, 2017), creating negative reactions in the film community and preventing visitors from other festivals from seeing the films. While heavy-handed intervention would prove detrimental, small steps could prove significant. Good subtitling is often a real issue, for example, as is an understanding of global cinema that can help to make informed decisions.

It is almost impossible to measure soft power but the Report (2016b: 7) suggests the need for a soft power matrix. However, India does not rank in Portland Communications Top 30 Global Soft Power impact nations. This may reflect the BJP government's instinctive autarky, or self-sufficiency and disinterest in what foreigners think of its social and economic programme. Many see the negative images of India in the Western press as anti-Indian, or 'Hinduphobic'. India's absence from the top thirty seems unnecessary, indicating that it squanders its huge soft power advantages. It is not the government that helps project India's soft power, which has been most successfully channelled through non-state organisations, with film the leading example. However, Bollywood is not making films that appeal abroad, except through the Indian diaspora, and in India's neighbouring countries and their diasporas too.

Soft power may well spread through the over-the-top (OTT) platforms, where Indian series are broadcast that conform to Western standards and styles, narratives and lengths, albeit via a familiar image of India in series such as *Sacred Games* (Series 1, 2018; Series 2, 2019; Netflix) and *Made in Heaven* (2019; Amazon Prime). Among the most successful series are those that are produced or directed by figures from the Indie/Hindi cinema. These OTT platforms allow filmmakers more creativity and less censorship as they explore issues that mainstream cinema avoids, such as homosexuality, marital infidelity and violence, including acts by state agents, that appeal more to the makers who understand international film and these series. The image of India that they create may be grittier and is certainly more realistic than Bollywood, but it is one which engages the wider world with contemporary India. Would Danny Boyle have made *Slumdog Millionaire* in the manner he did were he unaware of Anurag Kashyap's way of writing and shooting contemporary India (Kumar 2008)? Yet Kashyap had to struggle to get his films released in India, let alone seen overseas. It is hardly surprising that he was one of the first to move to the OTT platform with *Sacred Games*, even though he has since become a major movie producer. As the Report (2016b) notes throughout, while Bollywood is a major source of soft power, it is one that the government neglects. It seems that film and related industries find themselves hindered rather than helped by the state, whatever political party forms a government, and so they seek to bypass these controls by working in new media.

Works Cited

Athique, Adrian (2012), *Addressing the Nonresident: Soft Power, Bollywood and the Diasporic Audience*, in Anjali Gera Roy (ed.), *The Magic of Bollywood at Home and Abroad*. New Delhi: Sage, pp. 277–94.

Bajpai, Shruti (2019), 'China's Affair with Bollywood Is Now More Down Than Up. But Everybody Loves Mishu', *The Hindu*, <https://www.thehindu.com/entertainment/movies/chinas-affair-with-bollywood-is-now-more-down-than-up-but-everybody-loves-mishu/article26281614.ece> (last accessed 26 December 2019).

Bell, Chris (2017), 'Taj Mahal Left Out of an Indian Tourism Booklet', *BBC News*, <https://www.bbc.co.uk/news/blogs-trending-41482311> (last accessed 22 December 2019).

Business Standard (2020), '"Aatmanirbhar Bharat" Also Means "Making for the World", Says PM Modi', *Business Standard*, 15 August, <https://www.business-standard.com/article/current-affairs/corona-a-global-crisis-but-not-so-big-as-to-halt-india-s-juggernaut-modi-120081500228_1.html> (last accessed 15 August 2020).

Central Board of Film Certification (2018), 'Vision & Mission', <https://www.cbfcindia.gov.in/main/vision-and-mission.html> (last accessed 19 December 2019).

Dasgupta, Swapan (2018), Interview, 16 February.

Devasundaram, Ashwin (2016), 'Bollywood's Soft Power: Branding the Nation, Sustaining a Meta-hegemony', *New Cinemas: Journal of Contemporary Film*, 14:1, 51–70.

Dwyer, Rachel (2000), *All You Want Is Money: All You Need Is Love: Sex and Romance in Modern India*. London: Cassell.

Dwyer, Rachel. (2006), 'The Saffron Screen?: Hindi Movies and Hindu Nationalism', in Birgit Meyer and Annalies Moors (eds), *Religion, Media and the Public Sphere*. Bloomington: Indiana University Press, pp. 273–89.
Dwyer, Rachel. (2011a), 'The Case of the Missing Mahatma: Gandhi and the Hindi Cinema', *Public Culture*, 23:2, 349–76.
Dwyer, Rachel. (2011b), '*Zara hatke!*: The New Middle Classes and the Segmentation of Hindi Cinema', in Henrike Donner (ed.), *A Way of Life: Being Middle-class in Contemporary India*. London: Routledge, pp. 184–208.
Dwyer, Rachel (2013a), 'The Hindi Film Biopic', in Robert Rosenstone and Constantin Parvulescu (eds), *The Blackwell Companion to Historical Film*. Oxford: Blackwell, pp. 219–32.
Dwyer, Rachel (2013b), 'Bollywood's Empire', in Joya Chatterjee and David Washbrook (eds), *Routledge Handbook of the South Asia Diaspora*. London: Routledge, pp. 407–16.
Dwyer, Rachel (2014a), 'The Biopic of the New Middle Classes in Hindi Cinema', in Belen Vidal and Tom Brown (eds), *The Biopic in Contemporary Film Culture* American Film Institute readers, Edward Brannigan and Charles Wolfe (series eds). London and New York: Routledge, pp. 8–83.
Dwyer, Rachel (2014b), *Bollywood's India: Hindi Cinema as a Guide to Modern India*. London and Chicago: Reaktion Books.
Dwyer, Rachel (2015), 'Innocent Abroad: Shah Rukh Khan, Karan Johar and the Diasporic Star', in Elke Mader, Rajinder Dudrah and Bernhard Fuchs (eds), *Shah Rukh Khan and Global Bollywood*. Delhi: Oxford University Press, pp. 49–69.
Dwyer, Rachel (2017), 'Calling God on the Wrong Number: Hindu–Muslim Relations in *PK* (2014) and *Bajrangi Bhaijaan* (2015)', *Muslim World*. Special Issue: 'Hindu–Muslim Relations', ed. Lucinda Allen Mosher and Shaunaka Rishi Das, 107:2, pp. 256–70.
Dwyer, Rachel (2019), 'The National Spirit.' *Open*, 25 April, <https://openthemagazine.com/columns/the-rachel-papers/the-national-spirit/> (last accessed 26 December 2019).
Gehlawat, Ajay (2017a), *The 'Slumdog' Phenomenon: A Critical Anthology*, New Perspectives on World Cinema. London: Anthem Press.
Gehlawat, Ajay (2017b), 'The Metatext of *Bajirao Mastani* Intolerance in the Time of Modi', *South Asian History and Culture*, 8:30, 338–48.
Hayden, Craig (2011), *The Rhetoric of Soft Power: Public Diplomacy in Global Contexts* (Lexington Studies in Political Communication). Lanham, MD: Lexington Books.
HT Correspondent (2018), '*Padmavati* becomes *Padmaavat*: Here's How Film Changed After CBFC Modifications', *Hindustan Times*, 11 January, <https://www.hindustantimes.com/bollywood/padmavati-becomes-*Padmaavat*-here-is-how-the-film-has-changed-after-cbfc-modifications/story-xrLvCbOB-OFEwkmSUmI2yWO.html> (last accessed 19 December 2019).
Jaikumar, Priya (2006), *Cinema at the End of Empire: A Politics of Transition in Britain and India*. Durham, NC: Duke University Press.

Jalil, Rakhshanda (2018), 'How Bollywood's *Padmaavat* Distorted a Sufi Love Poem', *Aljazeera*, 1 February, <https://www.aljazeera.com/indepth/opinion/bollywood-*Padmaavat*-distorted-sufi-love-poem-180131135353836.html> (last accessed 19 December 2019).

Kumar, Amitava (2008), 'Slumdog Millionaire's Bollywood Ancestors', *Vanity Fair*, 23 December.

Kumar, Manoj R. (2018), 'This is the Real Problem with Sanjay Leela Bhansali's *Padmaavat*', *The Indian Express*, 31 January, <https://indianexpress.com/article/entertainment/opinion-entertainment/sanjay-leela-bhansali-*Padmaavat*-padmavati-5044875/> (last accessed 19 December 2019).

Nye, Joseph S., Jr (1990), *Bound to Lead: The Changing Nature of American Power*. New York: Basic Books.

Nye, Joseph S., Jr (2004), *Soft Power: The Means to Success in World Politics*. New York: Public Affairs.

Prasad, M. Madhava (1998), *Ideology of the Hindi Film: A Historical Construction*. Delhi: Oxford University Press.

Rajadhyaksha, Ashish (2003), 'The "Bollywoodization" of the Indian Cinema: Cultural Nationalism in a Global Arena', *Inter-Asia Cultural Studies*, 4:1, 25–39.

Rajagopalan, Sudha (2008), *Leave Disco Dancer Alone!: Indian Cinema and Soviet Movie-going After Stalin*. New Delhi: Yoda Press.

Ramnath, Nandini (2018), '*Padmaavat* Film Review: A Saga of Love, Honour and Death as Beautiful as it is Bloodless', *Scroll.in*, 24 January, <https://scroll.in/article/866152/*Padmaavat*-film-review-a-saga-of-love-honour-and-death-as-beautiful-as-it-is-bloodless> (last accessed 19 December 2019).

Report (2016a), Ministry of External Affairs, Thirteenth Standing Committee on External Affairs (2016–17) (Sixteenth Lok Sabha), 'India's Soft Power Diplomacy Including Role of Indian Council for Cultural Relations (ICCR) and Indian Diaspora', <http://164.100.47.193/lsscommittee/External%20Affairs/16_External_Affairs_13.pdf> (last accessed 19 December 2019).

Report (2016b), *Report of Committee of Experts Chaired by Shyam Benegal to Recommend Broad Guidelines [sic]/Procedure for Certification of Films by the Central Board of Film Certification (CBFC)*, 26 April, <https://mib.gov.in/sites/default/files/Shyam_Benegal_committee_Report.pdf> (last accessed 19 December 2019).

Robinson, Andrew (2003), *Satyajit Ray: The Inner Eye*. London: I. B. Tauris.

Roy, Arundhati (2017), *The Ministry of Utmost Happiness*. London: Hamish Hamilton.

Schaefer, David J., and Kavita Karan (2012), 'Bollywood and Soft Power: Content Trends and Hybridity in Popular Hindi Cinema', in Anjali Gera Roy (ed.), *The Magic of Bollywood at Home and Abroad*. New Delhi: Sage, pp. 57–80.

Siddique, Salma (2017), 'The Futility of Dreaming of the Padmavati–Khilji Dream Sequence', *The Wire*, 14 December, <https://thewire.in/communalism/futility-dreaming-padmavati-khiljis-dream-sequence> (last accessed 19 December 2019).

Tharoor, Shashi (2008), 'India's Bollywood Power', *Project Syndicate*, 16 January, <http://www.project-syndicate.org/commentary/india-s-bollywood-power> (last accessed 19 December 2019).

Tharoor, Shashi (2018), Interview, 16 February.

Thussu, Daya (2013), *Communicating India's Soft Power: Buddha to Bollywood*. London: Palgrave.

Zahran, Geraldo, and Leonardo Raos (2010), 'From Hegemony to Soft Power: Implications of a Conceptual Change', in Inderjeet Parmar and Michael Cox (eds), *Soft Power and US Foreign Policy: Theoretical, Historical and Contemporary Perspectives*. London: Routledge, pp. 12–31.

CHAPTER 10

Soft Power and National Cinema: James Bond, 'GREAT' Britain and Brexit

Andrew Higson

Introduction

The increasingly right-wing UK governments of the 2010s, backed by the right-wing media, sought to present Britain unequivocally as a global power. This process only intensified with the politicking around Brexit and the UK's departure from the European Union (EU) (Portland 2019). The official GREAT campaign, launched in 2011, promoted GREAT Britain throughout the decade as a brand that might attract and generate trade and investment. At the same time, the concept of Global Britain, 'the organising slogan of UK foreign policy in the age of Brexit' (Barber 2018; Global Britain 2018), became central to narratives about how the UK should perform on the international stage: this, too, was a nation-branding exercise.

There is no denying the prominence of the UK story globally. Thus the Anholt Nation Brands Index ranked the UK's overall 'National Brand' fourth in the world in 2019 (dropping from third the previous year), based on responses from 20,000 consumers in twenty countries (Ipsos 2019), while the 2018 edition of Portland Communication's *Soft Power 30* publication (McClory 2018) had the UK in the top spot in their annual league table. Despite the ongoing negotiations about Brexit, it was still in second place the following year (Portland 2019). The success of the GREAT campaign was cited as a key factor, while the pervasiveness of the Global Britain slogan was noted (McClory 2018: 46). But perhaps more important than both was the fact that 'Independent from the government, British art, film, music, fashion, and sport continue to flourish in highly competitive global markets' (ibid.: 44). The significance of the UK's cultural heritage and contemporary creative industries are repeatedly singled out for attention in commentary about the UK's soft power, their outputs identified as crucial soft power assets.

For Joseph Nye, the international relations expert who coined the term soft power, and for his followers, soft power is about the creation and circulation of compelling national stories, 'effectively communicating a winning global narrative' (McClory 2018: 12). This chapter reflects on the role cinema has been called on to play in communicating a compelling story about the UK in the 2010s, and on the role of one agent in particular: 007, James Bond. Those seeking to brand the UK as a global power also found it useful to invoke the iconic figure of James Bond, and the apparent ease with which Bond both asserts a British identity and moves around the world. Political discourse in and about the UK has positioned cinema, and the creative industries more generally, at the centre of the nation-branding process, and this chapter also charts the development of this discourse. At the end of the chapter, I consider the new configuration of national cinema that emerges from this discourse in this era of intense globalisation.

In identifying the UK as one of the world's leading soft power nations, two influential soft power reports, in *Monocle* magazine in 2014 and by Portland in 2015 (*Monocle* 2014; McClory 2015), cited the Bond films as prime contributors to that status. Around the same time, the Bond films were co-opted into the GREAT campaign, under the slogan 'Bond is GREAT Britain'. This was quite blatantly an exercise in nation branding for a global world, fully supported by the British government, and a deliberate attempt to project a particular national narrative. The nation branding at stake here also coincided with the visions of pro-Brexit campaigners in the run-up to the 2016 referendum about whether the UK should leave the EU: for them, too, Bond was a national hero.

James Bond's Soft Power

How, then, was James Bond, the leading character of one of the toughest and most violent action adventure film franchises in history, reframed as a cultural diplomat, an instrument of soft power? What part did the character play in formulating the Brexit narrative of GREAT Britain and how did he become a key component of a particular national brand? The focus here is on the first four Bond films featuring Daniel Craig in the lead role: *Casino Royale* (dir. Martin Campbell, 2006), *Quantum of Solace* (Marc Forster, 2008), *Skyfall* (Sam Mendes, 2012) and *Spectre* (Sam Mendes, 2015) (the fifth Craig/Bond film, *No Time to Die* (Cary Joji Fukunaga) was at the time of writing due to have a delayed released in 2021).

These are, at one level, British films, made by Eon Productions, but they depended on substantial inward investment from Hollywood, in this instance in the guise of MGM (Jones and Higson 2020). For most UK audiences, James Bond is a British agent, an identifiably British character – and

Figure 10.1 The Bond films are replete with British imagery, iconography, institutions, flags and characters: 007 meets the Queen, in a film made for the opening ceremony of the London 2012 Olympic Games (screengrab).

in the case of the five films in which Bond is played by Daniel Craig, he is, for UK audiences, a recognisably *English* character, given his southern, white, middle-class English accent (albeit with a Scottish upbringing, as revealed in *Skyfall*). The films are also replete with British imagery, iconography, institutions, flags and characters. Bond's British identity was further underlined when Daniel Craig appeared as Bond alongside the Queen in the short film made for the opening ceremony of the London Olympics in 2012 (Fig. 10.1).

The Bond films, then, are celebrated in the UK as very much national products, as Great British films about a Great British icon. At the same time, the films are also Great British exports – in both economic and cultural terms. Bond himself is also, of course, very much a global traveller, who inhabits a highly seductive narrative world filled with prestige consumer goods and a luxury lifestyle. This is a national narrative, but it is also a narrative of cosmopolitan globe-trotting adventure.

This serves to indicate that, if the Bond films are in some senses British, they are also very much global productions for global audiences. Indeed, Eon/MGM's Bond film franchise is, by any definition, a global phenomenon, and the films are very carefully packaged for worldwide markets. They are also very much transnational productions, in terms of the involvement of co-production partners, locations, creative personnel, crew, cast and actors from various different countries.

Despite the evident investment by Hollywood in the films and the transnationalism of their production, the Craig/Bond films were repeatedly mobilised as national totems in political debates about global Britain, co-opted into a soft power play that was designed to promote a persuasive and attractive image of the UK as a leading global player. In 2012, the year of the London Olympics as well as the hugely successful release of *Skyfall*, the magazine *Monocle* produced a soft power survey that put Britain at the top of the world table, 'thanks to the exploits of Bradley Wiggins, Andy Murray, James Bond, Adele and the Queen' (McClory 2012). The right-wing, populist British newspaper, the *Daily Mail*, was delighted: 'The sun may have set on the British Empire, but this country is once again the globe's most powerful nation by at least one yardstick' (Kelly 2012).

The 2015 *Soft Power 30* report claimed that Britain's combined hard military and political might, its economic strength and its soft diplomatic and cultural influence again made it the world's leading global power (McClory 2015). This, too, was picked up on the *Daily Mail*'s globally popular website, which proclaimed 'Britain as the world's ONLY global power – and we have the Royal Family, James Bond, Harry Potter and Sherlock Holmes to thank ... not to mention companies like Land Rover, Burberry and Topshop' (Drury 2015). James Rogers of the European GeoStrategy think tank was quoted approvingly: 'Brand UK has never been stronger' – and the Bond franchise, he argued, was key to that national brand (ibid.). With *Spectre* released that year, the British Deputy High Commissioner in India was moved to proclaim that 'Bond is back to show the world what makes Britain GREAT' (McAllister 2015).

The same theme was picked up in a report from a Select Committee on Soft Power in the UK's non-elected chamber of parliament, the House of Lords: 'UK cultural assets have a wide appeal that adds to the country's international recognition and reputation'. The global success of the Bond film franchise was cited by way of example (House of Lords 2014: 117). This passage was subsequently picked up in another report, commissioned by the British Film Institute (BFI), which concluded that 'British Film is a major generator of soft power for the UK', in which context the Bond franchise is 'particularly influential ... This is further underlined through the significant tourism and diplomatic value British film generates worldwide – by building interest and trust in the UK, they perform a role of great importance' (Olsberg-SPI 2015: 1–2).

This line of argument was also adopted in 2016 in the run-up to the Brexit referendum in a leaflet produced by the Brexit Leave Campaign, which articulated a vision of Britain going it alone as a global power freed from the shackles of the EU:

> The United Kingdom continues to punch above its weight in terms of 'hard power': the ability to control others through forces – usually economic or military – to do what you wish. . . . Yet it is in soft power that our influence is most remarkable. (Brexit Leave Campaign 2016)

How is that influence felt?

> From the Commonwealth to the G8, from the Hong Kong Sevens to Formula One, from gentlemen's clubs to the James Bond film franchise, the history of the British Empire and its expats is everywhere. Furthermore, there remains intense global media interest in Queen Elizabeth II and the wider Royal Family. . . . Come with us as we make a new future in this globalised world. (Brexit Leave Campaign 2016)

In a key speech by Michael Gove, then Justice Minister in the UK government and one of the leading Brexit campaigners, he argued that 'Britain is a great country, it's the world's fifth largest economy with the world's best Armed Forces, best health service and best broadcaster. We're first in the world for soft power, thanks to our language, culture and creativity' (Whale 2016).

The Brexit mythology of Britain as a great nation that is capable of standing alone plays heavily on popular memory of 1940 and Churchill's rhetoric of 'defend[ing] our Island . . . fight[ing] on the beaches . . . [and] never surrender[ing]' (Churchill 1940). This mythology of *Great* Britain was also played out in the UK government's GREAT tourist and trade promotional campaign. As Jeremy Hunt, then government Minister for Culture, put it, this was about 'putting great back into Britain' (quoted in Satherley 2011). This careful exercise in nation branding was a key early example of the UK government taking the soft power agenda seriously, and by 2016 it was being used in a highly coordinated fashion 'by 17 government departments and . . . actively branding the British diplomatic and trade presence in over 150 countries' (Pamment 2016a).

Launched by the Prime Minister, David Cameron, in 2011, the campaign co-opted a series of already very high-profile national brands, including the football Premier League, Jaguar, Aston Martin and James Bond. In his launch speech, Cameron explained, 'This campaign is simple. There are so many great things about Britain and we want to send out the message loud and proud that this is a great place to do business, to invest, to study and to visit' (BBC 2011). The involvement of the Bond franchise in the campaign (Fig. 10.2) was explained in an official government document:

Figure 10.2 One of the posters produced for the Bond/*Skyfall* tie-in with the GREAT campaign in 2012. Source: VisitBritain.

> VisitBritain, The Department of Culture, Media and Sport (DCMS) and the GREAT campaign partners saw an opportunity to use the globally recognised James Bond franchise to promote both tourism and the excellence of the UK's film-making expertise. (Hague 2014: 8)

The participation of two of the most powerful government departments, the Foreign and Commonwealth Office (FCO) and UK Trade and Industry, ensured that:

> over 20 Embassies and High Commissions held Bond-themed receptions and screenings to promote Britain as a world-class tourism destination to influential local audiences and highlight the strengths of the British film-making industry and Bond-related British products such as the new Jaguar. (ibid.: 8–9)

The 'Bond is GREAT Britain' campaign was renewed in 2015 with the release of *Spectre* and a new tagline, 'Live the Bond Lifestyle in Britain' (VisitBritain 2015). The objective was once again to 'utilis[e] 007's iconic international profile to show the world what makes Britain GREAT' (Bond Lifestyle 2015).

The politics of Bond's on-screen adventures equally present Britain as a sovereign global power. In the first four Craig/Bond films, British national security is threatened by a series of villainous global players, but protected almost single-handedly by Bond, with the support of the British secret service. There is little sense of international collaboration or cooperation as a positive force, even with the US. Indeed, the organisation SPECTRE, in the eponymously named 2015 film, is a multinational corporation, a metaphorical version of the G7, which seeks to privatise global cyber-security for its own sinister ends.

The Ironies of Bond's GREAT Britain

No wonder that the Brexit Leave Campaign invoked the Bond films: this is the perfect narrative for the post-Brexit vision of the UK as a sovereign global power. However, a closer inspection of the stories told in the first four Craig/Bond films, and of the circumstances of the production, distribution and reception of those films, throws up some challenging questions about nationhood in this period of intense globalisation. Indeed, there is much irony about the way the Bond films were wielded as instruments of soft power and nation branding, not least since Bond repeatedly exercises power through violent coercion rather than cultural diplomacy. And, of course, that power and the national narrative in which the Bond films participate depend on foreign investment in the UK's cultural economy, with the films heavily funded by Hollywood studios. This is the nature of national cinema in a neoliberal, globalised world, and indicative of how developed nations are mobilising commercial nationalism and soft power, and adjusting their presence in the global media landscape.

It is, of course, possible to read the Craig/Bond films in different ways to those in which the Brexiteers understand the films. Indeed, there is an explicit critique of the *Daily Mail* version of England at the heart of *Skyfall*, provided by Raoul Silva, the film's master villain: 'Oh, Mr. Bond. All that physical stuff is so dull. So dull. Chasing spies. So old-fashioned. . . . England, the Empire, MI6. You're living in a ruin, as well. You just don't know it yet' (Fig. 10.3). In the end, of course, Bond's traditional 'physical stuff', combined with the modernity of Q's computing mastery, proves successful. Change is there, too, in the reintroduction of Moneypenny in *Skyfall* as a black British character, and a woman with far greater agency than the previous incarnations of the character.

The same can be observed of the opening ceremony of the London Olympics, which was seen by commentators on both the left and the right as projecting an idea of Britain as a liberal, multicultural society. The involvement of Bond in this narrative suggests that Bond, too, has his

Figure 10.3 'Oh, Mr. Bond. All that physical stuff is so dull. So dull. Chasing spies. So old-fashioned. . . . England, the Empire, MI6. You're living in a ruin, as well. You just don't know it yet.' Raoul Silva to James Bond, in *Skyfall* (screengrab from *Skyfall*).

place in this modernised vision of Britain, which yet allows for the enduring nature of both the monarchy and an imperialist version of British masculinity.

Finally, in this list of ironies troubling the Brexit vision of Bond's soft power, there is the thorny issue of whether international audiences actually perceive Bond as British. Many such audiences are far less certain than British audiences about this matter: after all, in order to appeal to contemporary global audiences, the film franchise must and does look beyond a parochial sense of Britishness. Indeed, as Bond scholar James Chapman notes, Bond's Britishness has long been 'carefully packaged for the international market', by combining British signifiers with elements of internationalism and cosmopolitanism (Chapman 2003: 97).

The production and distribution of the Craig/Bond films is typical of how global capitalism operates – and in this case, how the same cultural products are exploited on a global scale. Glocalisation – investing global products with some sort of local flavour – is an important part of this work. Thus, each of the films was both set and shot in numerous locations around the world, while in many countries Bond fluently speaks the local language, thanks to the practice of dubbing. These global products are thus able to depict local places and speak to local audiences. This is neatly captured in a scene in *Spectre* when a meeting of the global organisation headed up by Blofeld is conducted by people from a variety of national, racial and ethnic groups speaking several different languages. Even in the English-language version of *Spectre*, the meeting of Blofeld's organisation requires subtitles to capture the meanings of the several different languages spoken.

For some viewers, the Craig/Bond films may be full of signifiers of Britishness, but their emphasis on action, big-budget special effects and international locations means they are seen by many non-British audiences as 'Hollywood' films rather than 'British' ones. This perspective is reinforced by the fact that the Craig/Bond narratives are prefaced in most markets by the MGM and Columbia studio logos. Taking such issues into account begs all sorts of questions about how audiences make sense of cultural products, spectacular or otherwise, questions that are rarely addressed by diplomats or politicians (Jones and Higson 2020; Clarke 2016; Albro 2015).

Unambiguous Nation Branding

The involvement of the Bond franchise in the GREAT campaign certainly did not entertain such ambiguities. As an official exercise in nation branding, this is hardly surprising. As Melissa Aronczyk (2014) points out, such official processes generally iron out diversity, plurality, internal national differences and competing ideas of the nation and national identity. On the basis of twelve case studies of nation branding around the world, she argues that only those 'aspects of a culture that are deemed economically viable are promoted as part of the branded national identity'.

Such branding exercises often produce and recirculate the most familiar, and therefore most stereotypical, images of a nation. As such, they play a key role in maintaining and promoting commercial, consumable national brands, providing reductive, non-complex images and narratives of the nation for consumption. As Janine Widler (2007: 148) notes, 'instead of fighting stereotypes [nation branding] reproduces and enhances them'. For many, this is clearly highly appropriate. As former diplomat Tom Fletcher (2016: 139) puts it, 'Successful country branding uses stereotypes and national symbols rather than fights them' because 'people want some familiarity'.

The Bond films themselves, in seeking to address diverse global audiences, are clearly more ambivalent in their use of traditional, nationally specific stereotypes and iconographies, since they also offer alternative images of a more diverse nation and allow audiences to read them non-nationally. The question of how actual audiences and consumers make sense of the sorts of national narratives and images circulated by campaigns such as GREAT is important. As Melissa Nisbet (2015) notes, 'those on the receiving end of soft power do not always respond in the way that politicians might expect them to'.

The Discourses of Soft Power

No doubt some will argue that I am using the terms soft power and nation branding too loosely, too interchangeably. Gary Rawnsley (2018), for instance, argues that 'soft power has become one of the most familiar, yet perhaps over-used and misunderstood concepts in international relations'. This may be a problem in terms of the rigours of academic scholarship and the protection of disciplinary boundaries. But in terms of how such concepts are used more widely, and how professional practices have developed around them, it is precisely this usage that is significant. What interests me in particular is the way that the concept has been used in debates about the creative industries, and especially film, in the UK.

Joseph Nye (2003) defines soft power as 'the ability to get what you want by attracting and persuading others to adopt your goals. It differs from hard power, the ability to use the carrots and sticks of economic and military might to make others follow your will.' Jonathan McClory (2010: 1), creator of the Soft Power 30 Index, explains that this is about 'relying . . . on the attractiveness of a nation's institutions, culture, politics and foreign policy, to shape the preferences of others'. Rawnsley (2018) provides a more succinct definition: 'Persuading publics in other countries to want what you want, or to want what you want them to want.'

This understanding of soft power is now a central pillar of many government foreign policies and diplomatic missions around the world, as they seek to project 'the attractiveness of their "national culture" . . . as a means to achieve competitive advantage over other nations' (Ang et al. 2015). James Pamment (2016b) has examined in detail how the UK government's Foreign and Commonwealth Office embraced the discourse of soft power in the 2010s, transforming how the FCO, the civil and diplomatic services and two key arm's-length organisations, the British Council and the BBC World Service, promoted the British national brand abroad. This was, Pamment notes, 'the re-imagining of British diplomacy in the light of the digital communication revolution' (ibid.: 2), and numerous public pronouncements along these lines can be found in the work of Parliament and in speeches by government ministers.

Thus, Lord Howell (2011), Foreign Office Minister, noted that 'The Government have been and are looking closely at how to improve the co-ordination across Whitehall of soft power resources.' In 2013–14, a House of Lords Select Committee examined the UK's soft power challenges and opportunities in some depth, producing a highly detailed and oft-cited report (Select Committee 2014). But it was not until 2018 that the government sought to establish a formal, cross-government soft power strategy, as part of its *National Security Capability Review* (2018: 32): 'How the UK is perceived matters'. Crucial to this work was the effort to secure the future but also to maintain 'the independence of the BBC World Service, British Council and the many British institutions and brands that contribute to our soft power'.

By the later 2010s, it also became necessary for the government to articulate 'what we mean by "Global Britain" as we navigate our way to leave the European Union' (Ellis 2018); or, as another commentator put it, 'Over the past few years, the HM Government has been pushing the "Global Britain" narrative aggressively as a response to claims of a more inward-looking post-Brexit Britain' (Portland 2019). In an official government statement, it was explained that 'Global Britain is about reinvesting in our relationships, championing the rules-based international order and demonstrating that the UK is open, outward-looking and confident on the world stage' (Global Britain 2018). For Jeremy Hunt (2019), by now Foreign Secretary, this was 'the story of a small nation playing a decisive and enlightened role in world affairs'.

Although the British Council and the BBC World Service were seen as crucial to the telling of this story, they were under threat at various times during the 2010s. One way in which the British Council sought to maintain its position was to intervene at some length in the soft power debate and demonstrate the significance of its cultural diplomacy work, notably in their *Influence and Attraction* report (Holden 2013). Following a major review of the Council in 2014, its purpose was redefined as 'soft power projection' (Foreign and Commonwealth Office et al. 2015). In so doing, there was an implicit alignment of soft power with cultural production, circulation and reach. Rawnsley is critical of what he sees as this reductionist alignment of soft power to the cultural attractiveness of a nation, arguing that this obscures the 'power' element in the equation. This is, however, probably the most widespread use of the term in UK public and political discourse, and as such, it maps neatly on to the idea of nation branding.

The GREAT campaign was a key product of this attempt to develop a coordinated approach to diplomacy, soft power and national security during the 2010s. The focus was on cultural projection, tourism and trade – with both cultural projection and tourism understood almost solely in terms of trade. If economic growth and new inward investment were the core goals of the GREAT campaign, the vehicle was cultural, in the form of striking stories and images. The GREAT campaign is thus not about securing a political agenda, or establishing the framework within which debate takes place, but about what Robert Albro (2015) calls 'a cultural policy of display – of showing or representing the nation through cultural spectacle', with 'governments promot[ing] spectacles of nationhood as forms of national aggrandizement'.

It is the impact of this spectacular storytelling that the various soft power and nation-branding league tables seek to measure. Such tables are taken seriously, by diplomats, politicians and the media, and widely regarded as 'authoritative, influential assessment[s] of the strengths and weaknesses of national brands and the changing cultural landscape' (Kramb 2017). Or as Tom Fletcher (2016: 138) conceives of it, 'this is a competition that should matter, and not just to diplomats'.

There is, then, a close relationship between the discourses and practices of soft power and those of nation branding. A soft power strategy in the digital age, Fletcher argues, 'comes down to three ideas: having a strong national story; knowing how to tell it; and knowing how and when to mix the tools at your disposal' (2016: 138). 'A nation needs to tell a good story,' he argues, one that is aspirational, inclusive and persuasive in terms of the values it expresses (ibid.: 138). It does not 'need to be sophisticated or detailed', he suggests, 'but it does have to be something that people can buy in to, and that other countries can take as an authentic and attractive vision' (ibid.: 139).

The Discourse of Nation Branding

Aronczyk (2013) has examined in some depth the ways in which nation branding has been legitimised as a business, following the work of Simon Anholt (1998). Governments all over the world now turn routinely to branding consultants, public relations advisers and strategic communications professionals to create and hone their national brand. In demonstrating this process, Aronczyk charts 'the political, cultural and economic rationales by which the nation has been made to matter in a twenty-first-century context of global integration', a context in which national borders often seem irrelevant to economic transactions (2013: 1). Nadia Kaneva (2011: 118, 120) argues something very similar, that nation branding is a means of 'reconstituting nationhood through marketing and branding paradigms', in order to 'enhance[e] a nation's competitive advantage in a global marketplace'. This is the benign reassertion of national distinctiveness, producing a nation brand as a marker of difference, in a period dominated by global businesses, global trade flows and neoliberal economic policies. It is thus about creating and promoting a specific, appealingly packaged and officially sanctioned idea of the nation that can be bought into and consumed in the global marketplace, an attractive destination for tourists, skilled workers, investors and businesses. Globalisation in its various forms supersedes the idea of the nation, unpicks its borders and adopts practices that are designed to sidestep national governance. Nation branding seeks to reassert an image of the nation that has some sort of purchase in this landscape.

This is what Zala Volcic and Mark Andrejevic (2016a) call commercial nationalism – producing a competitive brand for the nation, commodifying and selling it, but at the same time nationalising the sell, using that recognisable national brand to encourage inward investment and sell products. 'In the global economic context', they argue, 'the ability to channel and capture attention is a crucial one' (ibid.: 1). As can be seen in the UK government's GREAT campaign, this involves creating a 'relationship between state appropriation of marketing and branding strategies on the one hand, and, on the other, the commercial mobilization of nationalist discourses' (Volcic and Andrejevic 2016b: iv).

The nation is thus reforged as a commercial brand in the context of globally dominant neoliberal thinking. All of the analysts cited above situate nation branding in the context of 'competiveness policies, the commercialisation of culture, and the widening application of corporate strategy to non-market institutions' (Aronczyk 2014). Typically of neoliberal approaches, 'national wellbeing is defined primarily in terms of securing an economic competitive advantage, and nation-branding is expected to contribute to this by attracting investments, tourists, human capital, or trade' (Kaneva 2011: 122). The role of national governments in this context is to support enterprise and competition by creating a competitive national context in a global free market, and by creating an attractive image of the nation as a place to do business. That is the instrumentalist function of the so-called creative industries and the cultural products they produce. Indeed, the emergence of soft power doctrines and nation branding coincided with the establishment of neoliberal creative industries policies in the UK and elsewhere.

The UK Film Business, Nation Branding and Soft Power

While these different policies and practices emerged around the same time, in the late 1990s and early 2000s, it was only in the 2010s that the creative industries came to be understood in the UK as the producers of so-called soft power assets. This was in part thanks to the influence of the House of Lords Select Committee Report on Soft Power (Select Committee 2014), the British Council's *Influence and Attraction* report (Holden 2013) and the annual *Soft Power 30* Report (McClory 2015 and so on). Thus the latter stated that 'Brand Britain['s] . . . dynamic creative industries, from art, film, and music, to architecture, design, and fashion, are all critical to its soft power stores' (McClory 2017: 44), which are 'instrumental in spreading British influence and cultivating soft power' (McClory 2018: 44).

Around the same time, the UK Screen Sectors' Task Force (2017: 6) drew attention to 'the value [of] forging new economic relationships through the prism of cultural soft power, one of the UK's greatest assets'. To that end, one of the five cross-cutting priorities they identified for the government's emergent Industrial Strategy was the importance of 'Linking international trade with cultural "soft power" – harnessing the power of the stories which are told across all platforms through film and the moving image to influence hearts and minds' (ibid.: 3).

These sentiments were also picked up in the government-commissioned *Review of the Creative Industries*: 'The cultural and creative sectors are the engine of the UK's international image and soft power' (Bazalgette 2017: 4). By 2018, they had found their way into ministerial speeches, with Jeremy Wright (2018), the Culture Minister, arguing that the creative industries are 'pivotal to our economy and our standing as a nation', and 'at the heart of our soft power'. Even Theresa May (2018), then Prime Minister, contributed to the fanfare: 'every day our creative industries fly the flag for Britain on the global stage. . . . Our creative industries really are at the heart of what makes Britain great.' The discourse was mobilised again as the government sought to bolster these industries following the COVID-19 social and economic lockdown. Thus the new Prime Minister, Boris Johnson, described the 'cultural industry' as 'the beating heart of this country', with the Culture Minister adding that 'our arts and culture make our country great and are the lynchpin of our world-beating . . . creative industries' (Department for Digital, Culture, Media and Sport 2020).

A great deal of work had been done by the UK Film Council in the 2000s to establish a robust sense of the economic scope and impact of the film business and its value to the wider economy, in the hope of leveraging government support for the business. Inward investment was a key aspect of this work (Oxford Economics 2005–12). Another independent report by Olsberg-SPI (2012: 18) argued that two of the eight economic drivers for investment in the film production business were increased tourism and national brand building, which, they argued, were closely interrelated:

> Films contribute to a wider 'branding' of a country's inhabitants, society and culture. This can have a very strong influence on creating a desire to engage in business transactions as well as tourism visits. The same effects that are experienced by potential tourists about a destination are to be found also in the international business and trade community. This can assist in building export markets and inward investment There are also geo-political benefits to increasing the understanding of a nation worldwide as a result of a film's impact.

While the GREAT campaign plays out its soft power credentials through top-down, state-sponsored ideological work, few of the products of the UK's creative industries are developed in this way. Feature films, for instance, may receive state support in the form of tax credits or National Lottery funding, but are produced by private, non-state players whose activities are only loosely coordinated by the BFI. Once produced, the films may be co-opted by state agencies, as the Bond films were by VisitBritain for the GREAT Campaign. But as the discussion of the Bond films above demonstrates, films themselves are rarely straightforward in their ideological work. Texts, characters and narratives are often multivoiced, open-ended and ambivalent, and audiences read them in a variety of ways, depending on their own circumstances.

On the one hand, this is a problem for the soft power agenda. On the other, the independence of the media, and the arm's-length relationship that the government has with organisations such as the BBC, the BFI and the British Council, is an important part of the national story about the UK as an open, democratic society. Harnessing films for official soft power initiatives in the UK has, to date, been undertaken in a very abstract and generic manner. Hence the ministerial statements quoted above about the pivotal role that the creative industries play for the economy and by flying the flag for the nation on the global stage. With the exception of the campaigning in the run-up to the Brexit referendum, politicians have been wary of claiming that individual films project a preferred national image or story.

This relative independence created space for the BFI and the British Council to adopt an approach to the value of film, and to wider cultural activity and the creative industries, that was different to the government's. While both institutions have engaged with the soft power agenda, they have sought to change that agenda in certain ways. For them, cultural value cannot be reduced to economic value, but neither can it be reduced to a monocultural national brand. Both organisations have promoted the concept of cultural exchange rather than cultural projection.

The British Council's *Influence and Attraction* report (Holden 2013) argued for a new approach to international cultural relations, organised around interactive and inclusive networks, and designed to encourage an openness to other cultures. The soft power debate tends to imply a simple one-way projection of one's own culture, displaying it as if it were, in some way, singular, superior and beyond reproach. The Council instead argued for cultural exchange as a dialogue with others, which would enable comprehension of each other through mutual cultural understanding.

They also argued that culture and cultural exchange should not be seen in a purely instrumental sense but should be understood as valuable in their own right. Cultural exchange should then be seen as a means of stimulating creative responses to encounters with other cultures, enabling innovation and cultural dynamism:

> Culture itself develops through exchange. Culture is a 'good' in its own right, regardless of its political or economic effects, and develops through dialogue, either with past or contemporary practice. . . . Culture itself mutates through exchange, but cultural exchange also provokes new modes of thinking, doing, learning and sharing; in short, cultural exchange helps us to innovate. . . . Creativity happens where difference meets and contact between cultures is characterised by flux, stimulation, plurality and diversity. (Holden 2013: 32)

The BFI drew on the same set of arguments in various official pronouncements. Their plan for 2013–17, for instance, spoke of 'help[ing] the Foreign and Commonwealth Office . . . and Department for Culture, Media and Sport . . . engage more effectively on the world stage through UK film's cultural value', and 'maximis[ing] the cultural, creative and diplomatic impact of our cultural programme' through cultural exchange (2013: 3, 7). Their plan for 2017–22 (BFI 2016a) does not even mention the concept of soft power, again preferring the terminology of cultural value. Their annual report for 2018–19 reworks soft power in terms of cultural exchange as dialogue, rather than the one-way trajectory of projecting a national brand: 'there is nothing soft about so-called soft power. Cultural exchange initiates conversations, shows real intent to collaborate as partners, and opens the door for trade discussion in a way that is hard to beat' (BFI 2019: 6).

Cinema, Creative Industries Policy and the Neoliberal Political Agenda

The BFI's policies and pronouncements in the 2010s thus sought to round off the hard edges of neoliberal creative industries policies and carve out a space for valuing film as a cultural practice. But there can be no escaping the fact that the BFI has still had to operate in the context of a quarter-century of neoliberal thinking in the UK about the so-called creative industries. In 1998, the Government's Department of Culture, Media and Sport defined the creative industries as 'those industries which have their origin in individual creativity, skill and talent and which have a potential for wealth and job creation through the generation and exploitation of intellectual property' (Creative Industries Strategy Group 2001: 5). Building on that definition over the last two decades, policymakers have, with some success, sought to present the creative industries as vital contributors to the national economy.

Their goal was to establish the economic breadth and the dynamic growth potential of those industries and enterprises, a view that is now widely accepted within the UK and internationally. Thus, the United Nations *Creative Economy Report* (UNDP/UNESCO 2013: 10) demonstrated that 'world trade of creative goods and services . . . more than doubled from 2002 to 2011'. In establishing a new Industrial Strategy in 2017, the UK government identified the creative industries as one of five industries to drive economic growth in the UK (Department for Business, Energy and Industrial Strategy 2017). Margot James (2018: 4), Minister for Digital and the Creative Industries, described the creative industries as 'an engine of growth across the UK'. The Bazalgette Report (2017), too, signalled the vital place that the creative industries have in the contemporary UK political economy.

While a number of more progressive and democratic currents have fed into this policy agenda, it is shaped above all by neoliberal imperatives. At the heart of creative industries thinking is a market-led definition of cultural practice as industrial enterprise. The focus of this definition and of the broader policy agenda was and remains economic growth, competitive enterprise, job creation, the development of skills, talent and entrepreneurial leadership, the development of a production infrastructure, and an emphasis on investment rather than subsidy (Higson: forthcoming). From this perspective, cinema is to be valued above all for its economic rather than its cultural potential: 'Bond is GREAT Britain' because Bond films do excellent business around the world.

The perceived economic value of the creative industries, including the film business, means that national governments still invest in them. But the neoliberal view is that creative decisions should be market-led, in terms of which action is most competitively advantageous in a global free market. It is in this context that the appeal of ideas of soft power and nation branding should be understood, as a means of drawing attention to the enterprise and attractions of particular nations and achieving a competitive advantage over less well branded nations.

For the UK Government's Department for Digital, Culture, Media and Sport (2019), investing in the creative industries is justified in terms of boosting the image of the UK as a place to visit and to do business: 'We help to give the UK a unique advantage on the global stage, striving for economic success.' Meanwhile, a Treasury spokesperson justified tax breaks for the creative industries by noting that 'One of the ways the world sees Britain at its best is through world-class films and television made in Britain. They not only help us showcase the country but are also an important part of a dynamic and diversified economy' (quoted in Winnett 2012). The Bazalgette Report (2017: 12) brought in the concept of cultural enrichment, but the emphasis was again on economic contribution and reputational promotion:

> Alongside the Creative Industries' irrefutable economic contribution sit a number of intangible benefits: its outputs, particularly in our cultural sector, enrich the lives of UK citizens, and promote Britain around the world. There is evidence of a direct relationship between cultural assets and economic impact, with cultural investment creating an ecosystem of impacts.

Cultural enrichment is, then, simply a passing reference. The core theme is the economic impact gained by circulating cultural assets in the global marketplace. The cultural value of film in this context is its capacity to display an attractive national brand and thereby assert soft power.

Operating in this context, with the government as its masters, the BFI has embraced some of the central tenets of neoliberal policy. Their 2017–22 plan opens with the statement that 'The sustained Government commitment to the sector . . . ensures the UK's competitiveness as a business destination. Together film, animation, television and games make a significant contribution to the economy' (Berger and Nevill 2016: 2–3). Key goals identified in the plan include, 'working with Government to ensure the right conditions are in place for future growth', 'ensuring a globally competitive UK film industry' and 'ensuring inward investment remains a huge success story for the UK economy' (BFI 2016a: 24, 24, 25). The plan also identifies the challenges involved in addressing all filmmaking through this neoliberal lens:

> There are genuine questions for us to consider about how independent British film can be supported to take advantage of its creative success to scale up and better compete in what should be an age of opportunity. Future economic value will come from more and better UK content being created, owned and then exported by UK businesses. (Berger and Nevill 2016: 3)

The neoliberal agenda is, however, tempered by the BFI's cultural programme, 'the foundation of all our work' (ibid.: 2), and their commitment to diversity, to encouraging new talent and to the cultural value of film:

> Great filmmaking can change lives. Through stories from now, and from other times and other cultures, we learn to think differently and understand each other better. Great filmmaking is about revealing things we don't yet know, seeing the world in new ways, enriching our lives and making a vital contribution to our wellbeing. (BFI 2016a: 10)

This is a powerful statement about the soft, cultural and social benefits of film, but it is a rather different version of soft power to the one promoted by the government and the various league tables. Films are no longer reduced to mere economic or soft power assets. Simplistic nation branding, one-way cultural projection and bombastic assertions of soft power are replaced by the values of cultural exchange, difference and understanding. This is a much richer vision of storytelling than the one proposed by the Culture Minister who wanted to 'put . . . great back into Britain' (quoted in Satherley 2011), or the boastful, imperialistic comments of the *Daily Mail*. And it is a vision of the complexities of films as texts, even those produced for global markets, like the Bond films, that can move beyond the myopic, monocultural claims made for them by Brexiteering politicians.

Reasserting the National: A Place for National Cinema?

Neoliberal economic policies and the processes of globalisation have threatened the national in all sorts of ways. Two broad responses to this threat have developed. On the one hand, there is the re-emergence of populist nationalism, responding to a sense of insecurity in this global era; and on the other hand, the rise of soft power, nation branding and commercial nationalism, accepting the neoliberal logic of the market and seeking to create the most attractive image in that market. As Samanth Subramanian (2017) notes, 'both seek, in different ways, to regain or construct a more distinctive version of a country's self'.

The embracing by governments of ideas and practices of soft power is a means of reasserting the national – but still from a neoliberal perspective. National governments are keen to attract inward investment from foreign businesses to boost the local economy, in a perverse but actually typical mixing of the global and the local. The practice of nation branding also clearly reproduces the idea of nations and national identities in a globalised world. Once again, then, the national remains a meaningful entity in relation to audio-visual storytelling and the industrial structures and processes that support it. What emerges, though, is a reconfigured version of national cinema.

Looking back, we can see that, as Film Studies as an academic discipline slowly came to terms with the intense globalisation of cinema in the 1990s, we scholars felt we needed to move beyond the discourse of national cinema, and we adopted a new set of terms, such as the transnational, the postnational and world cinemas. But the national has not withered away, and as John Hill (2016) notes, 'discourses of the "national" . . . continue to structure and inform how films of various kinds are categorised, funded, promoted and made sense of by a range of social actors ranging from politicians and civil servants to filmmakers, critics and audiences'. But in the UK at least, national cinema is not a concept that seems to have much purchase at the level of policymaking.

If national cinema is understood as the totality of films made in a particular nation, contemporary British filmmaking is too diverse to be promoted as a simplistic national brand. This did not prevent the GREAT campaign from using the slogan, 'FILM IS GREAT BRITAIN', in a series of posters launched in 2013 (MacLeod 2013) (Fig. 10.4). The BFI (2016b) also created a promotional video using the same imagery and wording. This video celebrates individual British talent in front of and behind the camera, and films made using British facilities. The video flashes up some readily recognisable national iconography at the start – a view of Britain from space, St Paul's Cathedral, Tower Bridge, some green and pleasant heritage landscapes and a cityscape of postmodern London, with the Eye and Big Ben prominent. This is GREAT Britain, apparently. But there is otherwise no effort to brand the diverse achievements featured in the video as the products of a national cinema. In so far as one can discern national images, identities and values in outputs such as this, they are depoliticised, reduced to an attractive, competitive resource that can emphasise market differentiation in a so-called borderless, globalised world.

Figure 10.4 The title image from a promotional film produced by the British Film Institute as part of the GREAT campaign in 2016 (screengrab).

What is on offer is less a national cinema, more a national brand that can be consumed, hired or invested in. If there is a national cinema here, it is a loosely defined economic space carved out of the global market, and the talent, facilities and investment opportunities associated with that space. This is the plight of national cinema in the struggle to achieve 'national visibility and legitimacy amidst the multiple global flows of late modernity' (Aronczyk 2013: 3). The film business and the wider creative industries have, to that extent, been carefully co-opted into the neoliberal framework of the creative industries, nation branding and the assertion of soft power. James Bond may be GREAT Britain, but the very presence of the Bond films depends on inward investment, a global market, and stories and images that are both diverse and spectacular enough to appeal to audiences around the world.

Works Cited

Albro, R. (2015), 'The Disjunction of Image and Word in US and Chinese Soft Power Projection', *International Journal of Cultural Policy*, 21:4, <https://www.tandfonline.com/doi/full/10.1080/10286632.2015.1042471> (last accessed 9 February 2018).

Ang, I., Y. Raj Isar and P. Mar (2015), 'Cultural Diplomacy – Beyond the National Interest?', *International Journal of Cultural Policy*, 21:4, <http://www.tandfonline.com/doi/10.1080/10286632.2015.1042474> (last accessed 9 February 2018).

Anholt, S. (1998), 'Nation-brands of the Twenty-first Century', *Journal of Brand Management*, 5:6, 395–406.

Aronczyk, M. (2013), *Branding the Nation: The Global Business of National Identity*. Oxford: Oxford University Press.

Aronczyk, M. (2014), 'Nation 'Branding' to Promote States in the Global Market Has Serious Consequences for Social Diversity within European Countries', *LSE Europopp Blog*, 22 January, <https://blogs.lse.ac.uk/europpblog/2014/01/22/nation-branding-to-promote-states-in-the-global-market-has-serious-consequences-for-social-diversity-within-european-countries/> (last accessed 17 November 2020).

Barber, T. (2018), 'Spinning Global Britain', *Financial Times*, 13 March, <https://www.ft.com/content/4e1ec04c-26a8-11e8-b27e-cc62a39d57a0> (last accessed 2 January 2019).

Bazalgette, P. (2017), *Independent Review of the Creative Industries*, September, <https://assets.publishing.service.gov.uk/government/uploads/system/uploads/attachment_data/file/649980/Independent_Review_of_the_Creative_Industries.pdf> (last accessed 3 November 2017).

BBC (2011), 'London 2012: David Cameron launches "Great" campaign', 22 September, *BBC News*, <http://www.bbc.co.uk/news/uk-15019587> (last accessed 30.8.19.

Berger, J., and A. Nevill (2016), 'Introduction', in BFI, *BFI2022: Supporting UK Film, BFI Plan 2017–2022*, BFI: London, <https://www.bfi.org.uk/2022/> (last accessed 5 June 2017).

BFI (2013), *The Wide Angle: The BFI's International Strategy*, <https://www.bfi.org.uk/sites/bfi.org.uk/files/downloads/bfi-wide-angle-international-strategy-2013-v2.pdf> (last accessed 30 August 2019).

BFI (2016a), *BFI2022: Supporting UK Film, BFI Plan 2017–2022*, BFI: London, <https://www.bfi.org.uk/2022/> (last accessed 5 June 2017).

BFI (2016b), 'Film Is GREAT Britain', promotional video, *GREAT campaign* (Ambassadors webpage), <http://www.greatbritaincampaign.com/#!/ambassadors> (last accessed 30 August 2019).

BFI (2019), *BFI Annual Report and Financial Statements 2018–19*, <https://assets.publishing.service.gov.uk/government/uploads/system/uploads/attachment_data/file/822757/190716_BFI_Annual_Report_and_Financial_Statements_2018-19__Final_.pdf> (last accessed 30 August 2019).

Bond Lifestyle (2015), 'VisitBritain Launches Bond Is GREAT Campaign', 11 October, <http://www.jamesbondlifestyle.com/news/visitbritain-launches-bond-great-campaign> (last accessed 18 November 2020).

Brexit Leave Campaign (2016), 'Better Off Out', <http://www.betteroffout.net/wp-content/uploads/2016/05/soft-power-A5-booklet_Layout-1.pdf> (last accessed 5 February 2018).

Chapman, J. (2003), *Licence to Thrill: A Cultural History of the James Bond Films*. London: I. B. Tauris.

Churchill, W. (1940), 'We Shall Fight on the Beaches', speech in the House of Commons, *International Churchill Society*, 4 June, <https://winstonchurchill.org/resources/speeches/1940-the-finest-hour/we-shall-fight-on-the-beaches/> (last accessed 30 August 2019).

Clarke, D. (2016), 'Theorising the Role of Cultural Products in Cultural Diplomacy from a Cultural Studies Perspective', *International Journal of Cultural Policy*, 22:2, <https://www.tandfonline.com/doi/full/10.1080/10286632.2014.958481> (last accessed 9 February 2018).

Creative Industries Strategy Group (2001), *Creative Industries Mapping Document*, <https://www.gov.uk/government/uploads/system/uploads/attachment_data/file/183544/2001part1-foreword2001.pdf> (last accessed 5 February 2018).

Department for Business, Energy and Industrial Strategy (2017), *Industrial Strategy: Building a Britain Fit for the Future*. London: HM Government, <https://www.gov.uk/government/publications/industrial-strategy-building-a-britain-fit-for-the-future> (last accessed 5 February 2018).

Department for Digital, Culture, Media and Sport (2019), *gov.uk*, <https://www.gov.uk/government/organisations/department-for-digital-culture-media-sport> (last accessed 30 August 2019).

Department for Digital, Culture, Media and Sport (2020), '£1.57 Billion Investment to Protect Britain's World-class Cultural, Arts and Heritage Institutions', *gov.uk*, <https://www.gov.uk/government/news/157-billion-investment-to-protect-britains-world-class-cultural-arts-and-heritage-institutions> (last accessed 23 August 2020).

Drury, F. (2015), 'Britain is the World's ONLY Global Power – and We Have the Royal Family, James Bond, Harry Potter and Sherlock Holmes to Thank', *MailOnline*, 8 November, <https://www.dailymail.co.uk/news/article-3309040/Britain-world-s-global-power-Royal-Family-James-Bond-Harry-Potter-Sherlock-Holmes-thank.html#ixzz4TO4NTFZF> (last accessed 30 January 2019).

Ellis, M. (2018), Minister for Arts, Heritage and Tourism, speech at ministerial event on soft power, Department for Digital, Culture, Media and Sport, 24 July, <https://www.theculturediary.com/sites/default/files/soft_power_speech_michael_ellis_24_july_fin.pdf> (last accessed 30 August 2019).

Fletcher, T. (2016), *Naked Diplomacy: Power and Statecraft in the Digital Age*. London: William Collins.

Global Britain (2018), *gov.uk*, 13 June, <https://www.gov.uk/government/collections/global-britain-delivering-on-our-international-ambition> (last accessed 30 August 2019).

Hague, W. (2014), 'Government Response to the House of Lords Select Committee on Soft Power and the UK's Influence', CM8879, June, p. 8, <https://www.parliament.uk/documents/lords-committees/soft-power-uk-influence/Lords-Soft-Power-Government-Response.pdf> (last accessed 31 August 2019).

Higson, A. (forthcoming), 'Creative Industries Policy in the UK, Creative Clusters and Cultural Entrepreneurship'.

Hill, J. (2016), 'Living with Hollywood: British Film Policy and the Definition of "Nationality"', *International Journal of Cultural Policy*, 22:5, <http://www.tandfonline.com/doi/full/10.1080/10286632.2016.1223646> (last accessed 30 August 2019).

Holden, J. (2013), *Influence and Attraction: Culture and the Race for Soft Power in the 21st Century*, British Council/Demos, <https://www.britishcouncil.org/sites/default/files/influence-and-attraction-report.pdf> (last accessed 2 February 2016).

House of Lords (2014), Select Committee on Soft Power and the UK's Influence – First Report: Persuasion and Power in the Modern World', Report of Session 2013–14, HL150, <https://publications.parliament.uk/pa/ld201314/ldselect/ldsoftpower/150/15002.htm> (last accessed 30 August 2019).

Howell, Lord (2011), Speech in the House of Lords, 3 May, <https://www.gov.uk/government/speeches/foreign-office-minister-talks-of-using-soft-power-in-the-interests-of-the-uk> (last accessed 29 August 2019).

Hunt, J. (2019), Foreign Secretary, Speech at the Lord Mayor's Banquet, 14 May, <https://www.gov.uk/government/speeches/lord-mayors-banquet-2019-foreign-secretarys-speech> (last accessed 30 August 2019).

Ipsos (2019), 'Germany Retains Top "Nation Brand" Ranking, France and Canada Emerge to Round Out the Top Three', 18 November, <https://www.ipsos.com/en-us/news-polls/Germany-Retains-Top> (last accessed 23 August 2020).

James, M. (2018), 'Foreword', in J. Mateos Garcia, J. Klinger and K. Stathoulopoulos, *Creative Nation: How the Creative Industries are Powering the UK's Nations and Regions*. London: NESTA/CIC.

Jones, H. D., and A. Higson (2020), 'Bond Rebooted: The Transnational Appeal of the Daniel Craig Bond Films', in J. Verheul (ed.), *Beyond 007: James Bond Reconsidered*. Amsterdam University Press/Chicago University Press.

Kaneva, N. (2011), 'Nation Branding: Toward an Agenda for Critical Research', *International Journal of Communication*, 5, 117–141, <ijoc.org/index.php/ijoc/article/download/704/514> (last accessed 30 August 2019).

Kelly, T. (2012), 'Britain Ousts the U.S. as World's Most Influential Nation', *Daily Mail*, 18 November, <https://www.dailymail.co.uk/news/article-2234726/Britain-tops-global-soft-power-list.html> (last accessed 30 August 2019).

Kramb, D. (2017), 'UK Slips to Lowest Ever Ranking in Monocle's Annual Soft Power Survey – But the Arts Keep it Afloat', *FMcM*, 16 November, <http://fmcm.co.uk/news/2017/11/16/uk-slips-to-lowest-ever-ranking-in-monocles-annual-soft-power-survey-but-the-arts-keep-it-afloat> (last accessed 30 August 2019).

McAllister, D. (2015), British Deputy High Commissioner in India, speech at an event on 19 November, <https://www.gov.uk/government/speeches/bond-shows-the-world-what-makes-britain-great> (last accessed 28 August 2019).

McClory, J. (2010), *The New Persuaders: An International Ranking of Soft Power*, Institute for Government, <https://www.instituteforgovernment.org.uk/sites/default/files/publications/The%20new%20persuaders_0.pdf> (last accessed 30 August 2019).

McClory, J. (2012), 'Soft Central – Global', *Monocle*, 59:6, 46–54, <https://monocle.com/magazine/issues/59/soft-central/> (last accessed 30 August 2019).

McClory, J. (2015), *Soft Power 30: A Global Ranking of Soft Power 2015*. London: Portland PR, <https://portland-communications.com/pdf/The-Soft-Power_30.pdf> (last accessed 30 August 2019).

McClory, J. (2017), *Soft Power 30: A Global Ranking of Soft Power 2017*. London: Portland PR, <https://softpower30.com/wp-content/uploads/2017/07/The-Soft-Power-30-Report-2017-Web-1.pdf> (last accessed 30 August 2019).

McClory, J. (2018), *Soft Power 30: A Global Ranking of Soft Power 2018*. Portland PR, <https://softpower30.com/wp-content/uploads/2018/07/The-Soft-Power-30-Report-2018.pdf> (last accessed 18 November 2020).

Macleod, Ishbel (2013), 'UK Government Promotes Fact that Film is GREAT in New Campaign Stage with Radley Yeldar', *The Drum*, 30 August, <https://www.thedrum.com/news/2013/08/30/uk-government-promotes-fact-film-great-new-campaign-stage-radley-yeldar> (last accessed 24 November 2020).

May, T. (2018), 'PM Speaks at Creative Industries Reception: 8 May 2018', <https://www.gov.uk/government/speeches/pm-speaks-at-creative-industries-reception-8-may-2018> (last accessed 1 August 2018).

Monocle (2014), 'Soft Power Survey 2014/15', 16 November, <https://monocle.com/film/affairs/soft-power-survey-2014-15/> (last accessed 18 November 2020).

National Security Capability Review (2018), March, HM Government, <https://assets.publishing.service.gov.uk/government/uploads/system/uploads/attachment_data/file/705347/6.4391_CO_National-Security-Review_web.pdf> (last accessed 2 January 2019).

Nisbet, M. (2015), 'The Art of Attraction: Soft Power and the UK's Role in the World', *Cultural Trends*, 24:2, <https://www.tandfonline.com/doi/full/10.1080/09548963.2015.1031485?src=recsys> (last accessed 30 August 2019).

Nye, Joseph S., Jr (2003), 'Propaganda Isn't the Way: Soft Power', *International Herald Tribune*, 10 January, <https://www.belfercenter.org/publication/propaganda-isnt-way-soft-power> (last accessed 30 August 2019).

Olsberg-SPI (2012), *Building Sustainable Film Businesses: The Challenges for Industry and Government*, <http://www.o-spi.co.uk/wp-content/uploads/2013/09/Building-Sustainable-Film-Businesses.pdf> (last accessed 2 March 2018).

Olsberg-SPI (2015), *Cultural and Audience Contributions of the UK's Film, High-End TV, Video Games, and Animation*, 2 December, <https://www.bfi.org.uk/sites/bfi.org.uk/files/downloads/%20cultural-and-audience-contributions-of-the-uks-film-highend-tv-video-games-and-animation-programming-sectors-2016-01.pdf> (last accessed 28 August 2019).

Foreign and Commonwealth Office, HM Treasury, Philip Hammond and George Osborne (2015), 'Foreign Office's Settlement at the Spending Review 2015', 25 November, <https://www.gov.uk/government/news/foreign-offices-settlement-at-the-spending-review-2015> (last accessed 29 August 2019).

Oxford Economics (2005–12), *The Economic Impact of the UK Film Industry*. Oxford: Oxford Economics, 2005, 2007, 2010 and 2012.

Pamment, J. (2016a), 'GREAT: A Campaign Approach to Projecting Soft Power', *The Soft Power 30 Report: A Global Ranking of Soft Power, 2016*, London: Portland Communications, pp. 64–6, <https://portland-communications.com/pdf/The-Soft-Power-30-Report-2016.pdf> (last accessed 31 August 2019).

Pamment, J. (2016b), *British Public Diplomacy and Soft Power: Diplomatic Influence and the Digital Revolution*. Basingstoke: Palgrave Macmillan.

Portland (2019), *The Soft Power 30*, <https://softpower30.com/country/united-kingdom/> (last accessed 23 August 2020).

Rawnsley, G. D. (2018), 'Challenging the Snake-oil Salesmen: A Critique of British Approaches to Soft Power', *The Journal of International Communication*, 24:1, <https://www.tandfonline.com/doi/full/10.1080/13216597.2017.1422779> (last accessed 30 August 2019).

Satherley, J. (2011), 'Put the Great Back into "Great Britain": Government Announces Campaign to Promote Britain Abroad', *Daily Mail*, 22 September, <http://www.dailymail.co.uk/travel/article-2040322/David-Cameron-announces-GREAT-Britain-campaign-ahead-London-2012-Olympics.html> (last accessed 31 August 2019).

Subramanian, S. (2017), 'The Long Read, How to Sell a Country: The Booming Business of Nation Branding', *The Guardian*, 7 November, <https://www.theguardian.com/news/2017/nov/07/nation-branding-industry-how-to-sell-a-country> (last accessed 5 February 2018).

UK Screen Sectors' Task Force (2017), 'Submission to HM Government, Building our Industrial Strategy Green Paper', <www.bfi.org/bfi-uk-screen-sectors-task-force-submission-to-hm-government-building-our-industrial-strategy-green-paper-2017-04> (last accessed 30 August 2019).

UNDP/UNESCO (2013), *Creative Economy Report: Widening Local Development Pathways*. New York/Paris: UNDP/UNESCO, <http://www.unesco.org/culture/pdf/creative-economy-report-2013-en.pdf> (last accessed 3 August 2018).

VisitBritain (2015), Press Release, 11 October, <http://media.visitbritain.com/?service=feature&action=show_content_page&language=en&feature=11389> (last accessed 14 August 2016).

Volcic, Z., and M. Andrejevic (2016a), 'Introduction', in Z. Volcic and M. Andrejevic (eds), *Commercial Nationalism: Selling the Nation and Nationalizing the Sell*. Basingstoke: Palgrave.

Volcic, Z., and M. Andrejevic (eds) (2016b), *Commercial Nationalism: Selling the Nation and Nationalizing the Sell*. Basingstoke: Palgrave.

Whale, S. (2016), 'Michael Gove's Full Brexit Speech on Today Programme', 19 April, <https://www.politicshome.com/news/uk/foreign-affairs/news/73978/michael-goves-full-brexit-speech-today-programme> (last accessed 30 August 2019).

Widler, J. (2007), 'Nation Branding: With Pride Against Prejudice', *Place Branding and Public Diplomacy*, 3:2, 144–50.

Winnett, R. (2012), 'Budget 2012: Tax Breaks To End Exodus of Britain's Best Television Drama', *The Telegraph Online*, 16 March, <http://www.telegraph.co.uk/finance/budget/9146935/Tax-breaks-to-end-exodus-of-Britains-best-television-drama.html> (last accessed 30 August 2019).

Wright, J. (2018), Culture Minister, UK's Secretary of State for DCMS, speech at the Creative Industries Federation Summit, 9 October, <https://www.gov.uk/government/speeches/jeremy-wright-speech-at-the-creative-industries-federation-summit> (last accessed 30 August 2019).

Index

Andreasyan, Sarik, 142, 147
Anholt, Simon, 4, 6, 7, 43
Anima Mundi, 63–4, 69–70
animation festivals
   distribution strategies for
      O Menino e o Mundo (Abreu), 70–1
   international, 63, 64, 70
animation industry
   in Brazil, 63–6, 67–8
   co-production, 68–9
   distribution platforms, 67
   global value, 62–3
   intellectual property revenues, 64–5
   market demand for, 66
   Masha and the Bear (Kuzovkov), 78, 79, 82, 84–5, 86
   Masiania (Kuvaev), 87
   origin of resources, 65–6
   outsourcing, 68
   Salad Fingers (Firth), 87
   SEA (South America–Europe–Asia) Project, 69–70
   soft power potential of, 68–9, 71–2, 85–6
Aronczyk, Melissa, 122, 218, 221

Baron Cohen, Sacha, 42
Bollywood
   appeal to the diaspora, 195, 196, 203, 205
   audiences, 8
   Baahubali: The Beginning (Rajamouli), 190, 191, 204–5
   Chinese market for, 40, 52
   Dangal, 30, 40
   Half the Sky, 48
   Hindi film, 195–6
   historical biopics, 201–3
   hyper-nationalist films, 199, 200
   idealisation of Hindu women, 201–3
   India's national brand and, 39, 196–7
   Kung Fu Yoga (Tong), 44–5, 52
   Manikarnika (Jagarlamundi/Ranaut), 202–3
   National Film Development Corporation (NFDC), 197–8
   Newton (Masurkar), 44
   Padmaavat (Bhansali), 201–2
   relationship with the state, 197–8, 204
   Sino-Indian co-productions, 44–5
   soft power of, 4, 5, 40–1, 190–1, 198–9, 203, 205
   sports biopics, 199–201
   see also India
Bolsonaro, Jair, 45, 59–60, 61
Bond films
   alternative readings of, 216–17
   British identity and, 211–12, 214–15, 217
   British sovereign global power and, 215–16
   as global productions, 212–13, 217–18
   within the GREAT campaign, 211, 214–15, 218
   Hollywood funding, 211, 216
Bong Joon-ho, 4
Botha, Martin, 175
Bourdieu, Pierre, 88
Brazil
   the animation industry, 63–5
   animation origin of resources and intellectual property ownership, 65–6
   animation workforce, 64
   Brazil-Russo co-productions, 40
   Brazil-Sino relations, 45, 62
   distribution platforms for animated content, 67–8

INDEX

film culture, 4
fourth BRICS film festival, 45–6, 51
Gabriel e a Montanha (Gamaran Barbosa), 44
Half the Sky, 48–9
national brand, 58–9
national film industry, 39–40, 50, 53, 60
Nise: O Coração da Loucura (Berliner), 43–4, 52
O Menino e o Mundo (Abreu), 70–1
public diplomacy by, 38–9
reaction to the COVID-19 pandemic, 59
reputation management, 59
SEA (South America–Europe–Asia) Project, 69–70
socio-political challenges. 4, 39, 59–60, 61
soft power and foreign policy, 60, 61
soft power capacities, 2, 3, 38–9
soft power potential of the animation industry, 70–2
soft power potential of the film industry, 60–1
Where Has Time Gone?, 48–9
see also BRICS
BRICS (Brazil, Russia, India, China and South Africa)
adoption of soft power concept, 17–18
compilation films, 8, 44, 46–51
co-productions, 40, 44
cultural brand management, 38, 59
economic value of the creative industries, 61–2
film festivals, 38, 43–6, 50–2
foreign views on, 40–3
Half the Sky, 46, 47–9
Hollywood depictions of, 41–2, 96
impact of COVID-19 pandemic, 6–8
individual film cultures, 39–40, 53
Neighbors, 46, 51–2
soft power potential of, 2
term, 38
Where Has Time Gone?, 46, 47, 48–9
see also *individual countries*
British Council
film as a cultural practice, 224–5
Influence and Attraction report, 220, 222, 224
soft power and cultural production, 219, 220, 222–3, 224

British Film Institute (BFI)
film as a cultural practice, 224–5, 227–8
film as a soft power asset, 213
the GREAT campaign promo, 229
oversight of the British film industry, 224
brittle propaganda, 41

Chan, Jackie
Kung Fu Yoga (Tong), 44–5, 52
Skiptrace (Harlin), 43
China
becoming sameness narrative, 101–3, 105–6
Brazil-Sino relations, 45
at the BRICS film festivals, 50
challenges to Hollywood's China narratives, 97, 108–13
Confucius Institutes, 2, 26, 50, 110
distribution of *Nise: O Coração da Loucura* (Berliner), 43–4, 52
film culture, 2
film policies as propaganda, 28–9
global Chinese film hits, 29–30
'Going Out Policy, 95
The Great Wall (Zhang), 21–2, 23, 24–5, 28
Half the Sky, 48
in Hollywood science fiction films, 98–100
Hollywood's accommodation of China's strategic narratives, 97–106
Hollywood's soft power potential for, 96–7, 105–6
Indian films in, 40, 52
international image deficit, 7, 24, 26–7, 95–6
Kung Fu Yoga (Tong), 44–5, 52
national film industry, 30, 39–40
Neighbors, 51–2
peaceful rise strategic narrative, 98–100
public diplomacy, 27, 53
Russo-Sino co-productions, 40
second BRICS film festival, 43–4, 46
Sino-Indian co-productions, 44–5
Sinological orientalism in Hollywood, 41, 96, 101
Skiptrace (Harlin), 43
soft power and cinema, 27, 30–1, 95
soft power trajectories of, 2, 3, 4, 17–18, 22
soft power/hard power relationship, 27–8

China (cont.)
  South Park (Band in China), 111–13
  as a space power, 99
  US-China co-productions, 29–30, 43
  US-China relations, 7, 24, 106–8
  in Western media, 108
  Where Has Time Gone?, 47, *47*
  see also BRICS
Chitty, Naren, 1, 6, 17
Chua Beng Huat, 21
COVID-19 pandemic, 6–8, 108
creative industries
  cultural expression in, 61–2
  economic value of, 61–2, 225–8
  export of creative services, 62, 68–72
  as soft power assets, 210, 222–3
  see also animation industry
culture
  affect as cultural flow, 23
  cultural capital, 88–90
  foreign policy and, 60, 71–2
  Westerncentric bias to cultural production, 96

da Silva, Luiz Inácio (Lula), 3, 4, 39
Dalian Wanda Group, 21, 25, 28
Damon, Matt, 22, 29
digital technology
  in the animation industry, 87
  new forms of soft power and, 79–80
  Russian manipulative soft power and, 76–7
  symbolic capital of cultural products, 88–90

economics
  economic value of the creative industries, 61–2, 225–8
  exportation of creative services, 62, 68–72
  of the global animation industry, 62–3
Erkenov, Khusein, 125
Eurasian Economic Union (EAEU), 144, 158, 160

film festivals
  Bollywood's engagement with, 197
  BRICS film festivals, 38, 43–6, 50–2
  BRICS-made films, 44
  Crouching Tiger Hidden Dragon Film Festival, 46, 52–3
  future of, 50–1
  limitations of, 51–2
  success of Brazilian films, 60
  Tokyo International Film Festival, 52
  Venice Film Festival, 52
  see also animation festivals
film industry
  of the BRICS, 39–40
  China's national film industry, 30, 39–40
  discourses of national cinema, 228–30
  impact of COVID-19 pandemic, 7–8
  links with culture industries, 5–6
  nation branding and, 122
  Nollywood, 171, 174, 178, 183
  portrayals of India in international films, 195
  in Russia, 39–40, 53, 121–2, 143–4
  soft power potential of, 1, 4–5, 60–1, 223–4
  South Africa in international films, 173–4, 176
  US-China co-productions, 29–30, 43
Firth, David, 87
Fletcher, Tom, 218, 221

Getino, Octavio, 180–1, 183
Guardians (Andreasyan)
  characters/actors, 155–6
  conflict/action in, 158
  geo-political framing, 142, 153–4, 160–1
  narrative arc, 147–8, 151
  parallels with Hollywood superhero films, 149–50, 153–4
  resolution in, 160
  as soft power-based geo-political interventions, 154–60
  team member characteristics, 148–9
  territorial imaginary, 157

hard power
  combined with hard power, 75
  combined with soft power, 1, 24, 27–8, 83
  defined, 1
Hartig, Falk, 98, 110
Hollywood
  access to China's film market, 96, 101, 110–11
  China's strategic narratives and, 97–106
  Chinese women in films, 103–5
  Cold War era films, 121

INDEX   239

depictions of Britishness, 42–3
Independence Day: Resurgence, 99, 100
The Mask of Fu Manchu (Brabin), 41, 96
portrayals of China in science fiction films, 98–100
production of Bond films, 211, 216
representations of BRICS nations, 41–2, 96
sameness strategic narratives of China, 101–3, 105–6
Sinological orientalism in, 41, 96, 101
Sino-US co-productions, 43
Skiptrace (Harlin), 43
soft power potential of for China, 96–7, 105–6
Transformers: Age of Extinction, 99, 100–1, 103, 104–5, 110

India
first BRICS film festival, 43
Hindu nationalism, 191–2, 198, 199–203
international image deficit, 192, 194
national brand, 39, 196–7
national film industry, 39–40, 53
over-the-top (OTT) platforms for Indian series, 205–6
socio-political challenges, 39
soft power potential of, 191 193–4, 205
'Yoga Day,' 194
see also Bollywood; BRICS
Indian Council for Cultural Relations, 193

Ji, Li, 19, 20
Jia, Zhangke
BRICS compilation films, 8, 44, 46–7
Crouching Tiger Hidden Dragon Film Festival, 46, 52–3
Johnson, Matt, 3

Kazakhstan, 42
Kennedy, John F., 99
Korea, 4
Kravchuk, Andrei, 127, 128, 135, 144–5
Kuvaev, Oleg, 87
Kuzovkov, Oleg *see Masha and the Bear* (Kuzovkov)

Luruli, Ntshaveni Wa, 176

Mandela, Nelson, 170 173–4, 176
Masha and the Bear (Kuzovkov)
distribution on YouTube, 78, 79
neoliberal orientation, 82
popular geo-politics and, 84
Russian brand building through, 84–5
symbolic capital of, 78, 88–90
transmedia storytelling, 86–8
world-building potential of, 90–1
Mashatile, Paul, 173
Massumi, Brian, 30–1
McLuhan, Marshall, 24
Medinskii, Vladimir, 119, 120, 123–5, 126, 135, 136
Mexico, 5
Mindadze, Aleksandr, 123, 124, 125, 127
Miskimmon, Alister, 5, 6, 10, 97, 142, 154, 155, 171
Modi, Narendra, 30, 43, 191, 193
Morojele, Sechaba, 176
Murat, Lúcia, 43

national brands
Brazil, 58–9
commercial nationalism, 222
concept of Russianness, 76, 122
cultural brand management, 38, 59
defined, 122
film as a tool of nation building, 122, 174–5
impact of cultural/national stereotypes on, 41–3, 59
India, 39, 196–7
nation building strategies and, 172
neoliberal agendas and, 228
(re)branding of post-Soviet states, 77
Russian Federation (RF), 80–1, 84–5
Russian patriotic cinema, 120, 122 123, 127–8, 134–6
soft power and, 6, 140–1
South Africa, 39, 172
United Kingdom (UK), 210–11, 214–15, 218, 221–2
Nollywood, 171, 174, 178, 183
Norris, Stephen, 89, 142
Nye, Joseph
on animation, 68
brittle propaganda, 41
on China's soft power, 4
impact of COVID-19 pandemic, 7
on India's soft power, 4

Nye, Joseph (*cont.*)
  on Polish soft power, 82–3
  public diplomacy definition, 74
  role of strategic narratives, 97
  on Russian soft power, 4, 81, 82, 121
  self-criticism to establish credibility, 108
  soft power concept, 1, 17, 120–1, 140, 171, 190–1, 210–11, 219
  soft power flows, 19

Obama, Barack, 106–7
Ogunnubi, Olusola, 174
Okeke-Uzodike, Ufo, 174
O'Laughlin, Ben, 5, 6, 10, 97, 142, 154, 155, 171
Olympic Games
  Brazil 2016, 3
  London 2012, 212, 213, 216–17
  opening ceremonies, 3, 5
  Sochi 2014, 75, 120, 129, 132, 141
  Summer 2020, 52
O'Neill, Jim, 38
orientalism
  becoming sameness of China, 101–3, 105–6
  defined, 96
  gendering of, 103–5
  Hollywood's Sinological orientalism, 41, 96, 101
  othering of Russia, 77, 81–2
  in *Viking* (Kravchuk), 146

participatory video (PV)
  Changing the Story, 182
  community identity-formation through, 179–81
  the 'Fogo Process,' 179, 181
  Heaven Hugged Me, 183, 184, 185
  in South Africa, 181–5
  Tit for Tat, 182–3
  When You Strike a Woman You Strike a Rock, 183
People's Republic of China (PRC) *see* China
Poland, 82–3
popular geo-politics
  in *Guardians* (Andreasyan), 142, 153–61
  in *Masha and the Bear* (Kuzovkov) and, 79, 84–5
  role of popular culture, 77, 142
  of the Russian blockbuster, 143–4, 154–60
  space power discourses, 99
  in *Viking* (Kravchuk), 145, 146, 150–2

postcolonialism, 77, 91, 101, 192; *see also* orientalism
public diplomacy
  by Brazil, 38–9
  of the BRICS, 38–9
  by China, 27, 53
  culture as instrument of, 60, 71–2
  daily communications, 74
  defined, 74
  as government-led agency, 74
  non-governmental agency, 75, 81
  relationships with key individuals, 74, 75, 90
  by Russia, 74–5, 77–8
  soft power and, 5–6, 27, 74
  strategic communications, 74–5
Putin, Vladimir, 120, 122–3, 129, 141, 150–1, 155

Ramaphosa, Cyril, 169, 171
Rawnsley, Gary, 219, 220
Ray, Satyajit, 39, 195, 197
Rogers, Matt, 180
Roselle, Laura, 5, 6, 10, 97, 142, 154, 155, 171
Russian Military Historical Society (RVIO), 124
Russia/Russian Federation (RF)
  animation industry, 78, 79
  anti-corruption protests, 119–20
  Brazil-Russo co-productions, 40
  concept of Russianness, 76
  cultural industry, 88–9, 121
  daily communications, 74
  'Foundations of the State Cultural Policy,' 119–20, 123, 125
  geo-political power, 157–8
  Going Vertical (Megerdichev), 131–3
  government funding policy for historical films, 124–7
  hard power, 75
  impact of COVID-19 pandemic, 8
  international image of, 155
  international reputation, 141–2
  Legend No. 17 (Lebedev), 128–31, 134
  Leviathan (Zviagintsev), 75, 76, 143
  manipulative soft power, 76–8
  nation branding via patriotic cinema, 120, 122, 123, 127–8, 134–6
  national brand, 80–1, 84–5

national film industry, 39–40, 53, 88–9, 121–2, 143–4
non-governmental agents of soft power, 83–4
Panfilov's 28 (Druzhinin), 125–6, 135
patriotic Soviet sports films, 128–34
Penal Battalion (*Shtrafbat*) TV series, 124–5
popular geo-politics in blockbuster films, 143–4, 154–60
public diplomacy efforts, 74–5, 77–8
relationships with key individuals, 75, 90
Russian Federation, term, 80
Russo-Sino co-productions, 40
second Putin era, 122–3
Sochi Olympics, 75, 120, 129, 132, 141
soft power as multicentric, 78–9, 83–4, 90–1
soft power as world-building, 79–80, 84–5, 86, 90
soft power events, 75, 129, 132, 141
soft power potential of, 2–3, 4, 75–6, 81, 83, 119–20, 141
Spacewalk (Kiselev), 134–5
strategic communications, 74–5
Tanks (Druzhinin), 135–5
territorial imaginary, 142–3, 156–7
28 Panfilov guardsmen legend, 125–6
Where Has Time Gone?, 48
see also BRICS; *Guardians* (Andreasyan); *Masha and the Bear* (Kuzovkov); *Viking* (Kravchuk)

Said, Edward, 77, 96
Saks, Lucia, 175
Saunders, Robert A., 77
Shouse, Eric, 23
Sidiropoulos, Elizabeth, 172
Skiptrace (Harlin), 43
smart power, 1, 141, 154
social media, 77
soft power
 agents's role, 19, 20, 21
 animation industry and, 68–9, 71–2
 combined with hard power, 1, 24, 27–8, 83
 creative industries and, 210, 222–3
 defined, 1, 120–1, 140
 effects of, 19, 20–2, 23–6
 evaluations of the efficacy of, 6, 18–19, 20
 film industry and, 1, 4–5 60–1, 223–4
 impact of COVID-19 pandemic, 6–8

 national security and, 25
 as a network, 78–9
 Nye's concept of, 1, 17, 120–1, 140, 171, 190–1, 210–11, 219
 public diplomacy and, 5–6, 27, 74
 in relation to government/civil society, 3, 4
 socio-political vulnerability of, 4, 39, 59–60, 61
 strategic narratives and, 4–5, 143–4, 154–60, 171–2
 sustainability of, 4, 39
 vaccine diplomacy as, 7
Solanas, Fernando, 130–1, 183
South Africa
 audience development, 177–8
 authentic stories in South African film, 175–6
 Brand South Africa, 172
 Changing the Story (PV project), 182
 Community Video Education Trust (CVET), 181
 community-level, participatory video projects, 170–1, 181–5
 film as a tool of nation building, 174–5
 gender-based violence, 169–70, 171
 Heaven Hugged Me, 183, 184, 185
 impact of COVID-19 pandemic, 8
 MultiChoice Africa, 174
 national brand, 39, 172
 National Development Plan (NDP), 172–3
 National Film and Video Foundation (NFVF), 175, 176–8, 185
 national film industry, 39–40, 53, 173–4, 175–7
 portrayals of in international films, 173–4, 176, 195
 'Rainbow Nation' narratives, 170, 172
 socio-political challenges, 39
 soft power potential of, 171, 172–3, 174
 strategic narratives, 172, 174, 175, 176, 182–5
 third BRICS film festival, 44–5, 52
 Tit for Tat, 182–3
 When You Strike a Woman You Strike a Rock, 183
 Where Has Time Gone?, 48
 during the Zuma administration, 169–70
 see also BRICS
South Park (Band in China), 111–13

Stewart, Kathleen, 24
strategic narratives
  becoming sameness of China, 101–3, 105–6
  challenges to Hollywood's China narratives, 97, 108–13
  China's peaceful rise, 98–100
  defined, 97, 98
  in International Relations (IR), 154
  of Russian patriotic historical films, 122–7
  soft power and, 4–5, 143–4, 154–60, 171–2
  soft power-based geo-politics in Russian blockbusters, 143–4, 154–60
  of South Africa, 172, 174, 175, 176, 182–5

Trump, Donald, 107–8

United Kingdom (UK)
  audience development, 178
  Brexit mythology, 213–14, 216, 220
  creative industries as soft power assets, 210, 222–3
  cultural assets, 213
  economic value of the creative industries, 225–8
  government adoption of soft power strategies, 214–15, 219–20
  the GREAT campaign, 210, 211, 214–15, 218, 220–1, 222, 224, 229
  Hollywood depictions of, 42–3
  interest in BRICS soft power, 2
  London Olympics, 212, 213, 216–17
  nation-branding, 210–11, 214–15, 218, 221–2
  neoliberal agenda behind cultural production, 226–8
  Othering of Russia, 77
  participatory video (PV), 179–80
  perceptions of Russia's manipulative soft power, 76–8
  soft power agendas and the film industry, 223–4
  soft power potential of, 2, 213, 221
  sovereign global power discourses, 213, 215–16, 220
  see also Bond films; British Council; British Film Institute (BFI)
United States of America (USA)
  binary soft power interpretations, 81
  Dalian Wanda Group's investment in cinema infrastructure, 21, 25
  Othering of Russia, 77, 81
  perceptions of Russia's manipulative soft power, 76–8
  space power, 99
  US-China co-productions, 29–30
  US-China relations, 7, 24, 106–8
  see also Hollywood

Viking (Kravchuk)
  as a blockbuster historical film, 127
  characters/actors, 155
  conflict/action in, 158
  depictions of religion, 145–6, 151, 155
  geo-political framing, 145, 146, 150–2, 154–61
  historical accuracy/cultural fit of, 128, 135
  narrative arc, 144–5
  resolution in, 159–60
  soft power sources in, 147
  territorial imaginary, 156–7

women
  in Bollywood historical biopics, 201–3
  gender-based violence in South Africa, 169–70, 171
  gendered orientalism, 103–5
  in Russian patriotic cinema, 127–8

Xi, Jinping, 5, 27, 30

Zakharova, Maria, 74
Zviagintsev, Andrei, 75, 76, 143

EU representative:
Easy Access System Europe
Mustamäe tee 50, 10621 Tallinn, Estonia
Gpsr.requests@easproject.com